THE
COMPLETE IDIOT'S GUIDE® TO

Writing for Young Adults

by Deborah Perlberg

ALPHA

A member of Penguin Group (USA) Inc.

To my daughter Sara, who makes it all worthwhile.

ALPHA BOOKS

Published by the Penguin Group

Penguin Group (USA) Inc., 375 Hudson Street, New York, New York 10014, U.S.A.

Penguin Group (Canada), 10 Alcorn Avenue, Toronto, Ontario, Canada M4V 3B2 (a division of Pearson Penguin Canada Inc.)

Penguin Books Ltd, 80 Strand, London WC2R 0RL, England

Penguin Ireland, 25 St Stephen's Green, Dublin 2, Ireland (a division of Penguin Books Ltd)

Penguin Group (Australia), 250 Camberwell Road, Camberwell, Victoria 3124, Australia (a division of Pearson Australia Group Pty Ltd)

Penguin Books India Pvt Ltd, 11 Community Centre, Panchsheel Park, New Delhi—110 017, India

Penguin Group (NZ), cnr Airborne and Rosedale Roads, Albany, Auckland 1310, New Zealand (a division of Pearson New Zealand Ltd)

Penguin Books (South Africa) (Pty) Ltd, 24 Sturdee Avenue, Rosebank, Johannesburg 2196, South Africa

Penguin Books Ltd, Registered Offices: 80 Strand, London WC2R 0RL, England

International Standard Book Number: 1-59257-545-5
Library of Congress Catalog Card Number: 2006925728

08 07 06   8 7 6 5 4 3 2 1

Interpretation of the printing code: The rightmost number of the first series of numbers is the year of the book's printing; the rightmost number of the second series of numbers is the number of the book's printing. For example, a printing code of 06-1 shows that the first printing occurred in 2006.

Printed in the United States of America

Note: This publication contains the opinions and ideas of its author. It is intended to provide helpful and informative material on the subject matter covered. It is sold with the understanding that the author and publisher are not engaged in rendering professional services in the book. If the reader requires personal assistance or advice, a competent professional should be consulted.

The author and publisher specifically disclaim any responsibility for any liability, loss, or risk, personal or otherwise, which is incurred as a consequence, directly or indirectly, of the use and application of any of the contents of this book.

Excerpts from an interview with Cynthia Voigt from book.scholastic.com/teacher/authorsandbooks. Copyright © 2006 by Scholastic Inc. All rights reserved. Reprinted by permission.

Excerpt from *Catherine, Called Birdy* by Karen Cushman. Copyright © 1994 by Karen Cushman. Reprinted with permission of Clarion Books, an imprint of Houghton Mifflin Company. All rights reserved.

From *Fast Sam, Cool Clyde, and Stuff* by Walter Dean Myers, copyright © 1975 by Walter Dean Myers. Used by permission of Viking Penguin, A Division of Penguin Young Readers Group, A Member of Penguin Group (USA) Inc., 345 Hudson Street, New York, NY 10014. All rights reserved.

Excerpts from HOLES by Louis Sachar. Copyright © 1998 by Louis Sachar. Reprinted by permission of Farrar, Straus and Giroux, LLC.

All efforts have been made to contact the copyright owners for permission to use reprinted material.

Most Alpha books are available at special quantity discounts for bulk purchases for sales promotions, premiums, fund-raising, or educational use. Special books, or book excerpts, can also be created to fit specific needs.

For details, write: Special Markets, Alpha Books, 375 Hudson Street, New York, NY 10014.

Publisher: *Marie Butler-Knight*	**Cartoonist:** *Shannon Wheeler*
Editorial Director: *Mike Sanders*	**Book Designer:** *Trina Wurst*
Managing Editor: *Billy Fields*	**Cover Designer:** *Bill Thomas*
Acquisitions Editor: *Michele Wells*	**Indexer:** *Angie Bess*
Development Editor: *Nancy D. Lewis*	**Layout:** *Ayanna Lacey*
Senior Production Editor: *Janette Lynn, Kayla Dugger*	**Proofreading:** *John Etchison*
Copy Editor: *Keith Cline*	

Contents at a Glance

Contents

Introduction

Don't let the word *literature* scare you—your young adult (YA) novel doesn't need to be *War and Peace* to get published. It just needs to attract an audience of young readers interested in the story you have to tell. And they will be interested: there is no end to the variety of subjects and experiences that appeal to YA readers.

YA books are unique in the marketplace both because of their narrow focus (readers aged 12 and up) and because of their content, dealing frankly with the main issue that preoccupies young readers: themselves.

Don't take that the wrong way. Young adults are supposed to be preoccupied with themselves. It's their job. Your job as a YA writer is to help shape their understanding of who they are and how they fit into the world. And although YA readers are notoriously astute at finding—and rejecting—contrivance, condescension, or insincerity, they're also the most dedicated, passionate, and loyal fans. What you write may profoundly influence their futures. Perhaps that's why YA novels tend to have a long shelf life, beloved by generation after generation.

Afraid you can't write a YA? You can, because you were once a young adult yourself. Whether you're now a grandparent, a parent, a 20-30-40-something, or even a young adult, you've been through the challenges, conflicts, and experiences that are the raw material for good writing.

As an added bonus, the same skills that help you write a compelling story for young adults are the same skills that will strengthen all your writing, whoever the audience.

How to Use This Book

This book is divided into four parts, each tackling a different aspect of getting your story out into the world.

Part 1, "Laying the Foundation: The Basics," begins with an overview of the YA industry, to help you focus your goals and identify the type of novel you want to write. Then we plunge right into the practical elements of plot, character, and conflict, learning to craft a solid story from premise to resolution. We touch all the basics and even help you learn how to develop ideas.

Part 2, "Work in Progress," continues with the skills and techniques that separate the pros from the amateurs. Chapters on point of view, dialogue, and voice will help you expand your technical repertoire; sections on revision, outlines, and the writer's bible teach the practical skills to take your project from start to finish.

Part 3, "Advanced Class," tackles more abstract skills, showing through example how to get at the emotions that drive your story and engage your readers; how to create a classic by going beyond plot to convey deeper messages; and teaching you how to identify the rules of your fictional world to keep it consistent.

Part 4, "The Business of Writing," offers practical information that every writer wants—and needs—to know, from finding agents and publishers to learning about copyrights and permissions. You'll learn to put together queries and pitch letters, find answers to the most frequently asked questions, and even take a dip into the surprising world of YA nonfiction.

Bonus Boxes

Throughout this book, you'll find extra tidbits of information and advice to guide you on your writing journey.

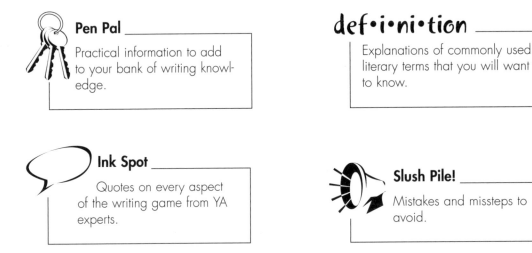

Pen Pal

Practical information to add to your bank of writing knowledge.

def•i•ni•tion

Explanations of commonly used literary terms that you will want to know.

Ink Spot

Quotes on every aspect of the writing game from YA experts.

Slush Pile!

Mistakes and missteps to avoid.

Acknowledgments

I'd like to report that no one was harmed during the making of this book—but first I'd need to check in with the family, friends, and pets that saw no sign of me for weeks on end. Special thanks to my special daughter for always being on my team, picking up the slack, and tolerating way too many frozen pizzas.

Many thanks to Marilyn Allen, agent extraordinaire, and Michele Wells at Alpha Books for their phenomenal patience, and gratitude to Gwen Moran, Bobbi Dempsey, Nancy Lewis, Marta Justak, and Keith Cline, consummate professionals, for lending their expertise and encouragement.

To all the folks at the Gotham Writers Workshop, especially Adam Sexton for letting me create the first children's book writing classes; wise and witty Dean of Students Alex Steele and the talented Dana Miller, writers all—ongoing thanks and appreciation; ditto to the dedicated staff at The Learning Center at Brown University.

To the writers, editors, assistants, and interns I've worked with over the years— especially those who've remained valued friends—thanks for helping me gather the knowledge and experience that went into this book. Last, but certainly not least, to my wonderful writing students in New York and Providence—thanks for constantly amazing me with your talent, insights, and creativity; you make it all worthwhile.

Special Thanks to the Technical Reviewer

The Complete Idiot's Guide to Writing for Young Adults was reviewed by an expert who double-checked the accuracy of what you'll learn here, to help us ensure that this book gives you everything you need to know about writing for young adults. Special thanks are extended to Marta Justak.

Trademarks

All terms mentioned in this book that are known to be or are suspected of being trademarks or service marks have been appropriately capitalized. Alpha Books and Penguin Group (USA) Inc. cannot attest to the accuracy of this information. Use of a term in this book should not be regarded as affecting the validity of any trademark or service mark.

Part 1

Laying the Foundation: The Basics

Sure, you're dying to jump in and start writing your best-selling YA novel—but where do you begin? Who's your main character? What's the plot *really* about? Do you have too many scene ideas—or hardly any? Yikes—writing novels is *hard!* Not to worry. This entire section—the longest part of the book—is devoted to getting your writing up and running. You'll get all the information you need—starting with an overview of the YA industry to help identify the type of novel you want to write and who you want to write it for!

What Is a YA, Anyway?

In This Chapter

- ◆ How to make sure your YA is a YA
- ◆ Why level matters
- ◆ Keeping it age appropriate

Check out any major bookstore these days and you'll find most young adult (YA) fiction in the children's section. I say *most* because the YA category is relatively new to juvenile literature. Before there was a YA designation, books for older children or teens could be found in the general fiction section.

Before the YA era, there were books that appealed to young adults, had main characters who were young adults, and were written in language that young adults could easily understand. Classic novels were published and marketed as fiction that appealed to both adults and children (e.g., *The Member of the Wedding* by Carson McCullers, *The Catcher in the Rye* by J. D. Salinger, *To Kill a Mockingbird* by Harper Lee, *A Separate Peace* by John Knowles, and the entire Tillerman family saga by Cynthia Voigt). For that reason, they could be displayed in both the children's book section and in general fiction, which was confusing and sometimes made them hard to find.

These particular books are still being read and enjoyed by children and adults, but today they are also classified as YA because they meet the following criteria for YA novels:

def•i•ni•tion

Reading level is the degree of difficulty of a book, suggesting the age and grade level of appropriate readers. Most children's books are assigned a reading level.

- The protagonist (the main character) is a young adult.

- The book's subject matter is of interest to young adults or within the experience of young adults; usually placing the protagonist into conflict with the larger world.

- The story is written at the *reading level* of a young adult (i.e., using a young adult's vocabulary).

All these books still appear on required reading lists for kids ranging from the upper grades of elementary school through middle and high school, and even into college. I remember reading *To Kill a Mockingbird* in sixth grade, way before I really understood what it was about or could appreciate the depth of its themes and messages. (And yes, I admit that was before the YA designation existed!)

But wherever and however they may be categorized today, they were all written and marketed to the general reader, young or old.

The YA category was developed as a marketing tool, connoting books written specifically for and about young readers. Don't get me wrong: adults read and enjoy YA books—I gravitate to them myself. Conversely, skilled young readers, whether they're 10 or 18, may read lots of adult fiction.

Pen Pal

Early YA novels (like Paul Zindel's *The Pigman*, Robert Cormier's *The Chocolate Wars*, and Judy Blume's *Forever*) scandalized many readers with their unflinching honesty. Even today, YA authors may find their books criticized—or even banned—for dealing with issues that offend some, but enlighten many.

YA or Adult?

What distinguishes YA fiction from adult fiction? Here are some distinctions:

- Adult fiction about a young person is told by an adult, with an adult's perspective and experience.

- Adult fiction about a young person often has a reminiscent tone, as if looking back on life's memorable moments.

♦ YA fiction is always told by a young adult, with no tinge of adult perspective or experience; instead, teens face adult problems for the first time.

♦ YA fiction contains no reminiscing about the past—unless the young adult protagonist is looking back on his or her own early childhood!

Calling All Bookstores!

Teens read YA novels because they speak to the problems in their lives. Even a light-hearted, escapist fantasy may have underlying themes that deal with young adult concerns such as gaining independence, first love, peer pressure, etc.

It's worth a field trip to your bookstore or library to get an idea of what's available in the YA category. Remember that YA books are generally shelved in the children's book section.

Most major booksellers separate the children's book section into further categories:

♦ Board books/read-aloud books

♦ Picture books

♦ Early readers (ages 6–9)

♦ Middle grades (ages 8–12)

♦ Young adult (ages 12 and up)

There may also be further sections, including mystery, horror, adventure, series books, biography, nonfiction, etc.

But what if the books aren't grouped into convenient categories? There's another way to identify books intended for YA readers.

Jackets, Flaps, and Back Cover Copy

Every word that appears in print on a published book is there for a reason—including any text on the cover.

Hardcover books wrapped with a paper jacket carry important information on the front, back, and inside flaps of the paper jacket that wraps around the book. On paperback books, similar information appears on the front and back covers.

Most children's books, including YAs, designate appropriate reading levels by age or grade somewhere in the *cover copy*.

Although the exact format of the listings may differ, the age range is generally given near the price or UPC code. For example, a book geared toward readers in grade seven and/or ages 12 and up, may use the following formats:

def•i•ni•tion ⎯⎯⎯⎯

> **Cover copy** is any text printed on the cover of paperback or hardcover books. Cover copy includes a blurb, or story summary; tag lines meant to capture attention; age, grade, and/or reading level; and price.

RL7 012+

1214

12–14

12+

Twelve and up

However it's presented, all of these formats indicate the book is ranked at reading level 7—appropriate for an average seventh-grade reader, or for readers ages 12 to 14, or for readers aged 12 and up.

Some YA books for older readers try not to call attention to their category. For instance, my hardcover copy of Chris Crutcher's award-winning novel *Chinese Handcuffs* shows no designated age level on the paper cover. How can you tell that it's YA level?

◆ The cover art shows an illustration of two older teens.

◆ Review excerpts on the back cover declare it "An ALA Best Book for Young Adults"—meaning it's highly rated by the American Library Association and recommended for young adult readers.

◆ In tiny print on the inside front cover flap: Ages 12 up.

The Importance of Reading Level to the YA Writer

Why should writers care about reading level?

Because, unlike adult books, YA books have a narrow focus. Although readers of any age might pick up and enjoy your YA story, your masterpiece will never make it to the editor's desk if you haven't done your research and learned how to write for your target audience. You also need to be aware of changing guidelines in this category. Newer categories in YA fiction include age levels of 10 to 14, and even 15 and up.

Professional writers are aware of their reader every step of the way. They know how to make each story age appropriate from their choice of subject matter to the way they approach the story to the length of their sentences and choice of vocabulary words.

Should that stop you from writing your story at this point, unsure whether it's for 12 and up or 14 and up? No way. You'll hear it now and often throughout this book: write your story first. Use all your enthusiasm and passion to get your ideas and characters down on paper.

I've seen entire manuscripts written before the author is sure about the protagonist's age. Or maybe the writer starts out exploring a subject from one character's point of view (POV) but then decides to take a more demanding approach and switch to another character's POV. Don't worry! Get your story down any way you can for your first draft and make adjustments later—that's what revising is for!

 Slush Pile! _____

Child development manuals and books on child (and teen) psychology usually list the main concerns of each individual age group. The specific conflict you create for your YA protagonist should reflect that character's place in the world: younger teens are still focused on themselves and conflicts closer to home. Older teens who drive, date, and work enter into conflicts within a broader sphere, reflecting their wider range of experience and responsibility.

Genres and Genders in Brief

The same genres that exist in mainstream literature exist in the YA category: mystery, romance, adventure, fantasy, science fiction, historical fiction, and the whole range of nonfiction topics.

What's different about YA genre books?

Simply that they must combine the conventions and concerns of their particular genre with the conventions and concerns of YA fiction. Above all, they must be age appropriate.

For instance, a YA romance follows the general pattern of an adult romance: attraction, complication, understanding, resolution. But within that broad form, the characters act, think, and speak according to their own age and experience.

Make it a historical romance and you must add authentic period details and make sure your characters conform to the social standards of the day.

If you're interested in writing within a specific genre, do your research about the genre form. Read mainstream mysteries or historical fiction; choose from the wealth of how-to writing books on science fiction or fantasy. Get to know your genre and how it affects plot, characters, and story structure—and then read a few YA novels in the same genre. Know the blueprint of your chosen genre and put your young characters into that format.

Genders: The Truth About Girls and Boys

Some of the traditional separation between books is disappearing, but for years books were thought to be either "girls" books or "boys" books. And there was very little crossover. (Think Nancy Drew vs. the Hardy Boys.)

Nowadays, juvenile bestsellers may be designed to appeal to both male and female readers (Harry Potter books; the Lemony Snicket series). Still, it's long been an accepted convention that girls will read boys' books, but boys won't read girls' books. If you really care about who reads your book, adjust accordingly!

The Golden Age Rule

Similarly, it's another accepted convention that young readers only read about characters their own age or older. It is true that the age of your main character has a hand in deciding who your reader will be. Younger kids always want to read about characters their own age or older.

Conventional wisdom has it that young adults won't read about younger characters—but there are exceptions. Harry Potter and Winnie the Pooh have reached cult status with the college crowd! And I've known teens who read and reread favorite middle-grade stories while also sampling YA and adult fiction. Still, if you want to enlarge your reading audience, make your main character as old as you can without destroying your credibility.

 Slush Pile!

If your subject really pertains to a 12- or 13-year-old, don't make your main character 18 in an attempt to capture a larger audience. YA readers can sense when they're being misled, and they'll stay away in droves.

Exceptions to the golden age rule are books written about older characters but aimed at younger readers. The Nancy Drew books are a good example: although Nancy and her friends are college age, the stories are geared toward the average 10-year-old reader. So feel free to break the rule as long as you understand why you're doing it and it makes sense for your particular story.

Getting Technical About Reading Levels

How do you know whether your writing is at the right level?

There are two ways to approach this problem.

- ◆ **By instinct.** Read books similar in content and structure to the book you want to write. Get a feeling for how they sound, the level of vocabulary words, and the complexity of structure.

- ◆ **By research.** Get help from teachers and librarians who may be able to get you copies of curriculum standards for specific grades. Although standards differ somewhat state by state, they all offer a wealth of information on the skills you can expect your readers to have at different grade levels.

Here's a sampling of one state's high-school reading curriculum standards:

- ◆ Students will be able to make inferences, make and support predictions, and analyze cause-and-effect relationships.

- ◆ Students will understand the use of story elements and their relationship to the meaning of the text (e.g., plot, mood, tone, POV, climax, and conflict).

- ◆ Students will apply word analysis and knowledge of word origins and word relationships to determine word meaning in literary texts; analyze idioms, dialect, word origins, analogies, and denotative and connotative meanings and their effect on the text.

Keeping It on the Level

Whether your approach is instinctive, technical, or both, all that really matters is how you use the information you gather.

You may have thought that content determined reading level. Not so. It's the way content is handled that matters. The older the target age group, the more demanding your text can be.

Confused? Let's look at a writing sample that contains the same basic information, modified for three distinct reading levels:

Picture-book level: *The sky was dark. The clouds were gray. Rain was on the way!*

Middle-grade level: *Molly shivered. Gray clouds filled the sky overhead. Would she make it home ahead of the rain?*

YA level: *With one hand, Molly gathered the collar of her flimsy coat tighter around her neck. Glancing apprehensively at the thickening storm clouds, she willed herself to move faster, ignoring the pain from her too-tight, hand-me-down shoes.*

Each version is progressively more sophisticated, matching the reading abilities of the intended age group:

◆ Sentences become longer and more complex.

◆ Vocabulary, although still age appropriate, becomes more sophisticated.

◆ Descriptions become more detailed; sensory information is added.

◆ Emotions and inner thoughts are introduced.

The simple declarative sentences of the picture-book version are one-dimensional.

Slush Pile! _____

Make sure your YA story uses all the age-appropriate story elements. Err on the side of simplicity, and you're writing a children's book. Err by writing from a too-experienced perspective, and you'll end up with an adult novel about a young character.

The middle-grade version offers descriptive details, shows cause and effect, and assumes the reader can make suppositions about what might happen next.

The complex prose of the YA version gives input of a more sensory nature. Take another look at the high school curriculum standards; see how they're put into action in the YA passage: no longer just a statement of facts, the YA version assumes the reader can assimilate impressions, anticipate consequences, attach a variety of emotions to physical conditions, make more-speculative inferences about cause and effect, and endure suspense.

How Far Can You Go?

Students always ask what subjects are taboo in YA books. The truth is, no subject is off limits. How you handle a topic determines how acceptable it is to publishers, booksellers, teachers, librarians, and readers.

In the '70s, "problem" books took hold of the YA market, and subjects that were previously taboo appeared in print for the first time. Suddenly books were exploring topics such as teen pregnancy, cliques, and blended families. Since then, YA books have kept pace with society and the media. Nowadays it's not only possible to find gay literature for teens, and ethnicity-based stories such as Latino and African American literature, but also books dealing with rape, incest, adultery, stalkers, terrorists—the whole range of human experience, horrific or not.

No manuscript will be rejected simply because of its subject matter, as long as that subject matter is handled with sensitivity, discretion, and integrity. Editors look for manuscripts with strong characterization, good dialogue, and a plot with honesty, believability, and authenticity—elements that will help make that sale.

Always remember that YA readers are unique. They have the option of choosing to read adult literature, to regress to childhood favorites, or to choose your YA novel. And despite the ways in which YA books differ from children's books and adult novels, there's one very important way in which they are all the same.

What could that possibly be?

The essentials, dear readers: a beginning, a middle, and an end.

> **Pen Pal**
>
> It might take a few tries to find your own YA voice. Choose a memorable event from your teen years, and try to describe the situation as if you were writing at the time it occurred.

The Least You Need to Know

- Before there was a YA category, there were books for and about young adults that remain classics today.

- A YA protagonist, subjects of particular interest to teens, and age-appropriate writing determines whether your book is a YA novel.

- Take time to familiarize yourself with publishing industry guidelines for age and reading levels.

- Don't be afraid to research curriculum guides, question teachers and parents, and spend time with teens to learn their concerns.

- If you approach your topic with integrity and sensitivity, no subject is taboo.

Chapter 2

Taking the Plunge: How to Begin

In This Chapter

- ◆ Facing the blank page without panic
- ◆ Creating character, conflict, and plot
- ◆ External vs. internal conflict
- ◆ Using conflicts to bring plots to life

Once upon a time, there was a writer who wanted to tell a story. This writer wasn't exactly sure which story to tell or exactly how to tell it. To be perfectly honest, the writer wasn't even sure there was a story worth telling. We've all been there.

Nothing is more intimidating than an unwritten story. The blank page (or the empty computer screen) is frightening to behold. Where do you begin? How do you convey the idea that caught your imagination? This chapter will help you get started.

Storytelling, or Story Writing?

Some people advise you to approach a written story the same way as you would when telling a story. But nothing is further from the truth. Telling a story is intuitive—writing down a story is another thing entirely.

Storytelling is fluid and organic; you see your audience and respond to it. You adjust your tone, your manner, even the details of the tale to suit the mood of your listeners. You might change your mind midsentence and go off in another direction; embellish the tale one day, but the next day you tell the same story starkly. Try to write down the same story, however, and everything changes.

You have no idea who your audience will be or what mood they'll be in when they read your work. There will be no instant feedback and no adjusting the telling to suit the reader. The story will no longer have an enchanting, shape-shifting form; committed to the page, it will remain the same each and every time someone reads it.

That's a scary thought, and a good reason for learning the craft of writing. I can't teach you to have an imagination; no one can. But I can teach you the tools of the writing trade so that you'll be able to get that story down on the page just the way you imagined it, enchantment and all.

The Blank Page

This chapter will launch you on your writing journey by starting at the beginning, with the three basic tools every writer must have: character, conflict, and plot.

Any number of how-to-write books will tell you that all stories spring from character. An equal number will declare that character comes from plot.

Pen Pal

All stories are built with the same basic building blocks: character, conflict, and plot, shaped into a beginning, middle, and end.

Truth is, it's a chicken-or-egg question: there is no definitive answer. And it doesn't matter.

In actual practice, the basic elements end up working together: character creates conflict, character suggests plot, conflict feeds back into character, which leads to plot.

That said, we have to begin somewhere, so we'll start with my personal favorite: character.

What Is Character?

Characters are the people who live in your story. Without characters, how would you begin to tell a tale? A girl, a boy, a dog, a fish, a stone … it all begins with a character—hopefully, a memorable one.

Character also refers to those traits (characteristics) that define the morals, attitude, and strengths and weaknesses of any individual.

In real life, a person's character is a multifaceted, often contradictory thing, formed from a swarming confluence of experience, environment, and personality, and tempered by learned beliefs, values, and behaviors. In fiction, however, you must decide which traits are necessary to your particular character in your particular story. And it doesn't matter whether the character is Cinderella trying to get to the ball, Hannibal Lecter in search of a good meal, Harry Potter out to vanquish Voldemort, or Peter Rabbit intent on escaping the wrath of Mr. McGregor. What matters in fiction is the way you use character to set up conflict.

Pen Pal

Character refers both to the people (characters) who fill your stories and to the essential traits (characteristics) that make each person a unique individual.

There is much, much more to say about characterization, but because it becomes so inextricably tied to conflict and plot, let's deal with it in relation to those elements first.

What Is Conflict?

Conflict is the stuff that drama is made of and it is central to every story. Without conflict, every day would be fine, every experience pleasant, and every person your friend. With conflict, each day becomes an unknown adventure, each experience fraught with danger, mystery, and endless possibility: in an instant, friend turns to foe.

Conflicts may be funny, exciting, frustrating, painful, excruciating, and even deadly—but never boring. Conflict results in struggle and strife of one kind or another and, more important, a well-constructed conflict becomes a rich source of plot events and scene ideas. In other words, conflict gives your characters something to do. Without it, they're like actors onstage with no lines to speak.

Pen Pal

Conflict is the fuel that propels the plot. Without it, your characters would have nothing to do.

Types of Conflict: Internal vs. External

Whenever there is disagreement or choice, conflict occurs. The source of the conflict determines whether it is internal or external.

Internal conflicts spring from moral dilemmas and personal quandaries. Often they cause inaction until the character can decide how to act. Here are some examples of internal conflict:

- Two teens befriend a lonely old man who makes his house their own. Are they taking advantage of him or making him happy? (*The Pigman* by Paul Zindel)

- A boy learns a shocking truth about his utopian community: imperfect children, like his new baby brother, are marked for termination. Can he let them destroy his brother or risk escaping into the unknown, outside world? (*The Giver* by Lois Lowry)

- An abused teen swears her best friend to secrecy. Should he remain silent or betray her trust in order to save her? (*Chinese Handcuffs* by Chris Crutcher)

External conflicts spring from outside factors—people or circumstances that force a character to take some kind of action. Here are some examples of external conflict:

- A boy sees his parents killed in an explosion. Traumatized and hospitalized, he's regularly interrogated by … a doctor? Or a government agent? Learning the truth might set him free—or drive him deeper into insanity. (*I Am the Cheese* by Robert Cormier)

- Abandoned by their mother, the oldest girl wants to keep her brothers and sisters together. The state wants to put them into separate foster homes. Can she shoulder the impossible burden of finding them a home? (*Homecoming* by Cynthia Voigt)

- Wrongly convicted of a crime, a boy yearning to prove his innocence must choose between friendship and self-preservation. (*Holes* by Louis Sachar)

Pen Pal

In well-crafted stories, big, overall plot conflicts have echoes in smaller subplots, every aspect of the story working together to create maximum story impact.

To be honest, I had to work hard to focus on a single conflict from each of these books. In fact, every one of them contains layers of conflicts: big, overall conflicts that drive the main plot; smaller conflicts that create subplots; and the kind of endless, tiny, everyday conflicts that fill our days and nights. And, inevitably, all the conflicts mingle and mix and make it hard to tell where internal ends and external begins, and vice versa.

Case study: *Chinese Handcuffs*

Things beyond his control are happening all around Dillon Hemenway. His life is a litany of loss—his mother abandoned his family. His older brother, adjusting to losing both legs in an accident, killed himself with Dillon watching, and Dillon is still recovering from the shock. He has romance problems with a fellow athlete, Jen, who starts pulling away just when Dillon wants them to get closer, leaving him feeling as if he's losing his best friend. He's in trouble with the school principal, who hates him for refusing to join a school team. His father is withdrawn and ineffectual, and a vicious motorcycle gang is after him.

There are plenty of subplots and complications in this melodramatic story, and Dillon, like Louise, faces them with self-righteous anger. It seems as if everyone in his life harbors dark secrets, and as Dillon attempts to unravel them, he uncovers a sickening history of abuse; abuse that's both done by, and done to, the people he loves.

But all these extreme events are foisted on Dillon by other people—the result of external conflicts. Dillon's character—pugnacious, obstinate, headstrong, caring, loyal, and blunt—has nothing to do with creating the situations he must face. His character is a factor in the story, as the source of the strength to handle crisis after crisis, and his character also influences the ending of the story, when Dillon must decide whether to keep Jen's secret or tell about the abuse in order to help her.

 Pen Pal _____

A special relationship exists between your characters and your story. When you begin writing, you arrange conflicts and orchestrate plot events. At some point, your characters take over and begin to create conflicts of their own.

In fact, Dillon does choose to tell about Jen in order to stop her suffering—even though he knows that she'll never be his girlfriend if he betrays her trust. With help, he devises a complicated plan to blackmail Jen's abusive stepfather to get him out of town (and keep him from preying on her younger sister). His character compels him to opt for compassion over selfishness. To help Jen, he must sacrifice what he wants the most: her.

This critical decision is just one of several internal conflicts Dillon faces throughout the story. It's clearly a pivotal conflict, but because it appears so late in the book it can't propel the plot. True to form, this internal conflict serves to deepen the complexity of the plot, but it does little to create plot events.

Creating External Actions for Internal Conflicts

It's easy to create situations as internal conflicts. Often you have the idea for the situation before you know what to do with it. But see how these interesting dilemmas, when posed as internal conflicts, soon become dreary:

♦ A bully attacks you. You ponder what to do about it.

♦ You get fired from your first job—and sit in your room, moping.

♦ Your car blows a tire, making you late to get your parents at the airport. You wait in the car for help to come.

So what do you do with these ideas to make them work for you and your plot? You find external actions to give the internal conflicts immediate, dramatic plot opportunities:

♦ A bully attacks you; you fight, or run—but you take some action.

♦ You get fired from your first job—you immediately look for another, or you file a complaint, or you write a fantastic letter to your local paper and end up getting a job there—but you take some action.

♦ Your car blows a tire, making you late to get your parents at the airport. You flag down a passing cab, stay with the car until a tow truck comes and page your parents, or abandon the car and hitch to the airport ... wise or foolish, you take some action.

Pen Pal

Actions lead to actions and plot developments. As your story progresses, make sure to look for opportunities to make internal conflicts into external actions.

The point is that you must make every event as active as possible to keep your plot moving and to keep your reader interested. When you choose an action—any action—for your character, it immediately leads to another possible action.

For instance, take the last example. Suppose your character flags down a passing cab ... is the cab empty? If not, who's in it? An accountant? A rock star? What do they do to help? Or not to help? Do they become an important figure in the story, etc.?

Acting Up

To put it even more bluntly, a character may face a gut-wrenching, life-changing moral decision—but how many pages can you write about that? How many pages could anyone stand to read about it? A character agonizing over a moral dilemma is, essentially, a passive activity—not something memorable scenes are made of.

Although internal conflicts may be critical to your overall story, by, say, illustrating a person's character, or suggesting how he might act, they do little to forward the plot on their own. So how do you dramatize internal conflicts? By creating external conflicts that represent your moral dilemma.

Stories work best when there are flesh-and-blood antagonists who come into direct conflict with your protagonist. It's fine to create characters with strong opinions and moral indignation—as long as they get into trouble expressing those opinions at the wrong time and place or to the wrong person. If your impulse is to write about a teen bucking the system, or questioning society's conventions, you need to create a suitable antagonist to represent the other side of the story.

Pen Pal _____

Abstract, moral, or philosophical dilemmas are essentially passive—and hard to write about. But create a dynamic character to represent the dilemma and you give yourself a rich source of plot events.

What Is a Plot?

My dictionary has more than a dozen definitions for *plot* and a surprising number of them make references to evil schemes—as in "plot to overthrow the government." My definition of plot is more benign: a planned sequence of events leading up to a resolution. (I can hear some of you protesting that not all stories have a tidy resolution, but I'd counter that even unresolved endings can be part of an overall plan.)

def•i•ni•tion _____

Plot is a planned sequence of events leading up to a resolution.

Let's depart from YA for a minute to take a look at a classic children's picture book.

Picture books—especially the classics—are great for studying plot because they feature simply constructed stories without distracting subplots and a clearly recognizable beginning, middle, and end. With their swift characterizations and straightforward conflicts, it's possible to examine the complete structure of a picture book in a few paragraphs.

Case study: *Ferdinand the Bull*

This beloved story by Munro Leaf is a beautiful example of character combined with external conflict to set the plot into motion.

The story: Ferdinand, a young bull in Spain, wants only to laze around the meadow and smell the flowers. He's laid back, sweet natured, and essentially passive. One day, Ferdinand's idyll is interrupted by a group of bullfight promoters searching for the perfect bull for their next bullfight.

They ignore Ferdinand until he sits on a bee. Stung, Ferdinand leaps into the air, bucking and kicking and snorting wildly. Thinking they've found the fiercest bull around, the promoters hastily transport Ferdinand to the city to prepare him for the ring.

The big day arrives; the packed stadium bursts with people anxious to see the vicious Ferdinand. Enter the matador, fearing for his life. Excitedly, the ladies in the crowd toss roses at the matador. Ferdinand takes one look—then ignores the matador and settles down to sniff the flowers, thereupon completely ruining the bullfight (and the careers of the greedy promoters).

Ferdinand is sent home in disgrace, but he could care less; all he wanted was to stay home and smell the flowers, and he gets exactly what he wanted.

Here's how external conflict makes this plot spring to life:

1. Main character Ferdinand is established as placid and gentle, wanting only to be left alone to smell the roses. There is no conflict in his life.

2. Greedy promoter antagonists appear, creating conflict when they mistakenly assume Ferdinand to be a fierce fighter who will attract record crowds.

3. The promoters' plans are foiled when Ferdinand's true nature is revealed. The bullfight is a disaster; Ferdinand happily returns home.

Conflict is inflicted upon Ferdinand, who remains essentially passive throughout. In fact, the charm and humor of the story spring from the promoters' misunderstanding of Ferdinand's essential nature. Their mounting frustration is funny because the reader knows all along that what they expect is impossible: Ferdinand's character makes him incapable of doing what they want.

The difference between the plot of a YA and a picture book is obvious: picture-book plots are simple and direct; YA plots can be as sophisticated or complex as you like, with multiple main characters and any number of minor characters with subplots of their own. Yet the truth is, plot ideas are simply the basic blueprint for any level of story. You can adjust the complexity of its structure to suit your audience.

Ferdinand the Bull as a YA novel

Let's see what happens if we take the exact same plot steps as outlined for Ferdinand but change the protagonist to a teenage boy:

1. Main character Fernando is established as a placid and gentle boy who wants only to be left alone to play video games. There is no conflict in his life.

2. Greedy video game developers appear, creating conflict when they mistakenly assume Fernando to be a competitive player who will represent their products at an upcoming convention, hopefully attracting record crowds.

3. The promoters' plans are foiled when Fernando's true nature is revealed (he ignores the throngs of interested conventioneers). The convention is a disaster; Fernando happily returns home.

To make this story long enough to fill the 200+ pages of a typical YA novel, you might need to throw in a subplot or two, and you'll definitely need to develop many plot events. But the core plot of the story remains exactly the same.

Different Covers, Same Book

Interestingly, this basic plot is not terribly different from the plot of Jerzy Kosinski's controversial 1971 adult novel *Being There*, which was made into a 1979 movie starring Peter Sellers. The plot goes roughly like this …

Through a series of comical mix-ups, a simple-minded gardener named Chance, raised largely by watching television, is perceived as a wise, distinguished, and worldly gentleman named Chauncey Gardiner.

Chance's cryptic statements elevate him to the status of a national prophet, a trusted advisor to the president of the United States, and a possible presidential candidate himself. Amid the media frenzy surrounding him, no one stops to consider the fact that his deceptively simple-minded pronouncements are, in fact, the statements of a simpleton.

Kosinski's novel is deeply satirical, and you could summarize its message as "people believe what they want to believe."

In each case, the fact that important characters believe the wrong thing leads to the plot complications. My point is that the same plot that serves an adult book can serve a children's book or a YA novel. The level is determined by the embellishments, not the core plot structure.

Now that we have an understanding of how plots work, it's time to start actively building a story.

Creating Internal and External Conflict

Go to your own bookshelf, the library, or a bookstore. Pull out YA titles—hopefully, some from books you've already read—and, reading the cover blurbs, identify the internal and external conflicts.

Find a quiet space to work. Begin by rewriting one or two of the blurbs with different characters, using the same or similar conflicts.

Finally, create different external conflicts for your new characters. Combine the elements into a story blurb of your own.

Here's a melodramatic example of what I mean.

Cover blurb:

Luke has always been known as a "bad boy"—but meeting Bernadette changes everything. For the first time in his life, Luke understands the urge to put someone else's needs first. And what Bernie needs is to get away from her narrow-minded, oppressive, overbearing father.

But when Luke rescues Bernie, everything goes wrong. Now Bernie's dad is hospitalized, fighting for his life. Will Bernie hate him forever? There's no chance to worry about that now, because Luke and Bernie are on the run, in the biggest trouble of their young lives.

Internal conflicts:

Luke is bad but wants to be good.

Bernie loves her dad, but she also loves Luke.

External conflicts:

Luke hurts Bernie's father.

Luke and Bernie are in trouble with the law.

Here are the same internal conflicts, rewritten for different characters. Luke becomes Lisa. Bernie becomes Brandon:

Lisa is bad but wants to be good.

Brandon loves his family, but he also loves Lisa.

Here are the external conflicts, rewritten:

Lisa steals money from her parents to buy Brandon a hot car.

Brandon crashes the car, and then learns about the stolen money.

Lisa didn't know it, but the car was stolen. Now Lisa and Brandon are in double trouble.

Here's how the new blurb might be written:

Lisa would do anything to get Brandon's love—even buy it, if she can. Desperate, Lisa steals money from her parents to buy Brandon a hot car, but when he learns Lisa stole the money to buy it, will he still want Lisa?

Before she can find out, Brandon crashes the car—and they both learn the car was stolen. Now Lisa and Brandon are in double trouble—with each other, and the law.

The Least You Need to Know

- ◆ Conflict is at the core of all successful fiction.
- ◆ Conflicts can be internal or external.
- ◆ External conflicts are more useful for creating plots.
- ◆ You can convert internal conflicts into external actions.

Plots in a Nutshell

In This Chapter

- How to create an instant plot
- Using the plot formula
- Creating big stories from small conflicts
- Think personal and specific

You've seen that whether central conflicts are internal or external, they both fit into similar plot structures. That's because any basic plot is composed of the same four simple elements:

1. A main character (the protagonist)
2. A "villain" (the antagonist)
3. Conflict (the plot events)
4. Resolution

In this chapter, you learn how to use those four elements to form a story idea into an instant plot by using a simple plot formula. Remember, the details of your story separate it from every other story. Just as two houses might share the same inner structure but look completely different from the outside, quite different stories can be built on the same foundation.

The Formula for a Workable, Instant Plot

Your first job is to get your four basic elements straight. Don't laugh: it's harder than it seems (because your second job is to take those four elements and rephrase them so there is enough action in your basic idea to turn it into an instant plot):

1. Hero needs A.

2. Villain needs B.

3. Conflict erupts (plot events).

4. Conflict resolves.

I know it sounds obvious, or simplistic, but the more active your basic story idea or premise, the easier it is to create enough plot events to make your story work.

Restating the formula as actions rather than things has a profound impact on your thinking, and will let you know whether your instant plot is worthy of becoming a workable plot. If it helps, you might also make those four statements into questions:

1. What does my hero want or need?

2. What does my villain want or need?

3. What could happen as a result of their conflicting needs?

4. How would it all end?

Slush Pile!

Take your time at the planning stage! It's easier to fix basic plot problems now than to revise a completed manuscript that was built on a shaky foundation.

You'd be surprised how often people think they have a foolproof story idea, but can't answer these simple questions. In fact, I've seen completed manuscripts (and sometimes printed books) in which those underlying questions aren't clearly answered. When that happens, you end up with a story that may have countless strong points and accomplishments but doesn't quite fly the way it should. Or you may end up with a total mess. It's a lot easier to work out your basic plot points at the earliest stage than to force a whole manuscript into a shape it never had.

The Instant Plot Formula at Work

Let's look again at the condensed plot summaries I used to define internal and external conflicts. With a little tweaking, you can see how they work according to the instant plot formula.

The Pigman by Paul Zindel

Conflict summary: Two teens befriend a lonely old man who makes his house their own. Are they taking advantage of him or making him happy?

Plot formula:

1. John and Lorraine, two teens from repressive families, need a place to call their own.

2. Grieving and aging Mr. Pignati (the Pigman) needs to fill the gap left in his life when his wife died.

3. The three form an odd family until John and Lorraine betray the Pigman. Heartbroken, he suffers a heart attack and dies.

4. John and Lorraine realize they can't blame this one on their parents; their own actions have consequences, and it's time they take control of their lives.

The Giver by Lois Lowry

Conflict summary: A boy learns a shocking truth about his utopian community: imperfect children, like his new baby brother, are marked for termination. Can he let the child be destroyed or risk escape into the unknown, outside world?

Plot formula:

1. At his "turning-12 ceremony," Jonas hopes for a good job—the right job—as he begins preparing for his future in a seemingly perfect community.

2. The community appoints Jonas the new Receiver of Memories.

3. Learning what his job entails, Jonas uncovers disturbing truths about his society's hypocrisies. Should he stay, or escape with his baby brother?

4. Jonas chooses to save his brother's life and, escaping with the boy to an uncertain future, strikes out on his own.

I Am the Cheese by Robert Cormier

Conflict summary: A boy sees his parents killed in an explosion. Traumatized and hospitalized, he's regularly interrogated by ... a doctor? Or a government agent? Learning the truth might set him free—or drive him deeper into insanity.

Plot formula:

1. Adam Farmer wants to visit his father in the hospital but can't break through his hazy memories to learn the truth—is his father already dead?

2. The man who questions him wants to pick Adam's brain about his parents.

3. Though Adam also wants to fill in the blanks of his life, he senses his interrogator might be an enemy.

4. Adam is trapped in his past—and in his mind, endlessly cycling to a destination he'll never reach.

Homecoming by Cynthia Voigt

Conflict summary: Abandoned by their mother, the oldest girl in the family wants to keep her brothers and sisters together. The state wants to put them into separate foster homes. Can she shoulder the impossible burden of finding them a home?

Plot formula:

1. Dicey Tillerman needs to get her three siblings to the safety of a relative's house.

2. The state wants to put the children into foster homes.

3. Will Dicey be able to keep them safe and sound on their long walk from Cape Cod to Maryland?

4. After many adventures, Dicey finds their grandmother and slowly convinces her to take them in.

Holes by Louis Sachar

Conflict summary: Wrongly convicted of a crime, a boy yearning to prove his innocence must choose between friendship and self-preservation.

Plot formula:

1. Stanley Yelnats needs to prove his innocence so he can get out of the youth detention camp.

2. The warden needs the campers to keep digging holes.

3. Overcoming his fears, Stanley gets closer to fellow camper Zero and discovers the real reason for digging the holes—and the connection between his family and Zero's.

4. Stanley exposes the warden, ends the curse on his family, and is reunited with his parents.

Of course, these plots are being summarized from completed books; a very different experience from using the formula to create a plot from scratch. Finished plots from finished books are much more complex than the bare-bones formula they begin with. Writing these conflict summaries proved the point: a few of the finished stories had plots that were so complex they couldn't be reduced to simple terms, so I had to leave them out. Even the books that I wrote conflict summaries for had many more plot elements than are listed here; it was often hard to figure out which elements were the most important.

That's because the finished plot of a typical YA novel has multiple layers of plot and subplot, and there are, inevitably, more story events than you could possibly note in a summary. It also shows that when you're beginning your story you can't possibly predict all the events that will happen along the way.

Trouble with Specific Conflicts

Here's a dilemma that students often ask me about: "I'm having a hard time creating an appropriate conflict for my character, Maxie (13). There are too many choices! Her family, her age, her size, her ego, school … help!"

This student was working from a character exercise and had no trouble writing perceptive descriptions of Maxie at various stages in her life. She wanted to create an instant plot for a funny book for a younger YA audience. Her writing showed a lively imagination, and she'd created some situations for Maxie that were both believable and hilarious. Yet she was totally bogged down at taking the next step.

She was having a typical new-writer problem; she had trouble creating a plot conflict because she was thinking too large. She needed to bring her character's conflict down to a manageable size and keep it age dependent.

Maxie was basically a good kid, but impulsive—the kind of girl who got herself into one funny scrape after another. We needed to create one overall conflict that could last throughout the book while other funny incidents were going on. Because Maxie was the type who meant to be good, it was important to show her getting into trouble for a good reason—in other words, we needed a setup showing that Maxie had the best of intentions, but outside forces made her act badly.

We decided to make Maxie do something forbidden. At 13, she was too young to drive, but she could get in trouble because of … a bicycle. Suppose she needed a bike to get somewhere in a hurry—say, in time to compete in a game, give an audition, perform in a school play, bring her best friend the money to buy a concert ticket …. Whatever it was, Maxie would do it to keep a promise or help a friend.

The particulars really didn't matter yet; brainstorming was more important. So we decided that Maxie didn't have a bike; maybe she'd had one, maybe she was totally into off-track racing, but crashed her bike and was on probation to show she could care for the really expensive replacement she wanted. So maybe she had to borrow a bike … and then was caught and accused of stealing it. That's an example of an age-appropriate need and a conflict big enough to lead to some meaningful consequences.

Maybe the bike belonged to a kid who turned around and blackmailed Maxie; or maybe he'd stolen it in the first place. Or maybe it was Maxie's bike, but she'd been grounded for smashing into another kid's bike … or for failing her English final … or forgetting to have her parent sign a discipline report from school … see how the ideas start flowing?

If Maxie were an older teen, you could use a similar setup, adjust the need accordingly, and maybe, instead of a bike, have her borrow a car to stop her best friend from going to an older guy's apartment, or race to catch a bus that's bringing her friend to an unwise rendezvous. Or maybe she forges a check when her friend needs money, or shoplifts on a dare—whatever she does, she'll have to face much more dire consequences, appropriate to her age.

Slush Pile!

Your story needs flesh-and-blood antagonists. A teen may rail against society, but society can't have an argument with your protagonist. Create a character to represent society's injustices.

Trouble with Overall Messages

Here's another concern I'm often asked about: "My character is an older teen fighting against racial prejudice after a terrorist attack. I know the big, overall message I want to send, but I'm having trouble coming up with smaller conflicts for plot events."

When doing instant plots, students often say that the protagonist's enemy is society, or bigotry, or that "nobody will listen to her," etc.

Trouble is, in a story or book, "society" needs to have some dialogue with the main character! Which is why I always say you need to construct flesh-and-blood antagonists, even if they are there to represent all of society, or bigotry, or bullying behavior, etc.

What I like to see is an antagonist who forces a conflict, who creates an event that makes trouble for the main character. When both characters are launched into the plot, make sure that the original conflict leads to some specific consequences.

Plot Do's and Don'ts

It is always easier, more dramatic, and more effective to write about specifics than about general ideas. The best specifics are related to …

♦ A specific person.

♦ A specific event.

Specifically, don't construct a plot based on a general premise:

♦ A boy is constantly thwarted by society.

♦ Girl genius can't fit into her family or school.

♦ Girl in foster care tries to find love in all the wrong ways.

> **Ink Spot**
>
> The man who writes about himself and his own time is the man who writes about all people and all time.
>
> —George Bernard Shaw

Do construct a plot based on specifics:

♦ A high-school boy wants to run for political office despite the fact that no teen has ever run before.

♦ Girl genius who can't fit into her family or school gets involved with people who accept and admire her; but are they actually luring her into a cult?

♦ Lonely girl in foster care tries to get a young caseworker to marry her.

None of these, by the way, are taken from existing stories, so don't bother looking for them in your local library.

Does Your Story Fit a Category?

Although I just got through telling you to be specific, lots of stories can fit into general categories:

- A coming-of-age story

- A buddy story in which two enemies learn to love and respect one another

- A relationship story in which a misunderstood teen finds a surprising mentor and reconciles with her family

There's nothing wrong with writing another book that falls within a plot category. No one expects you to create an entirely new category—and it isn't necessary. The best stories comfortably fit within the existing categories.

The Pigman, for instance, is another coming-of-age story in which unhappy teens create a surrogate family. But in this particular story, the head of their new family dies, "murdered" by their unintended callowness.

You could categorize *The Catcher in the Rye*, J. D. Salinger's long-lived classic, as another coming-of-age story. And although the impact of the once-shocking language has certainly diminished with the years, the wonderful quirkiness of the language and Holden Caulfield's character continue to draw readers into the story.

Pen Pal _____

The smaller and more focused your story idea is, the easier it will be for you to create situations and characters for your plot.

"Boy Fights Society" is a perfectly valid starting point, but it gives you absolutely no direction for creating characters or plot events. Create Henry Mason, an idealist with a stubborn streak, and pit him against the well-respected but smug, bullying owner of a local store with a large workforce, and you can begin imagining scenes and events.

Similarly, "Misfit Yearns to Fit In" is an entirely valid premise, yet offers you nothing to create a story from. But create a protagonist with a specific problem (Alita Jefferson with a terrible lisp), and an antagonist you can love to hate (Ernest, the needy, arrogant school tyrant), and you can begin to define your heroine's character, devise scenes that show Alita suffering because of her lisp, give her a best friend who tries to help, and maybe a surprising ally, who delights in thwarting Ernest at every turn.

When you create a best friend, ally, or enemy, your main character has someone to talk to and argue with, so you can write exciting, funny, and poignant dialogue instead of relying on endless narrative or exposition. And that means you can show us the story instead of explaining it to us.

Create an antagonist who represents society, or family, or the idea of any obstacle at all, and you also begin to create a fascinating character that your protagonist can argue and fight with.

Pen Pal

Exposition is that part of a story which sets forth or explains things to the reader—as opposed to dramatization, which shows information through dialogue.

Create any two specific characters and one or two plot events, and your story can begin to develop pacing, and dramatic highpoints, and twists and turns, and suspense, and ultimately a fabulous climax.

How Specifics Lead to Plots

You may be wondering why I'd say that generalities are bad, but generic story ideas aren't so bad. That's because you can create specifics within a generic idea to create plot events. As is, a generic story line can make a perfectly valid story premise, but without specifics, it gives you nothing to create a story from.

- ◆ Misfit yearns to fit in = dead-end premise
- ◆ Alita Jefferson learns to speak without a lisp in time to win the school debate, defeating rival Earnest Threadhole, the school tyrant = beginning of a plot

With specifics, you get …

- ◆ A heroine whose character you can begin to define.
- ◆ Plot ideas to show Alita suffering because of her lisp.
- ◆ A friend you can create to help Alita overcome the lisp.
- ◆ A worthy antagonist who will try to thwart her at every turn.

Specifics Bring Conflicts to Life

Using specific plot ideas makes a generic story fresh. By adding specifics, you can create suspense; develop pacing; and add dramatic highpoints, twists, and turns to your plot. And, ultimately, adding specifics will lead to plot events that lead to your fabulous climax.

◆ Create a specific event that encapsulates your conflict, and you can develop plot ideas.

◆ Create a friend or ally for your main character to talk to, and you can write exciting, funny, poignant dialogue instead of long, boring narrative passages.

◆ Create an antagonist who represents society, or family, or the idea of any obstacle at all, and you also can begin to create a fascinating foil who brings your protagonist to life.

And that means you can show us the story instead of explaining it to us.

So take another look at your own story ideas and find opportunities to make them entirely specific.

Small Stories Deliver Big Messages

Don't be afraid to scale back; think personal and specific. Let's say you create that plot about the owner of a local specific store, his policies of discriminatory hiring, and the effect of those policies on one or two specific people. You will still make your point about discrimination—just on a smaller, more personal scale.

Pen Pal _____

Choose two distinct characters from a memorable event during your teen years and make one the protagonist, the other the antagonist. Create a conflict that reflects the character traits of each one. Use the plot formula to create an instant plot.

Trust your readers: they'll get the idea that one kind of bigotry could very well manifest as another kind of bigotry. You can't be expected to write about all kinds of discrimination in one story—but the discrimination against one specific person in one specific workplace will resonate with your readers as a universal situation, not an isolated incident.

Besides, writing about one specific situation leaves you free to write about another specific situation, perhaps with the same or a similar theme. Just as there's no end to the ways we discriminate against one another, there is no end to the number of stories waiting to be written about them. As long as there are millions of people in the world, there will be millions of stories to tell about them. You won't use up your best ideas in any one story. So don't be afraid to tackle one particular story at a time, starring one very specific character.

The Least You Need to Know

♦ The same basic plot elements are used to begin a story, whether it's funny or serious, for older or younger readers.

♦ Adding active verbs to the plot formula changes a basic idea into an instant plot.

♦ Although YA books may contain multiple plot lines, one main story line runs throughout the book and defines an underlying theme.

♦ Basic story conflicts should relate to character and be age appropriate, with age-appropriate consequences.

♦ Never use general ideas as an antagonist; your main character needs someone to argue with!

♦ Above all, be specific in plot, conflict, and character.

Chapter 4

The Importance of an Active Premise

In This Chapter

- Why your premise should be active
- A method for creating active wants
- How premise turns into plot
- Underlying themes: how to get them and use them

We've talked briefly about taking the four basic story elements and making them more active by expressing them as wants or needs: Protagonist wants A. Antagonist wants B. Conflict erupts. Resolution.

The idea of using active wants, or an active voice, or active verbs, is repeated in almost every writing book I've seen. It covers every aspect of writing, whether it's referring to writing text or dialogue, narration or description. The idea of keeping your writing active is applied to everything from grammar (using verbs instead of nouns) to creating active character motivations and active plot ideas.

I've read books on writing fiction, screenplays, librettos, soap operas, radio plays—you name it. Every single one offers some kind of advice on how to make your writing active rather than passive. If so many accomplished authors feel it's that important an idea, it's worth exploring the idea a little bit more, even at this early stage.

How to Make Nouns and Verbs Work Harder—the Mamet Method

One piece of advice you'll see over and over is to limit your use of adjectives and adverbs. We visit this topic again when we get to Chapter 9 on writing description, but it also has a special meaning when you're just starting to build your story.

Exactly what are all these teachers and writers getting at when they harp on active vs. passive?

- Active words create a sense of excitement.

- Active words create a sense of momentum.

- Active words create conflicts that transform themes into actions.

For me, the explanation that helps the most at this stage of a project comes from playwright and director David Mamet. In his book *On Directing Film*, Mamet goes on at great length about the importance of creating active wants by replacing nouns with verbs:

- "Jack wants a boat" vs. "Jack needs to earn money to buy a boat."

- "Jill wants success" vs. "Jill wants to invest in real estate to become a financial success."

- "George wants a girlfriend" vs. "George wants to fascinate Megan so she'll go out with him."

Mamet happens to be speaking about writing for the screen. Cinematic characters don't have the luxury of time and space to give full descriptions of people, places, and things. Because film is a visual medium, they don't really have to. Filmgoers can see things that a novelist has to convey in written description. It's both a blessing and a curse; unlike their fictional counterparts, film characters can't take page after page to explain themselves to the audience. Things have to keep moving onscreen.

Yet, in a sense, fiction writers are just like film directors. Novelists also cast their characters by creating their background, motivations, and the words they speak. Through description, novelists set the stage and choose props and settings just as carefully as any art director or set designer. Novelists decide how we view each scene, who's in it, and how long it should last, as well as designing the mood, tone, and atmosphere that supports each scene. The list goes on and on.

Mamet's advice is geared toward making the most of each moment of screen time. Well, guess what? Things also have to keep moving on the written page, or your readers get bored. So Mamet advises replacing nouns with verbs as a technique to keep your writing active from the very beginning.

Using Nouns and Verbs for Plot Conflicts

Let's look at one of those sample phrases again:

Jack wants a boat.

The noun (a boat) is what we commonly mistake as a want or need.

What does Jack want?

Why, he wants a shiny new boat.

Seems like a sound enough idea, until you realize that so stated, the phrase implies absolutely no action. And therefore no conflict. In fact, "Jack wants a boat" is a statement, not a story premise.

Now look at this phrase:

Jack wants to earn money to buy a boat.

Replacing the noun with a verb (to earn) implies not only the main action (earning money) but an immediate string of possible events and consequences.

How Premise Turns into Plot

After you create an active situation (Jack trying to earn money), you need to get specific. Creating specifics leads you to an endless string of questions. And asking questions is the first step toward transforming a premise into a plot:

- ◆ How will Jack earn money?
- ◆ Has he ever had a job before?

- Does he have any talents or skills?

- Would he be able to keep a job if he found one?

- Is he incompetent, dishonest, or lazy?

- Is he cursed with such a strong dislike for authority figures that he can't bear working for anyone?

- Does this spring from Jack's frequent conflicts with his overbearing dad?

- Or does it trace back to misunderstandings with teachers over the years, who misinterpreted Jack's hyperactivity as disobedience?

- What are his options?

- What's his background … can his family lend him the money?

- Can his uncle hire him at the used car lot?

- Can his dad find a job for Jack at his office?

- Or is Jack in this world alone … does he even have a family?

Slush Pile!

Watch out for dead-end plot ideas. If your basic premise doesn't lead to endless questions about your character, his background, and his motivations, it's certainly not going to lead you to an effective plot.

When your premise leads to endless questions, you know you've got a workable idea—and a lot to learn about your own character. Which starts you thinking and choosing and developing his specific background and motivations. And that creates endless possible plot events—and develops the story in a way that will help you, not defeat you. All as a result of changing a noun to a verb!

Amazing, isn't it?

Mamet goes one step further: restate your idea, connecting the character's want to the person who is the object of the want, and add the result your character is hoping for.

We'd start with the phrase "Jack needs to earn money to buy a boat" but continue the action:

Jack needs to earn money to buy a boat … so he can win the boat race … thereby earning Ella's admiration.

What you've done now is to change that original, dead-end statement (Jack wants a boat) into an active need, which leads to a motivation, which culminates in the desired consequence of his need. From stating a possible plot idea, you've advanced to the much more productive step of developing an active premise.

Underlying Themes and the Active Premise

Well-respected author Lajos Egri writes extensively about the importance of an active premise in his book *The Art of Dramatic Writing*. Approaching the idea from a slightly different angle than Mamet, Egri stresses the importance of identifying your story's main theme to see whether it's active enough to support a plot.

Egri's point is that it takes more than plot to make a book a lasting success; it should also have a moral purpose, or a meaning bigger and more resonant than the actual plot alone.

Egri's method offers another way to view the underlying structure of a dramatic conflict. (Although he's actually writing about crafting strong stage plays, what he says is completely applicable to YA fiction.)

According to Egri, before you can test the soundness of your story, you first need to identify its underlying theme. For instance, let's say my theme is "don't judge a book by its cover."

Egri's second step is to take the underlying theme and phrase it in the most active way, which will show whether your plot is active enough. If it isn't, you can fix it before you submit that disgraceful manuscript to your dream publisher and get rejected.

The way to make your premise active is to combine the theme with the active phrase "leads to" or "brings about."

Example: Judging a book by its cover leads to ... heartache and misunderstandings.

A Shameless Instant Story

I'm going to make up a mythical book as an example. And I'm going to say I thought of the story first and then realized it had the theme of "don't judge a book by its cover."

(And, by the way, as an editor of series fiction, we often brainstormed ideas for individual titles [books] by first choosing exactly these kind of clichés or themes. There was always an underlying theme or moral in every book, because such themes help to create plot ideas. Curious how you can write 94 books and disguise the themes so that they can be repeated endlessly!) But I digress.

My mythical book's plot (shamelessly simplistic, I'm afraid) comes to me as this: Rachel is new in town. She's bookish and dedicated to playing the violin. In her old high school, she was totally accepted and admired for her musical talent and creativity.

But her new school is huge and emphasizes sports. Rachel feels totally left out. Even worse, her next-door neighbor, Brittnee (same age, same grade), is super popular. Rachel's mom desperately wants Rachel to make friends with Brittnee so that Rachel can also be popular. (We'll deal with Mom's shallow reasons in a subplot.)

Brittnee wears ultra-trendy clothes and makeup and seems obsessed with boys. She's into cheerleading tryouts (she missed trying out for the squad last year because of a sprained ankle). She constantly and obsessively reads fan magazines. Rachel assumes Brittnee is the last person on Earth she could ever be friends with. They are total opposites and have nothing in common. Rachel's mom does not agree; she does every-thing she can to throw the girls together; Rachel does everything she can to avoid Brittnee—but tells her mom they're getting along fine.

Hugely comic plot complications ensue, structured around some big central conflict. Cheerleading! Of course. (Yes, this is stream of consciousness. I'm making it up as I go. That's what years in this business will do to you.) Okay, everything builds to the day of the big cheerleading tryouts when Rachel's mom discovers the horribly ratty things Rachel has done to avoid Brittnee, not least of which is constantly lying to her mother about their "growing friendship." Rachel's mom is furious. Rachel is grounded for life and forced to go to the tryouts herself, for her mom's sake. To everyone's amazement, Rachel is great (hidden genetic talents).

When it's Brittnee's turn to try out, she pretends to pull a muscle, and then admits to Rachel that she's actually terrified, the whole cheering thing is her mom's idea, she lied last year about her sprained ankle. What's more, the trendy clothes and makeup are also her mom's idea, and Brittnee only pretends to be boy crazy to cover her very real insecurities, which is why she has no "steady," but is, rather, "good friends" with tons of guys. (Paradoxically, of course, this is why she's so popular, because the guys are all insecure, too.)

Rachel realizes she judged Brittnee totally wrong, discovers hidden depths in Brittnee (and a possibly horrible or comically tender personal story about Brittnee's home life—another riveting subplot).

The girls work together to get Brittnee another chance at trying out, they end up as partners or cheering squad co-leaders, Rachel sees the value in athletics, discovers that Brittnee secretly longs to be a singer, they work on an act together, neatly tying up all subplot threads culminating in a big happy ending.

Now that you know the story, let's use Egri's method to see whether my original premise leads to an active plot:

When Rachel judges Brittnee based only on superficial details, it leads to Rachel acting in a devious and dishonest manner, causing heartache and misunderstandings with her mother and Brittnee.

Works for me!

Testing for an Active Premise

You can apply this method to a book you already like or admire to see how it compares. For now, let's try it out on *Chinese Handcuffs* and *The Pigman*.

Chinese Handcuffs: Dillon's need to learn the circumstances of his brother's suicide leads him into trouble with a vicious motorcycle gang … leads to him learning about secrets he isn't prepared to face … leads to him learning about the depths a human being can sink to … and ultimately gives him the courage to betray Jen in order to help her.

I already knew there were a confusing number of plot lines in this book, but listing all of them leaves no doubt that there's plenty of active plot possibilities here.

The Pigman: John and Lorraine's need to be accepted for who they are leads them to invade Mr. Pignati's house and life, bringing about his destruction.

Not only is this plot easy to summarize, but reducing it to an active premise verifies that there's enough going on to create a satisfying plot. The actual book is far more complex than the summary indicates, first showing the kids building their friendship with the Pigman, then taking advantage of his kindness, and then unwittingly crushing his fragile dreams.

But instead of testing for an active premise in published, successful books, why don't I let a former student speak about her own story?

Another student asks:

"Now, applying it to my own story about Daniel in Charlestown, I started writing, 'When Daniel tries to assert his rights before raising his level of responsibility, it leads to ….' Aha! I had not really led the story along the lines of the theme! I should have put in more examples of Daniel acting in a more uneducated way, leading to consequences. As it is, I did not include personal consequences for Daniel. Am I correct in this?"

She was definitely correct. Not only did she get the point of the exercise, she found what might have been a real stumbling block to her own story. Before, she'd created a solid character and interesting, historically accurate scenes, but there was no feeling of rising tension, no sense of where the story was heading or what was at stake for Daniel, the main character.

After completing the exercise, she was able to reshape her opening chapters so that each plot event was there for a reason. The structure became clear: protagonist Daniel needed to learn to read so that he could take on a higher station in life, befitting his age and experience. The restructuring showed what was at stake for Daniel and emphasized the repercussions if he should fail to reach his goal.

The increased tension between what Daniel wants and what might keep him from getting it created effective suspense and made us care more about Daniel and about the plot. By clarifying her active premise, this author was able to see that her original plot events seemed haphazard or random; reorganizing events so they all related to Daniel's active need turned the story around.

Try the Egri Method

Apply Egri's method to some of your favorite stories—books, plays, or movies. To begin you may need to break things down by steps, first identifying the antagonist's main need or want and then reducing plots to only the most important events. It's harder than it sounds!

The Least You Need to Know

- Using active wants helps you create an active premise.

- Replacing nouns with verbs has a huge impact on your writing, your basic idea, and ultimately your plot.

- A premise is not the same as a story idea.

- An active premise puts your plot into motion; an inactive premise is a dead end.

- Identifying your story's underlying theme helps to focus your writing and clarify your plot.

- A cohesive story contains plot events that build to an inevitable conclusion.

Chapter

5

Getting to Know Your Characters

In This Chapter

♦ Let your characters develop the plot

♦ Character + circumstance = actions

♦ Stereotypes can be useful!

♦ Let's get physical: character and appearance

Begin to read any story, and if it captures your immediate interest, chances are it's because you're already asking "why?" Why would this happen, why would anyone do that, what will he/she do next, what's going to happen as a result?

These are the same questions you, the writer, need to be asking as you develop your characters. Or perhaps I should say, as your characters develop the plot.

Writers are always quoted about the ways characters take over the story and make them change the plot. I'm a firm believer in outlines, and you can plan every scene of your book if you'd like, but I'd be amazed if it ended up exactly as you planned it. Which is a good thing—you want your characters to spring to life and take control of your story. If you understand from the start that you'll likely do at least a second draft, you'll be more open to your own creative impulses.

I repeat this (continually) when we talk about outlines, and about revision, and probably in a few other places, but your writing life will be so much easier if you accept the need for doing at least an entire first draft manuscript just to get to know your characters.

I wish I could say that it's an easy process—that it's possible to create a character whose traits lead inevitably to your plot events and ultimate resolution—but it's a tricky business. Creating character traits is a process, and you need to grant yourself permission to relax. Take the time to let your characters develop, and they'll give your story authenticity.

Characters Evolve

If plot grows from character, where do you find those motivations, dreams, and desires that become the best characters?

Don't expect your characters to spring to life on the page, fully formed. It's perfectly fine to begin a story with vague, hazy, or unfinished characters. Invariably, they will change and grow as you work on your story. Don't be afraid to let them change; be happy to let your characters take the reins and point your plot in unexpected directions.

Half the battle in writing a novel is being flexible enough to let the characters evolve with your story—and if that means adjusting their motives and actions, or your plot, so be it.

Direct vs. Indirect Motivation

Until your characters begin writing your book, however, it's up to you to create motives for them. How you do that may be totally instinctive. But let's identify a few technical possibilities:

In *direct motivation*, a character's underlying motives are fully explicit, clearly laid out from page one:

"Wilfred Boyer was killed without rhyme or reason by an out-of-control garbage truck. After plowing over Wilfred as if he were no more than a banana peel, the truck plunged into the filthy river, drowning the hapless driver. Watching incredulously, Roman Boyer, Wilfred's younger brother, was left orphaned at age 17, thus beginning his adult life. Stunned beyond words, Roman fixated on a single idea: someone would pay."

You can't get more blatant than this. Although there's no way of knowing how the story might develop from this point on, Roman's motivation is crystal clear—and it sets the entire plot into motion. If this were a real book, we might expect Roman to start out with an overwhelming need to avenge his brother's senseless death; but we'd also expect that this unrealistic and one-dimensional need would change during the course of the story, as the plot—and Roman's character—became more complex.

Indirect motivation propels the majority of stories (which aren't structured in such a contrived manner). In most stories, we understand someone's character through indirect motivation after reading countless pages and observing their actions and reactions, the way they handle success, failure, disappointment, and envy. We experience their character as an accumulation of information about them. If other characters describe what the main character is really like, we are free to agree or disagree, based on what we've seen and heard. Make sure your characters are doing what you need them to do in your story.

> **Slush Pile!**
>
> An author may tell readers what to think about a character, but if the character's thoughts and actions don't match what the author's saying, readers are going to form their own opinions and ignore the author—even though he created the character in the first place.

Character by Implication

Even though the opening passage is deliberately structured to show how a blatant motive can set a story into motion, it also gives us important character information by implication. Most stories develop character in this indirect way, showing us a character in life and gently pointing us toward inevitable conclusions.

In those few short lines, we already perceive that Roman is deeply emotional, quick to make decisions without rational thought, perhaps narrow-minded, and closed to the possibility of change.

Through inference, we also know a lot about Roman's personal history (his *backstory*):

◆ Roman has already suffered the major loss of the rest of his family. (Wilfred's death leaves him orphaned.)

def•i•ni•tion

Backstory is the events that occurred before the present action takes place; a character's personal history.

◆ Roman's relationship with his brother was a close one (hence his extreme grief).

◆ Roman feels alone and lost. (He's stunned.)

◆ Roman has the strength of will to assign himself a task to keep him functioning (revenge).

Character Formula: Character + Circumstance = Actions

Before we pass final judgment on Roman's character, we also need to consider additional implied evidence:

◆ Roman is an unwitting victim of circumstances.

◆ Roman is likely to be suffering survivor's guilt.

◆ Roman faces the formidable task of making sense of a senseless, random, and catastrophic misfortune.

Given all of these circumstances, we can approach Roman as a pitiable and sympathetic character, floundering in reaction to extreme events. Without the benefit of a loving family to counsel him through his grief, Roman still finds a way (however misguided) to give meaning to his life.

Objectively speaking, Roman chooses a path (revenge) that is neither admirable nor noble, and he makes a decision that reeks of youth and inexperience and involves the kind of mindless violence that would alienate most feeling people.

Yet it's all perfectly understandable, even forgivable, given the circumstances. Even though his thinking may be deeply flawed and his plan of action distasteful and doomed to fail, Roman is a sympathetic character.

Why? Because Roman's motivation arises from circumstances beyond his control.

What would happen if Roman came up against an antagonist who didn't know the circumstances influencing his behavior and decisions?

Suppose that in his grief and bewilderment, Roman finds a knife or a gun and randomly threatens an innocent bystander? Suppose a policeman happens by, sees Roman's threatening behavior, and shoots him?

Besides the fact that I've just described the basic premise of *The Fugitive* (and other books, TV shows, and movies), I've also described a tragic, believable, and understandable scenario given the fact that the cop knows nothing about Roman's circumstances.

Taking actions out of context—not knowing a character's motivation—can lead to disaster or tragedy. In fact, this is exactly what happens to Stanley Yelnats in *Holes* when he finds himself in the wrong place at the wrong time with a smoking gun (in this case, holding a pair of famous—stolen—sneakers). Stanley finds himself arrested, convicted, and incarcerated, based purely on circumstantial evidence—all because the policeman didn't know the facts about Stanley.

A Vote for Stereotypes

I'm sure you've never seen this advice before! I routinely advise students to use stereotypes when creating characters. That's right—I ask them to create characters defined by a single word: the nosy one, the boss, the whiner. My justification is that it's easier to start creating a character from one specific angle than to try to make them spring forth fully complex and multidimensional.

My favorite example of building on stereotypes is *Little Women*, Louisa May Alcott's classic novel. (Luckily, it was written decades before there was a YA category, so I don't have to justify using a middle-grade or children's book as an example—as far as I'm concerned, this is one of many books that transcends age. Anyone can enjoy it!)

Looking at the character traits of the four sisters, it's easy to reduce each one to a single word:

> Meg = ladylike
>
> Jo = tomboy
>
> Beth = shy
>
> Amy = vain

I encourage students to think in such broad terms when beginning a project. It's an easy way to get a handle on your characters before you really know them. Hopefully, you'll add complexity and depth as you're writing, and at the end of your efforts, your characters will emerge as full-fledged, multidimensional people.

Accurate as those bare-bones descriptions may be, if you add the characteristics that each of the sisters displays throughout the story, you'll end up with far more complex descriptions:

Meg = ladylike; also quiet, decorous, responsible, generous, prone to worry about appearances and propriety, conventional, good-natured, steady, and grounded

Jo = tomboy; also impetuous, vibrant, forceful, opinionated, rebellious, stubborn, imaginative, loyal, honest, industrious, shortsighted, and changeable

Beth = shy; also sweet, gentle, fragile, nonjudgmental, self-sacrificing, musical, brave (given the limitations of her shyness), consistent, helpful, and noncomplaining

Amy = vain; also artistic, impulsive, quick-tempered, proud, stylish, and concerned with doing things the right way

Creating Characters When You Know Nothing About Them

One student asked me about a common dilemma, worrying that he couldn't use characters to forward the plot—because he didn't know what his plot was.

That's why they call it "creative" writing. You don't have to know your plot from beginning to end before developing your characters. In fact, you might have wanted to write a story just because you fell in love with a compelling character.

Stories can spring from either plot or character. But let's say you need to begin with character because you're not sure of your plot. No problem!

You might start by keeping a notebook or computer files or envelopes where you collect character ideas, interesting phrases, pictures, written descriptions, or snatches of overheard dialogue: anything that strikes your fancy.

Keep everything, because at some point you'll want to create dossiers on your characters: files or folders that contain enough information to create a character's complete biography. (For suggestions and sample character questionnaires, see Chapter 16.)

In my classes, I give various exercises to get students thinking in terms of outward appearance and inner character.

In one exercise, I hand out photos of people, torn from magazine ads. Students are asked to write down a few lines about each person in the photo, in answer to these three questions:

◆ What were they like as a child?

◆ What are they like now?

◆ What are they likely to become?

It's always fascinating to see how much character description comes out of studying someone's hairstyle or clothing along with their physical features—the lines on their faces, their expressions, the tired, hopeless, or zestful look in their eyes, etc. It's even more fascinating to see how similar students' descriptions can be—reinforcing the notion that we all judge character based on appearance, forming opinions about people from hasty first impressions, employing a cultural shorthand that translates external information into character information: that, plus an instinct for who to approach and who to steer clear of.

In exercises such as these, it obviously doesn't matter whether the character traits you come up with are close to the truth or not—especially because you'll never know the "truth." What matters is that it assures students that it's second nature to create characters: we make character judgments based on appearances dozens of times a day. That knowledge somehow makes writing down character descriptions a lot less daunting.

A variation on the exercise is to ask the same three questions about any person students had noticed on their way to class that day: someone in line at the ATM or on the bus or subway, perhaps someone in a building lobby or passing on the street.

Getting to Know Your Character Through Specifics

The following "homework" is a great example of using specific character information to jump-start a story:

1. Choose a main character. Describe what that character was like as a very young child.

   Sim was a sensitive child with a soft heart and sad, lonely eyes. He was so skinny you could see the curve of every rib beneath his skin.

2. Describe what the character was like at the time you knew him or her.

   Sim was a shy boy, with dark, smooth skin and brilliant white teeth, a Vietnamese refugee who had made it across the ocean to freedom. But his vivid pastel paintings revealed tortured, searing memories of his wild escape from his homeland, emotions he could not express in foreign words.

3. Describe what the character is likely to become later in life.

   Sim is a photojournalist now, recording others' experiences at lens-length distance. He focuses on immigrant poverty in America, and although to the world he documents these images as an observer, he himself is the true subject.

4. What does this character want more than anything else in the world?

   More than anything, Sim wants to be able to sleep through a night without his haunting childhood memories of the war, the boats, his family and his people dying all around him.

5. Who or what is preventing him or her from getting it?

   Sim is afraid that letting go of the past means letting go of not only the bad but also the good memories—memories of his mother, his home, his heart.

6. What is she or he going to do about that?

   Sim will travel back to Vietnam, as a grown adult, to give his mother a proper burial in their old village. He will photograph everything he once knew and loved to commemorate the past, while he forges new memories for the future.

What I like best is how this assignment develops from the general to the specific in a way that gives potential plot events.

Pen Pal

Don't ever think you can't create believable characters. For most of us, making up information about people is second nature. Every day, we notice people around us and make judgments about them based on their looks, their behavior, their speech. Why? What is it about them that caught your attention? What do you remember about their face, their clothing, their body language? Whatever it is, use those details as character description in a story.

Exercises to Establish Character

The Gotham Writers' Workshop assigns this task to beginning fiction writers: *Make a list of everyone you've ever known.*

It doesn't matter if you ever actually finish the list. It would take years to do so! The point is that we remember some people vividly. Why? Whatever it is that makes us remember them is valuable information about creating fictional characters.

Sometimes we remember people because they're connected to an emotion: the way Susie Q embarrassed us in gym class or a drama teacher who made us weep over a haunting poem. Paradoxically, it's often easier to remember bad experiences than good ones. Which do you remember more clearly—birthdays on which things went smoothly and you liked your gifts, or birthdays that were disasters?

People affect us for a reason; if you remember someone, find out why. Write down quick impressions, a few adjectives, a phrase or two—don't dismiss the list lightly. It's a valuable resource when you need to come up with a character and want them to be memorable in some way.

Physiology vs. Psychology

In fiction, as in life, someone's outer appearance often reflects their inner qualities:

> Neatly groomed = careful, methodical
>
> Unusual clothing = impulsive, eccentric

Not too long ago there was a TV special examining the influence of physical beauty on people's lives. Footage proved that beautiful babies received much more positive attention than not-beautiful babies. The impact of all that admiration was astounding: the attractive babies were more responsive, outgoing, enjoyed people more—in short, they thrived.

The inference was that babies (and adults) who received less attention, and had less positive reinforcement, would develop less self-confidence, and, if treated badly enough, might develop ugly personalities built on resentment and anger.

In *Chinese Handcuffs*, Preston Hemenway's legs are amputated after a horrific motorcycle accident. Preston, physically small and unimposing, already felt deeply inadequate. Post-accident, confined to a wheelchair, his outward appearance mirrored his inner character: an unfinished man capable of startling cruelty.

Author Crutcher establishes Preston's stunted soul through a disturbing act of childhood violence that also sets Preston's story line into motion. (I won't give away what it is because I expect you to run out and read the book!)

At the time of the incident, protagonist and younger brother Dillon follows his big brother's lead—at first out of false bravado—but then, to his own horror, out of perverse enjoyment.

Years later, big brother Preston comes full circle when he initiates another brutal act. Sickened by his own actions (and under the weight of other serious pressures), Preston shoots himself.

In contrast to Preston, Dillon, tall, fit, and a superb athlete, never forgives himself for the childhood violence; unlike Preston, he goes on to express his humanity through deep concern for his friends and family, his compulsion to learn the truth about his brother, and the actions he takes to prevent violence against the ones he loves.

Crutcher takes a situation where brothers share some traits and pivotal events and uses outward appearance to illuminate their very different characters, which in turn creates very different life choices—and a deeply riveting plot.

Character Exercise

Answer the questions that follow using a story you'd like to write—be sure to include as many specifics as you can.

1. Choose a main character. Describe what they were like as a very young child.

2. Describe what they were like at the time you knew them.

3. Describe what they are likely to become later in life.

4. What does this character want more than anything else in the world?

5. Who or what is preventing him or her from getting it?

6. What is she or he going to do about that?

The Least You Need to Know

◆ Understanding a character's motives helps establish believable plots.

◆ Characters act from a combination of circumstance and personality traits.

◆ Fictional characters can be created from the outside in; give them time and space to evolve.

◆ In fiction, physical traits can translate into character traits.

Chapter 6

Conflict: The Core of the Story

In This Chapter

- ◆ Creating conflicts that move plots forward
- ◆ Engaging emotions: the reader's, and the character's
- ◆ How to create a memorable reading experience
- ◆ Enhancing plots with predictability

Maybe you're familiar with the famous line from *Annie Hall*, Woody Allen's classic film on relationships. Toward the end of the film, lovers Alvy and Annie, realizing they're at a crossroads, stop to examine what's gone wrong between them. Relationships, he tells her, are like sharks, which need to constantly move forward or die. Their relationship has ceased moving forward. What they've got on their hands now is a dead shark.

Stories also need to constantly move forward, the conflicts evolving and deepening in impact, the stakes rising higher and higher. This chapter shows how to build conflicts to keep your story from being a dead shark.

Build Conflicts to Keep Plots from Dying

Back in Chapter 3 you learned to create compelling conflicts as the basis for strong plots. You know that conflicts should spring from character, and that they should be as specific as possible.

But let's say you're deep into your story summary, outline, or first draft, generally following this advice, yet something is lacking—the energy is fading, even though you carefully created enough plot events to fill a trilogy.

Before you shred pages or start cursing my name, stop! Do a story checkup. In my experience, excitement lags when conflicts sag. To keep your story moving, ask yourself these questions:

- Are you building suspense?

- Are you engaging the reader's emotions?

- Are you engaging the character's emotions?

- Have you established clear motivations for the actions now taking place?

Story Conflict, Story Structure: The Master Plan

Screenwriters are taught to construct screenplays using several visual models. The structure of the model influences the placement of conflicts throughout the story. Here's my version of the three most useful models.

Straight Rising Conflicts

These keep plots moving continuously forward, building conflicts to increase tension until plot events reach a climax.

Visualize a skate park jump: a skater launches himself onto a steep, inclined ramp, starting at ground level and rising smoothly in one unbroken line to its highest point, where the platform abruptly ends. Sent aloft, the skater either flies like an angel, soars like a jet plane, or drops piteously, crashing to the ground.

Stories that feature straight rising conflicts build logically from beginning to end. In such a plot, readers may be able to guess the ending and even predict some of the steps that will lead there.

Peaks and Valleys

These present conflicts in a jagged pattern of fits and starts, moving forward in bursts of intense, rising action, then stopping abruptly by hitting plot barriers or dead ends. Valleys may represent moments of panic, indecision, calm, reflection, or total inaction, until some event triggers another rising conflict, which hits another barrier or stopping point—perhaps with an AHA! moment this time—before dropping, then rising, etc.

The "skate park" equivalent would be a series of inclined ramps set end-to-end.

Stories with peaks and valleys exploit the element of surprise, constantly pulling the rug out from under readers with unexpected plot twists and turns, making it harder to guess the ending or to predict when and how conflicts will resolve.

Rolling Conflicts

These provide a gentle template with continuity and soft transitions between events, represented by a model of rounded peaks and valleys. Picture a fat, fluffy, cumulous cloud, or a series of gentle hills; there is progression from hillock to hillock, but no sudden surprises, no jutting crags to interrupt the flow.

There is no "skate park" equivalent for this; maybe a kiddies playroom filled with soft plastic balls …

Rolling conflicts provide the least dramatic ride, mirroring real life more closely than the other two forms. There may or may not be an overall conflict designed to tie together plot events, but there will certainly be many small conflicts that resolve with few discernable bumps and bruises along the way.

> **Slush Pile!**
>
> Readers expect—and deserve—consistency. While it's perfectly fine to begin a story gently and then build conflicts with mounting intensity, don't begin a story with the excitement of startling peaks and valleys only to suddenly switch to a story built of gently rolling conflicts.

Models in Action

Every story model is designed to keep plots moving. But must you stick strictly to one model or the other? For the answer, check out our sample stories.

Straight Rising Conflicts:

◆ *The Pigman:* We know from the start that the Pigman dies. The entire story is a flashback, retelling events as they happened. Suspense builds through the reader's mixed dread and anticipation of that unavoidable moment.

◆ *Holes:* The plot begins with Stanley's arrest and ends with his release.

◆ *Peter Pan:* Does anyone *not* expect Wendy and her brothers to go back home?

Peaks and Valleys:

◆ *Chinese Handcuffs:* Information is given in a mix of flashbacks and present-time action. Though we expect Dillon will put the puzzle pieces together, we can't guess how he'll do it, or predict what the ultimate crisis will be, especially as the story begins with brother Preston's suicide, but resolves with friend/love interest Jen's rescue.

◆ *Holes:* Stanley's incarceration provides the overall plot structure, but the story-within-the-story proceeds in fits and starts, presenting entire subplots involving characters from the past.

Rolling Conflicts:

◆ *Homecoming:* The Tillermans' search for a home leads them from one adventure to another, and events continue to develop even after reaching their grandmother's homestead, where a whole separate batch of conflicts arises as the kids attempt to settle in. The overall plot culminates only when Gran finally extends an official welcome.

◆ *Little Women:* With a focus on main character Jo, the daily domestic conflicts of all the family members provide the meat of the story. Intrusions by death, Civil War, engagements, marriages, and travel provide dramatic highpoints along the way.

Successful stories may mix-and-match elements of different conflict models, but all maintain a consistency of pattern.

◆ Do maintain a balance between flashbacks and present-day actions.

◆ Do avoid jarring transitions.

◆ Do create structural patterns that are predictable enough for readers to accept your mix-and-match.

Slush Pile!

Predictability—good or evil? Face it: most readers love a good story whether or not they can guess the ending. People read a book or see a movie the first time to *find out what happens*. They read it again or rent the DVD to *enjoy the way it happens*.

Surprise endings satisfy readers only when events are foreshadowed throughout the plot and have story logic. Surprise isn't crucial; satisfaction is. Make sure your story elements add up. Don't create endings that confuse or irritate; do construct stories that make endings inevitable.

Readers expect story logic. They'll accept any format you throw at them, as long as you don't skimp on the basics. Check for strong logic in planning your story, as you're writing, and while revising:

◆ Endings should validate premises.

◆ Setups should equal payoffs.

◆ Openings should ask questions; endings should answer them.

Preparing for Battle

As our old friend Lajos Egri writes, "No conflict ever existed without first foreshadowing itself."

Let's just accept the fact that conflicts should rise in dramatic intensity. Whether events are big or small, emotional and intellectual, or external, action-thriller, larger-than-life apocalyptic physical events, the stakes need to constantly rise.

In *The Art of Dramatic Writing*, Egri describes several critical aspects of conflict development. I've paraphrased four main definitions:

◆ Static conflict is when a character fails to take action. A character frozen by indecision creates static conflict and bogs down the action.

◆ Jumping conflict occurs when there hasn't been enough preparation for an event.

◆ Slowly rising conflicts develop out of the story premise, setting up character motives that result in logical actions, which forward the plot to its inevitable conclusion.

◆ Foreshadowing conflicts synthesize character, motivation, and action into the most successful and satisfying plots.

In other words, improper preparation confuses the reader and stops the logical progression of plot events. For example:

Improper foreshadowing:

An animal-loving jockey suddenly puts a beloved, healthy horse to sleep.

Proper foreshadowing:

A jockey realizes that riding a beloved horse to victory will destroy his only son's career and shatter the boy's fragile will to live. Tragically, he ends the animal's life.

Forming Emotional Engagements

We know that stories falter when conflicts don't develop logically and when the stakes stay the same. You can prevent both by creating conflicts that engage two sets of emotions—the character's and the reader's.

Engaging Readers' Emotions

Before readers choose to take your book home from the store or the library, they go through a process of selection. Here's how my process goes: I read a title, glance at the cover art, then flip the book over and read the story blurb or jacket flap.

Elements that grab me first usually reflect my personal interests—for instance, stories about musicians or artists, mothers and daughters. If the topic isn't of particular interest, I still might relate strongly to the main conflict. For instance, soccer doesn't especially grab me, but I could relate to a story about a talented soccer player going overboard, abusing the sport to work through grief over her mother's suicide (Bridget in *Sisterhood of the Traveling Pants*). Will Bridget ruin her soccer game, thereby losing yet another thing she loves?

Subject matter or a unique setting might draw me in, but a strong central conflict trumps both. Underdog stories, beating the odds, character transformations ... the bigger the conflict, the more extreme the change, the better.

Living the Story Experience

Different genres promise different reading experiences. Readers enter a story expecting its structure to reflect and reinforce their expectations of the experience—and they expect a visceral experience. That's why book covers and movie ads tell you how a story will make you *feel*.

You'll grip the edge of your seat. Experience a roller-coaster ride of heart-stopping, blood-thumping, nonstop thrills.

You'll laugh, you'll cry, you'll find renewed hope. You'll travel to places you've only dreamed about, burn with tropical fever and survive arctic chill.

The story will warm your heart, tingle your toes, touch your soul, reduce you to tears, dash you to the depths of despair, and lift you to heights of sublime faith and passion. From head to toes, you'll *experience* what you've never experienced before.

Pen Pal

Three categories of change propel most stories:

Outward change: switching from tea to coffee, changing careers, moving, death, divorce.

Physical change: football player paralyzed, a painter going blind, a gender change.

Intellectual change: learning to forgive, overcoming a deeply entrenched racial, cultural, or social belief, and accepting that a trusted friend/lover/colleague has become an enemy.

No matter what the trappings, one element links them all: emotional upheaval.

Accepting the Fantastic: Suspension of Disbelief

Suspension of disbelief is the phenomenon by which we willingly "believe" illogical or impossible actions, events, or beings in a work of fiction. That includes accepting stories about talking animals, the English-speaking aliens of *Star Trek*, or tales about mermaids who miraculously sprout legs when they're on land and fall in love with humans.

Why does someone snigger at the fact that a flimsy pair of glasses is supposed to totally disguise Clark Kent—yet accept without question the fact that Superman flies? Flying is equally ludicrous—but it's an intrinsic part of who Superman is. So we scoff at the smaller detail, but suspend rational thought in order to enjoy the bigger fantasy. Why? To fulfill our basic needs.

Pen Pal _____

Neurologists and psychologists have studied the way the human brain reacts to stories, linking suspension of disbelief (our willingness to accept the illogical, fantastic, or impossible) to various brain functions.

For instance, we get "lost" in a story because the part of our brain that governs movement is turned off when we settle down to read or to watch TV or a movie. The moment we get up again, the "active" part of the brain takes over and that intense connection is lost.

Predictability of Structure = Comfort = Intimacy

Experts say the average person experiences only thirteen minutes of true intimacy in a lifetime.

We seek out stories to find that missing intimacy. Loosely speaking, we're able to weep over fictional characters because of the same phenomenon that lets us lose ourselves in a story. Temporarily, "real life" is put on hold, and our innermost brain duplicates the intense emotional bonding we experienced with our mothers in infancy. Only this time, the bond links us with a fictional character.

Basically, scientists are saying that we humans will do almost anything to recapture that primal bond of intimacy. That's why predictability plays a part in every story. Think about childhood stories or nursery rhymes—they're designed with repetitive structures, rhythms, and catch phrases, the more predictable the better. We know that predictability makes children feel secure. As we age, the stories we crave increase in complexity, but we never quite lose our need for predictability.

When a romantic story introduces a threesome, say, one guy and two girls, we've been conditioned to assume that there will be lots of conflicts until the guy falls for one of the girls. Predictable. Yet we enjoy variations of that plot over and over again.

When a thriller, adventure, or mystery introduces our favorite spy, explorer, or sleuth to his arch enemy, we're conditioned to believe the hero will triumph in the end—yet that doesn't stop us from rooting for the hero, or feeling actual tension or fear when he or she is in trouble.

Readers approach stories expecting—and needing—to be emotionally involved in conflicts big or small. But what about the characters themselves?

Engaging Your Character's Emotions

Conflicts present dilemmas and ask characters to choose actions. The pressure to choose and act creates a character's discomfort or dissatisfaction. Feeling uncomfortable or dissatisfied, characters hope for a way to resolve the conflict so they can return to normal (that is, the absence of conflict and a return to comfort).

In plot terms, this emotional conflict can be expressed as:

Hope leads to action leads to reaction leads to resolution.

Nice formula, but, as we know, drama is created when things *don't* go smoothly. So, to be more dramatic, let's put it this way:

Hope leads to *unwise action*, which leads to *disappointment* which leads to *turnaround*, which leads to *renewed hope*, which leads to *resolution*.

Let's revisit our friends from the writing exercise in Chapter 2: Luke and Bernadette.

Here are the bones of the plot:

Luke comes to Pop's store, knowing that Bernadette works there. He's surprised to see Pop. He doesn't know Pop is Bernadette's father until Bernadette appears. Luke asks her to go off with him, Pop says no, they argue, it escalates, they scuffle, and Pop goes down. Luke grabs Bernadette, grabs the money from the counter, they run.

[Middle plot happens, with various escalating conflicts between Luke and Bernadette, who's torn between her love for Pop, attraction to Luke, and anger and disappointment of her own that Luke hurt Pop, whose life is now in danger. Cops pursue Luke, things build to a big crisis.]

Luke turns himself in, and it's revealed that Pop suffered a stroke; Luke didn't injure him. Charges dropped, Luke vows eternal devotion to Bernadette and her father, leading to renewed hope and resolution.

Here's the plot with the formula attached:

Hoping to win Bernadette's love, Luke goes to Pop's store and unwisely asks her to go off with him. Pop says no and Luke's disappointment leads to argument, which escalates to scuffle, and Pop goes down. Luke grabs money and Bernadette, they run.

[Middle plot happens, with various escalating conflicts between Luke and Bernadette, who's torn between her love for Pop, attraction to Luke, and anger and disappointment of her own that Luke hurt Pop, whose life is now in danger. Cops pursue Luke, things build to a big crisis.]

Which leads to turnaround. Luke turns himself in, and it's revealed that Pop suffered a stroke; Luke didn't injure him. Charges dropped, Luke vows eternal devotion to Bernadette and her father, leading to renewed hope, leading to resolution.

The Big Fix: Characters and Emotional Upheaval

In a thriller or mystery, there are lots of plot events and lots of subconflicts going on. But for the protagonist, the biggest dilemma always asks the same question: Can I fix it?

Can our hero or heroine find the killer, save the innocent, thwart the terrorist, and return things to normal? It's a yes-or-no question that raises the highest stakes for the protagonist. At stake is their very credibility and self-worth.

Are we rooting for the good guy to win? Absolutely. Will we accept their defeat? Absolutely—as long as that defeat is foreshadowed so that the failure makes logical story sense. Will we be disappointed? Probably, but only until we're given the faintest glimmer of hope that things will turn around again.

Yes, part of us is crushed that Wendy leaves Neverland, but we're comforted by the knowledge that it was inevitable—and because we know that Wendy's children, and their children, and theirs, will continue to visit Neverland. We don't really need Wendy to stay with Peter in Neverland. We just need Neverland to exist.

We've examined some pretty complicated mechanisms in this chapter, but they all boil down to one main idea: readers don't care that stories aren't real. Whether their plots offer soothing nostalgia or tooth-gnashing, fingernail-biting terror and suspense, stories are the ultimate comfort food.

The Least You Need to Know

- Stories rely on rising conflicts to keep plots moving forward.

- Three models keep stories moving forward: Straight rising conflicts, peaks and valleys, and rolling conflicts.

- Stories succeed by engaging emotions: the reader's and the character's.

- Understanding how predictability enhances plots will prepare readers (and characters) for a satisfying ending.

Chapter 7

Plots Till You Plotz

In This Chapter

- ◆ Building plots according to plan
- ◆ Myths and fairy tales
- ◆ Components of a well-crafted plot
- ◆ Steps to a satisfying ending

A plot is a structure that ties events together into a story. After all, what is a story without a plot? A random series of events that might not ever come to a resolution.

There are numerous techniques and models designed to help you develop a story from start to finish. Let's call them plot plans. In this chapter we take a look at the three best known, most commonly used plans: The Hero's Journey, Fairy-Tale Form, and Three-Act Plots).

The Hero's Journey: A Method of Myth

The *Star Wars* movies are always cited as having this format. In summary form, this journey involves four main elements:

◆ Hero (protagonist) leaves home.

◆ Ten steps lead from one dilemma to another.

◆ Hero conquers, outwits, or outmaneuvers all antagonists.

◆ Wiser, hero returns home to acclaim.

The full journey takes 12 specific steps:

1. Establish the ordinary world

2. The call to adventure

3. The refusal of the call

4. The meeting with the mentor

5. Crossing the first threshold

6. Tests, allies, and enemies

7. The approach to the inmost cave

8. The ordeal (the ultimate test)

9. The reward

10. The road back

11. The resurrection (testing the lessons learned)

12. Return with the elixir

A classic but complicated plot formula, The Hero's Journey often takes the form of a saga, in which the hero overcomes seemingly endless obstacles and reversals until finally vanquishing all enemies, overcoming adversity, and returning home to acclaim.

def•i•ni•tion

Episodic is a story consisting of a series of events (episodes) not necessarily related by theme or chronological order and whose resolution doesn't necessarily depend on them.

Leaving and returning home are essential ingredients of this plot model, which can also function as a symbolic journey of self-discovery. Based on myth, followed in ancient Greek sagas such as the *Iliad* and the *Odyssey*, the hero's journey often leads to *episodic* stories, where a long string of events occurs.

The situations themselves may not add up to one climactic moment, and in fact, all the events may not need to happen so that the story can come to its ultimate resolution.

Little Women is also heavily episodic; although there are mini-plots within the overall story, and different conflicts are resolved as they arise, overall it is a chronicle of a family's everyday life, carried out according to a strict code of ethics and beliefs established by the parents.

Each character has a journey to take, but there is no sense of suspense, no taut thread of tension that draws the reader breathlessly toward a particular climax that heralds the end of the story.

On the other hand, Stanley Yelnats in *Holes* is forced to leave home (he's arrested and sentenced to work camp) and to endure multiple hardships (back-breaking labor, thirst, hunger; the sadistic whims of the warden and Mr. Sir; some initial threats from the other boys).

Near the climax of the story, Stanley and Zero take a literal journey, unknowingly retracing the steps of their forefathers. Along the way, Stanley musters his wit and determination not only to survive but also to solve a long-standing riddle—which brings down his enemies and wins Stanley his freedom. Odyssey ended, Stanley returns home a hero.

> **Pen Pal**
>
> In *Holes*, Stanley takes a hero's journey with some variations: forced to leave home and wander among enemies, he relies on wit and resourcefulness to defeat his foes and solve an ancient riddle. His return home brings success to his family and wins him personal acclaim.

Fairy-Tale Form

The Fairy-Tale Form is another familiar plot structure where the protagonist must overcome obstacles—often of mounting difficulty—before proving herself and earning a reward or prize. Even modern-day stories may conform to the Fairy-Tale Form. The children in *Homecoming*, like the heroines of so many fairy tales, have lost their mother. Big sister Dicey leads them on a literal journey from Massachusetts to Connecticut, testing her wit and resourcefulness while enduring sore feet, bad weather, hunger, and the constant threat of being discovered by the police and sent to foster homes.

> **Pen Pal**
>
> In *Homecoming*, as in many classic fairy tales, Dicey leads her siblings on a journey to find a true mother, encountering adversity along the way. After vanquishing an evil stepmother, they must prove their worth to their grandmother. Their hard work, goodness, and honor secure them their reward: love and a permanent home.

Arriving at their destination, Dicey finds their Aunt Eunice, a perfect stand-in for the ubiquitous evil stepmother, cruelly misunderstanding the children, using their plight to gain sympathy for herself and conspiring to split them up. Overcoming this threat involves a daring escape and a final journey to the Maryland home of their grandmother, where the four kids work as hard as seven dwarves to prove their usefulness—eventually softening their grandmother's heart and winning themselves a permanent home.

The Classically Crafted Three-Act Plot

Think of it this way: a tightly plotted story begins with a question and ends when the question is answered. Usually, a classic plot follows the familiar three-act structure of beginning, middle, and end. Act I asks the question when it sets up the problem and gives necessary information; Act II shows the developments linking the initial problem and the ultimate resolution; and Act III answers the question by tying up all the loose ends, showing the ramifications of choices made, and providing the final resolution.

In the main plot of *Chinese Handcuffs*, for instance, Dillon begins with the question of why his brother committed suicide. Dillon's need to learn why Preston took his own life compels him to take actions to save his friend Jen's life. On the way, Dillon comes to terms with his brother's death, his mother's leaving, and his father's ineffectualness, and establishes his own reason for living.

Several subplots run parallel to the main plot, each resolving in due time, each existing as ancillary story lines feeding the main story. The lengths Dillon goes to protect Jen serves as evidence of his own sterling character, proving that, unlike his brother, Dillon saves those he loves; Preston hurt them.

When Dillon learns the details of Preston's suicide and discovers what really brought it about, he can acknowledge how Preston's lifelong self-doubts and problems set him on an inevitable path to self-destruction. The differences in their characters ensure Dillon's survival. When the initial question (why suicide?) has been answered to Dillon's satisfaction, the story ends.

What is at stake? Dillon's sanity and Jen's life.

What's at stake for the sisters in *Little Women?* They each contribute to their family's functioning during good times and bad, and ultimately each wants to get married, but they are not driven by either a need to help or to get married. Their stories are presented as entertainment, hopefully to amuse and to inspire by example. But the plot could just as easily stop sooner or end later.

In a classically plotted story, nothing is arbitrary. No outcome is left to chance, and no event is completely insignificant: character, event, and theme cross-pollinate to bring about the final resolution.

Pen Pal

I chose to go into detail with the Three-Act Plots because, in our culture, it's the most familiar story format. The advantages of each plan become clear according to the story you want to write. It would be easier to write about an epic adventure using The Hero's Journey; a lighthearted romance might lend itself beautifully to the Fairy-Tale Form. You could even combine elements of each plan, using the idea of a fairy-tale quest in a three-act plot.

Crossovers

Hopefully, you're already thinking that there's a lot of crossover in our sample books. Maybe *Holes* is closer to fairy-tale form; maybe *Chinese Handcuffs* presents a hero's journey. The good news is, there's no quiz coming, and no one's going to demand that you give definitive labels to any piece of writing.

To me, the main purpose of any of these formats is to illustrate how many elements you need in a satisfying story. Whether you use more steps or less, you can develop a satisfying plot to suit your need—no matter which form it takes.

However, most of us are already conditioned to think of stories in three acts, however vaguely defined those acts may be. For that reason, I recommend the following plot plan—especially if you're new to writing or have writing experience but still have trouble bringing a story to a satisfying conclusion.

The ABCs of Plot

This method is featured in many writing programs—and is the preferred method taught at New York's esteemed Gotham Writers' Workshop. It uses an alphabetic breakdown to help students remember the five components of a well-crafted plot:

A = action

B = background

C = conflict

D = development

E = ending

I've always used the story of Peter Rabbit by Beatrix Potter as a model to teach classic plot structure. I see no reason to stop using it; so instead of explaining and defining the plot components in a vacuum, I'll walk you through the story, which shows a beautifully structured plot in action.

A = Action, or Inciting Incident

Momma Rabbit tells her bunny children that they may go out, but warns them to stay away from Mr. McGregor's garden.

All stories begin with some *inciting incident:*

def•i•ni•tion

The **inciting incident** is the particular event that sets the plot in motion.

- A unique action that makes this day different from all other days

- An event that sets the ball rolling and puts your plot into action

Whatever event occurs, big or small, internal or external, something about it is the reason your story exists. It also enforces the rule of thumb that it's best to begin all stories in an action, or with an active line of dialogue, as opposed to opening with a narrated history or a lot of explanation.

You may disagree with this rule, and because we're talking about creativity here, how you begin a story is your choice—and a matter of style and taste. But start paying attention to first paragraphs in books you admire. How do they begin?

In the case of Peter Rabbit, Momma's warning to stay out of the garden is the inciting incident. Contrary Peter immediately does exactly what he's warned not to do, and that begins the action.

B = Background

Mr. McGregor, who owns the garden next door, put Poppa Rabbit in a pie. It could happen to Peter or his sisters!

Most new writers have trouble deciding when, where, and how to convey *background* or *backstory*. Backstory runs amok when it becomes exposition—those unfortunate passages where all action stops and long-winded explanations set in. The rule of thumb is to give only the amount of backstory needed at any particular moment to understand that scene.

If you've ever read a story to a young child, you know how they interrupt whenever something isn't immediately clear; kids need to know exactly who, what, where, when, and how at every moment.

def•i•ni•tion

Background (also known as **backstory**) is crucial or historical information about characters or events that happened before the current scene takes place. It includes any information necessary for readers to understand the story.

Writing backstory is easy when you're targeting little kids—each time something new is introduced, you clarify immediately. If "Jack" enters the room, you stop and explain right away who he is: friend, brother, teacher, etc.

Young adults, on the other hand, have the patience and the intellectual skill necessary to hold information in mind, saving questions until they come across the answers in the text. Still, if a particular piece of backstory is crucial, you need to give it as soon as possible—hopefully, integrating it into the scene.

For instance, Maybeth, the younger sister in *Homecoming*, is characterized as slow and speaks so little that Aunt Eunice asks point blank if she's retarded. But we don't get the definitive answer (she's not) until much later in the story. So, for instance, although we might need to know in Chapter 1 that Herman is adopted to understand his caution when he's invited to spend Christmas with a big, happy family, we don't need to know how he became orphaned. Rather than bog the story down in lengthy explanations, you can save that information and insert it later on—perhaps as the basis for an emotional scene with plenty of dialogue.

Slush Pile!

Backstory is necessary to understand a character's motivation, but knowing where, when, and how much to put in makes many writers stumble. Try not to overload readers with too much backstory at once: it's always better to establish characters first, so background information will be meaningful—and memorable.

C = Conflict

Peter's character compels him to disobey Momma's orders. Straightaway, he goes into that garden.

Conflict comes in the form of a choice: should Peter obey Momma, or disobey and put himself in danger?

Character leads to conflict, and conflict (the way your character answers the question posed by the conflict) leads to development.

D = Development

Development encompasses all actions up to the moment of crisis, such as the following:

1. Peter eats, feels sick, hunts for parsley to make him feel better, but instead meets Mr. McGregor.

2. Peter is chased with a rake.

3. Peter loses his shoes but keeps going.

4. Peter's jacket buttons catch on a gooseberry net. He sobs: all is lost!

5. A bird encourages Peter to try harder. Peter escapes.

6. Peter rushes to the toolshed, jumps into a watering can, and sneezes. Mr. McGregor finds him!

7. Mr. McGregor tries to stomp him, but Peter is smaller and quicker and gets away.

8. Mr. McGregor gives up and goes back to work.

9. Peter rests. He finds the garden gate, but it's locked. He asks a mouse for another way out, but the mouse doesn't help. Peter loses heart again.

10. Peter wanders, lost, stumbles across the White Cat and begins a retreat when he hears a noise. It's Mr. McGregor, standing between Peter and the garden gate—the only path to freedom.

Pen Pal

Most people consider S. E. Hinton's classic novel *The Outsiders* to be the first well-known YA novel. The book, published in 1967, was seen as the first novel to launch the YA fiction trend. The market quickly picked up steam and has only continued to grow since then.

E = Ending

Surprise! The ending isn't the end; it's the beginning of the end. For example:

- Endings wrap up the action.

- Endings indicate how other characters are affected by the main character's actions.

- Endings draw a conclusion by establishing a lesson learned, or showing how the main character has changed as a result of his or her journey.

That's a lot to accomplish, and accordingly we break endings down into several components. In this plan, there are four steps to a satisfying ending, and they all begin with the letter *C*:

- Crisis

- Climax

- Consequences

- Conclusion

C = crisis

What should Peter do?

Like all crises, this one asks a question. The answer determines the way the story will play out.

Choices the author could have made include the following:

- Peter tries to find another way out of the garden.

- Peter lays low in the toolshed until Mr. McGregor goes home to bed.

- Peter accepts his destiny (like father like son) and swears he'll be the best bunny pie ever.

- Peter digs a bunny burrow and tries to tunnel home.

Any of these are viable options, but instead, the author brilliantly chooses an ending that is both believable for an actual rabbit and also springs directly from Peter's character. Plus, it is the most dramatic.

C = climax

Peter runs.

Because he isn't quite sensible, or self-sacrificial, or a quitter, Peter makes a break for it. Again, he does what his nature compels him to do: he takes the biggest risk, hoping for the biggest payoff—his freedom or his life!

Foolish? Yes, but it's also the one action that makes us want to stand up and cheer.

Are we done? Was that the ending? Oh no! It's time for the consequences.

C = consequences

Mr. McGregor hangs up Peter's jacket and shoes to use as a scarecrow.

Peter arrives home, exhausted and feeling sick.

Mom's unhappy at the loss of Peter's shoes and jacket—again!

C = conclusion

Peter falls ill. Mom puts him to bed, and, to add insult to injury, gives him some awful chamomile tea as medicine.

Pen Pal

Conclusions—the denouement, where all the pieces of the story fall together—may teach a moral lesson or sum up how the protagonist has changed as a result of his or her journey.

Flopsy, Mopsy, and Cotton-tail, virtuous bunnies who obeyed Momma, are awarded their just desserts: bread, milk, and berries!

Note that it takes five steps to bring this story to a satisfying conclusion—proving that endings are far more complex than you may have suspected.

Satisfying endings accomplish many tasks and take more time—and space—than you might suspect. Follow the four Cs to keep from skimping on the necessary steps to a successful conclusion.

Try It Yourself

Choosing a story that's familiar to you, see if you can pinpoint the major plot points using the information from the section "The ABCs of Plot."

The Least You Need to Know

- ◆ Follow any of the three main plot types to construct your story from start to finish.
- ◆ Every plot type follows a different plan but contains the same basic elements.
- ◆ Endings have their own set of rules—and are more complicated than you might think.

Chapter 8

The YA Voice: What It Is and How to Get It

In This Chapter

- The basic elements of an authentic YA voice
- How to avoid adult-itis
- The right way to use reading level
- How to create a blockbuster series

YA readers are at the top of the children's book spectrum—able to handle sophisticated vocabulary and writing styles. Still, they respond best to stories with a young adult voice: text that feels as if it were written by another teen—even if that teen is older, wiser, and has an exceptional command of language.

Let's make a distinction right now—an adult voice and an adult narrator are two very different things. An adult narrator means your story is being told by an adult, and that knocks your book right out of the YA category—even if your topic is mainly of interest to teens.

An adult-sounding voice is a subtle thing; a combination of the words you choose and the tone, perspective, and feeling behind the words.

So how do you create a YA voice? And exactly how does it differ from an adult voice? That's the topic of this chapter. Read on.

Creating an Authentic YA Voice

First of all, don't confuse an adult narrator with an adult voice. Avoid adult narrators in any YA material! Even if your narrator is a teen, and your story is written from a teen's point of view (POV), the words you use, your tone, and your attitude can unconsciously mirror an adult's perspective.

The following are elements that contribute to voice:

♦ Verb tense

♦ Vocabulary

♦ Sentence construction and/or phrasing

♦ Attitude

Verb Tense

Let's make a distinction right now between deliberately manipulating verb tense and simply being grammatically correct.

With experience, you'll be able to instinctively choose the tense that works best. While there are no hard-and-fast rules about which tense to use when, once you make a choice, be consistent.

Do choose a tense that works best for each incident, passage, or chapter.

Don't arbitrarily switch tenses within an incident, passage, or chapter.

Vocabulary

There are lists and guidelines galore for age-appropriate vocabulary words. But it's more important to choose words that make sense for the story you're writing.

Do use vocabulary words that reflect the time and place you're writing about.

Do choose vocabulary that reflects the background of your characters. Especially when writing dialogue, the words your characters speak should reflect their individuality. The more distinctive their speech, the easier it is for readers to remember them.

Don't use the same language or figures of speech for every character. Varying vocabulary, rhythm, and construction of sentences creates contrast and interest.

Don't confuse the way your characters speak with the way you, the author, "speak" in your narrative passages. Let's look at these elements one by one in a sample passage, purposely written in an adult voice.

Example 1: Adult Voice/Past Tense

Albert Klein ruled our street. A short, scraggly boy with a permanently sour expression, somehow, the combination of his size and shape and that formidable grimace created an effect of power.

Albert mellowed into adulthood, but I feared him when I was 5, and 9, and 12. Now, at 15, although I seethed with secret resentment, I became his personal slave.

This passage is written in past tense, which, in this case, contributes to the adult feeling by automatically setting up an air of nostalgia, with the narrator reminiscing about earlier times. So let's change to present tense and see what happens.

Example 2: Past Tense vs. Present Tense

Albert Klein rules our street. A short, scraggly boy with a permanently sour expression, somehow, the combination of his size and shape and that formidable grimace create an effect of power.

Albert mellowed into adulthood, but I feared him when I was 5, and 9, and 12. Now, at 15, although I seethe with secret resentment, I have just become his personal slave.

Using present tense does make the passage feel a bit more like it's happening now, but it doesn't do much to change the adult tone.

Slush Pile!

Watch your voice! Failing to distinguish between the way you, the author, think and talk and the way your characters think and talk is one of the most common reasons manuscripts get rejected. Try putting yourself into your character's head when you write. If you need help getting started, borrow some basic acting techniques: try wearing different hats (literally!) for each of your characters. Pretend you're onstage, portraying your character in an important scene. Read scenes out loud and tape yourself to "hear" your voice. Find a way to "be" the character—and your writing will stand out from the crowd.

Example 3: Vocabulary and Structure: Formal vs. Casual

Formidable, permanent, grimace, mellowed, seethed, and *resentment.* Although these particular vocabulary words are at a high-school reading level, younger or less-adept YA readers might still be able to decipher their meanings in context.

However, these words are more formal than words we typically use in everyday speech. Although you might get away with using one or two such words, there are far too many of them in this short passage.

Sentence Construction and/or Phrasing

The higher the reading level, the more you can use complex and varied sentence construction. Generally speaking, any sentence with clauses, parenthetical expressions, or asides is considered complex.

But sentences with complicated structures not only raise the reading level, they also tend to sound less like everyday, spoken language. Writing that mimics spoken language automatically feels less formal—and although casual language can still sound adult, being less formal is the first place to start.

Don't forget the distinction between your character's voice and your authorial voice. Don't use complex sentence construction in a character's speech unless it mirrors the way he or she acts in "real life."

Do construct sentences that match the reading skills of your target audience. For younger readers, keep sentences shorter and simpler. For older teens, feel free to use more complex forms.

Do pay attention to the formality of your language and sentence construction.

Formal: I feared him when ....

Less formal: I was afraid of him.

Least formal: He scared me.

Formal: ... although I seethed with secret resentment ....

Less formal: Secretly, I resented him.

Least formal: I hated him.

Formal: A short, scraggly boy with a permanently sour expression, somehow, the combination of his size and shape and that formidable grimace created an effect of power.

Less formal: He was short and scraggly and always had a sour expression. But somehow, the combination of his size and shape and the grimace on his face created an effect of power.

Least formal: He was short and scraggly and always looked like he just ate a lemon. But he had power.

Note that the less formal examples change drastically. Not only did I streamline the sentence structure but I also eliminated some phrases altogether and generally used much simpler language.

Attitude

Adult-itis sneaks up on writers all the time, and it's usually completely unconscious. Anything that feels as if it comes from an adult's perspective, any comments that imply prior knowledge, or anything that can only be known through experience reek of adult-itis.

Do check your work for subtle intrusions by an adult voice.

Example 4: Attitude and the YA Voice

For instance, this line could only come from an adult, looking back on childhood: Albert mellowed into adulthood ….

There is no way the 15-year-old narrator could know what Albert would be like as an adult, so this phrase has to go.

Adult-itis is sometimes blatant, sometimes subtle, and includes using outdated slang or dialogue that kids just wouldn't use or even sentence constructions that feel adult.

Adult: Nevertheless, Josh attended the dance.

YA: Josh went anyway.

There are endless ways to revise the sample passage to give it a more YA voice, but here's one attempt:

Albert Klein ruled our street. He was short and scraggly and always looked like he just bit into a really sour lemon. But he had power.

He scared me when I was 5. And 9 … and 12.

And now that I'm 15—I hate to admit this—he still scares me. And it gets worse: I've just become his personal slave.

I kind of miss the line "I seethed with secret resentment," but it really doesn't sound like a kid. So out it came. Vocabulary became more vernacular, sentences got shorter, more direct, and loosened up to imitate spoken language.

Slush Pile!

Don't be afraid of second opinions. Experienced writers know that the subtle intrusion of adult tone or voice can ruin a submission and make editors question your ability to produce a professional manuscript. It's nearly impossible to see every slip-up in your own work, so be brave: ask friends, family, or other writers to give you targeted feedback on your YA voice. If they say the writing doesn't "feel" authentic or doesn't sound like real kids, make the effort to correct it before submitting.

More About Reading Level

Vocabulary choice has an enormous impact on determining reading level. Some publishers keep lists of grade- and/or age-appropriate vocabulary words to help writers gauge their material. You can also get a feel for level by reading lots of books written for the level you think you're writing for.

Does this mean you should limit your vocabulary to the simplest words possible?

Not at all; challenging words help educate readers. Be mindful of the words you use, but don't hesitate to use occasional words that may be unfamiliar. Instead, find a way to imply the word's meaning in context.

Although you should make reasonable efforts to keep your vocabulary at the appropriate age level, inappropriate words may sneak in. Don't worry too much; your about-to-be-published manuscript will go through a thorough editorial process, during which above-level words will be revised.

Blockbusters and Other Role Models

With experience, you'll become more aware of using too-adult elements and get better and better at creating a believable YA voice. Until then, one of the best ways to get familiar with the YA voice is to read series books—any current bestseller should do the trick.

While researching this book, I plowed through list after list of favorite YAs, most written by girls, most of those girls ages 13 or 14, although there were a fair number of lists from readers as old as 18. Actually, there were also quite a few lists submitted by adults—usually teachers or people working with teens who have a special interest in what kinds of books they're reading.

Most of my case studies examine classic YA novels with literary merit—and to give young readers credit, these books frequently appeared on their own lists of favorites. In fact, it was interesting to see how many kids had to read these books for school—and were surprised they actually liked them!

Still, I'd be lying if I didn't report that the majority of the top 10 favorites were light, breezy chick lit ranging from beautifully written, well-crafted, entertaining, and dramatic series books to some lurid soap opera-type series—all of them dealing with teen problems ranging from the shallow to the deeply emotional.

> **Pen Pal** _____
>
> Excellent sources of popular YA books include the Internet, your local library, and your local high school. Check Amazon.com for lists posted by young readers. Most libraries keep binders filled with different categories of YA titles to make your search easier. And don't forget to check the Sunday best-seller lists!

Popular series books are usually shot through with plenty of teen attitude and slang-filled, stylized language. Several are in diary format; all are easy to read, with lots of white space on the page. Their main characters are easy to relate to, and though they face plenty of bumps and scrapes are basically resilient, cheerful, and optimistic.

Series Stars and Other Heroines

There's an art to creating characters so likeable that readers demand title after title. In fact, we should all be so lucky! It's a gift to be able to write books that touch vast numbers of readers; books that are enjoyable while at the same time offering readers comfort, support, or validation.

If you've ever struggled through a lesser book that's trying desperately hard to be funny and wise and real but isn't, you'll admire the talent behind the genre even more.

At the time this book is being written, a typical top 10 YA list might include more substantial books by the authors represented here (Cormier, Crutcher, Lowry, Paterson, Sachar, Zindel, etc.) as well as wildly popular titles intended for teens, adults, and even middle-grade readers.

Typical top 10 books chosen by teens include the following:

- The Sisterhood of the Traveling Pants books by Ann Brashares

- The Princess Diary books by Meg Cabot

- Georgia Nicholson books (ex. *Angus, Thongs,* and *Full Frontal Snogging*) by Louise Rennison

- The Shopaholic books by Sophie Kinsella

- The Bridget Jones books by Helen Fielding

- The Harry Potter books by J. K. Rowling

- A Series of Unfortunate Events series by Lemony Snickett

- *Sloppy Firsts* and *Second Helpings* by Megan McCafferty

- Gossip Girls series by Cecily Von Ziegesar

- The A List series by Zoey Dean

Have Spunk Will Travel

Bestsellers don't happen by accident. A few common threads run through these titles. Maybe your book will be listed next—if your epic has these required elements:

- An immensely appealing main character

- A diverse supporting cast of friends

- Complications from family

- Inventive, funny, and/or heartbreaking events

- Effective subplots

- A deceptively casual tone

- A heavy dose of reality

If you take the best of these books and describe their heroines by one quality, it would be "spunk." Whether their story lines are funny or dramatic, these leading ladies share huge reserves of determination. They may fumble through life, making mistakes and getting things wrong, but they always bounce back and find a way to turn troubles into triumphs.

Overall, these protagonists are deeply involved with friends and family and school, and their problems cover the full range of teen experience, from being terminally geeky and trying to fit in, to coming to terms with abuse, addiction, death, divorce, drugs, gender issues, racism, single parenthood, step–siblings, suicide … you name it.

Pen Pal

Lots of writers hate going to bookstores. Seeing all those other books in print incites feelings of envy, jealousy, resentment, or hopelessness. But take heart! Fact is, success breeds success. The sheer number and diversity of books out there means *your* book has a shot at stardom, too: there's a reader waiting for your style. Never compare your writing to anyone else's or you'll begin to question your ideas and your talent. Instead, learn as much about your craft as you can, then go for it!

Adult vs. Teen Protagonists

The main difference between the popular YA series books and their adult counterparts is that whereas the characters in both deal with relationship problems and the conflicting demands of family and friends, the adults' struggles are centered more on external conflicts than internal ones.

- Bridget Jones suffers through intolerable jobs and intolerable bosses while she deals with varied friends, her mother's infidelities, and the quest for Mr. Right.

- Shopaholic series star Becky Bloomwood, also deeply committed to friends and family, struggles to overcome her shopping obsession and balance her checkbook while searching for Mr. Right.

One reason both these adult series appear on lists of teen's favorite books may be the basic likeability of their main characters: Bridget and Becky are endearing, sometimes flighty, big-hearted and kind characters who get into one hilarious jam after another, always rescued by a combination of charm, native intelligence, and an uncanny knack for finding the silver lining in any disaster. But for the most part, they already know who they are; they're not searching for an identity as much as trying to get things right. (And they both find Mr. Right.)

Let's look at top-selling YA series heroines to see how they capture the teen reader's interest:

- Mia Thermopolous, teen star of The Princess Diaries books, gets into one scrape after another with foes at school, her friends and family, and the quest for Mr. Right Teen while suffering teenage angst.

♦ Georgia Nicholson, heroine of Louise Rennison's British series (also in diary format) gets entangled with friends, family, and boys while searching for Mr. Right Teen, and enduring teenage angst.

At first glance, these YA heroines are very similar to their adult counterparts. But there's an essential difference between them: the search for inner identity.

Here's a brief description of the kinds of conflicts suffered by our teen heroines:

Mia Thermopolous, *The Princess Diaries*, Book I:

Mia undergoes a Cinderella-like transformation in Book I, going from geeky outcast loner to well-groomed and poised girl-with-a-boyfriend loner. She also happens to become the ruler of a small principality. Along the way, she espouses a personal philosophy embracing vegetarianism, saving the planet, loving animals, and fighting corporate greed.

Georgia Nicholson, *Angus*, *Thons*, and *Full-Frontal Snogging*:

Georgia speaks in vivid, catchy slang, casts a hilariously ironic eye on everyone and everything, and generally pursues her dream-boy-of-the-moment in one misadventure after another.

> **Ink Spot**
>
> The slang I use is partly made up and partly what we used at school and partly what me and my friends use now … the expression as thick as two short planks, or mad as a loon, or two short loons is from me and my mates now … it can take us years to get to the end of a sentence when we are in the mood. It's fantastic actually because it has become a real cult over here, all over the country girls are calling their dads Vati and asking if they can go to the piddly diddly department. Even more fab is that I have now started getting letters from American girls saying that they are "practicing being British" and can I send them anymore British words so that they can get really good at it!!! Fab!
>
> —Louise Rennison, creator of Georgia Nicholson

Bridget, Lena, Carmen, and Tibby, *The Sisterhood of the Traveling Pants*:

In the more dramatic of the series books, the four main characters of The Sisterhood of the Traveling Pants face multiple gut-wrenching situations, including a mother's suicide and the death of a terminally ill young friend, while enduring torn loyalties, broken families, first love, first sex, first broken heart, and an array of betrayals and reversals … a smorgasbord of teen troubles.

While all the teen heroines blunder into more dilemmas and mishaps than the average girl, they're all in the process of defining themselves and figuring out how they want to live in the world, while mired—appropriately—in self-obsession and confusion. Teen readers will always pick and choose from both adult and YA books, but only the YA novels focus on true teenage concerns.

 Pen Pal _____

Whatever the subject matter, whether somber in tone or zany and playful, the underlying themes of YA books center on the main task of adolescence: the perilous journey toward self-image and identity.

Adult book heroine Bridget Jones may suffer over her fluctuating weight and every disaster that befalls her, but she's already out in the world pursuing a career that reflects her interests and strengths.

Her teen counterparts are still struggling to define and identify their interests and strengths, and this quest plays a hugely important part in every plot and subplot of a YA book.

When Princess Diaries' YA heroine Mia learns she's a real, live princess, her identity struggle becomes an extreme example of the universal adolescent identity struggle. Mia's story lines show her constantly defining and redefining what it means to be a princess.

Accepting or rejecting the values, ideals, and moral choices thrown at her from every angle, Mia's story includes delightfully eccentric specifics: her free-spirited, social rebel artist mother provides a totally different role model than her ostentatiously rich, conventional, and rule-driven grandmother. Her friend Tina Hakim-Baba freely indulges in romance novels and fantasy while her super-genius, intellectual, TV-cable-show host and long-time best friend Lily Moskovitz disparages anyone not dedicated to political activism and moral outrage.

Chameleon-like, Mia's burgeoning personality borrows and reflects and rejects different aspects of these outside influences until she finds a way to embrace her own contradictory impulses: relishing both a totally flattering makeover while wielding her princess power to create social justice.

With adult heroines, we already know their characters, quirks, and general moral stance; the fun is in seeing them react when they're thrown into zany or serious situations. Watching *I Love Lucy*, we already know that Lucy Ricardo will make the worst possible choice and get in over her head. Hubbie Ricky Ricardo will find out, explode, then lovingly forgive her.

With YA heroines like Mia, or Georgia Nicholson, or the heroines of the Sisterhood of the Travelling Pants, the fun and suspense comes from *not* knowing how they'll react in any given situation. When vegetarian Mia realizes she can use her royal authority to protect animals, the reader is as surprised and thrilled as Mia herself at this discovery.

Getting Practical

Before you start writing your own teen series, keep in mind that, unless you have a track record, you're far more likely to sell a single title than an entire book series. But don't worry; if your single title is successful and has series potential, editors and agents will flock to you with offers.

But first concentrate on creating your own memorable characters—and polish up those writing skills. Because books such as these are really, really hard to write. And even if you're blessed with a rare talent for breezy language and plots that flow effortlessly from one enthralling situation to the next, you'll be competing with the best.

The Least You Need to Know

- Word choice, sentence structure, and tone affect the voice of your story.
- Formal and stilted language discourages YA readers.
- Paying attention to reading level pays off because you'll attract more readers with appropriate "mechanics": vocabulary, construction, and tone.
- Don't underestimate the skill level of popular YA series, because their authors have lessons to teach about creating vivid, engaging characters and plots that draw readers in, and keep them coming back. No easy feat!
- Whatever the subject matter, YA books always center on self-image and identity.

Chapter 9

Description: Where Are We and What Was He Wearing?

In This Chapter

◆ Why good books need good descriptions

◆ How and when to use description

◆ Description dangers to avoid

Description. The very word sends chills down my spine—chills of dismay. I'm one of those people who dreads writing descriptive passages, who's terrified by the thought of writing metaphors, similes, or anything vaguely approaching poetic imagery. Okay, I admit it—I can't even understand poetry unless it's read out loud.

Unfortunately, you simply can't write fiction without writing description. So I'm sharing the tricks I've learned to get over my fears and put description to work. And work it does—you'll probably be surprised by the many roles description plays in creative fiction. This chapter examines those roles to show how and when to use description—and how to avoid common descriptive mistakes.

Why Is Description So Important?

Reading is an active, visual process. Although writing is a form of verbal communication, the written word actually creates visual images in the reader's mind. The more vivid the images are, the more a reader feels involved with the story.

When I read a novel, I find myself continually flipping to the front cover to see what the characters look like. In fact, most YA book covers feature faces—not abstract designs or graphics. This emphasizes, yet again, the fact that YA fiction is so thoroughly immersed in character and intimacy. Most young readers share the need to "see" the people, places, and things in your story, and it's your job to supply them with the necessary details.

Show, Don't Tell

The main reason for including descriptive details in a story boils down to that cardinal rule of writing fiction: show, don't tell.

What does that mean, exactly?

Well, when you tell the reader something, you simply lay it out there, spoon-feeding information to the reader in a passive, easy, and probably not very exciting or imaginative way. On the other hand, when you "show" a reader something, you paint a vivid picture by using visual images that really help the reader get your point. Here's an example:

Telling: Mary's family was very poor.

Showing: Mary walked gingerly up the front stairs of her family home, careful to skip the broken and cracked steps. She gazed toward the porch's faded blue paint, which was peeling in more places than Mary could count. As she reached for the front door, she noticed a familiar sight on the doorknob—the bright orange tag left by the gas company, a not-so-friendly reminder that the service was about to be terminated due to nonpayment.

Signs That You Are a "No-Show" Writer

Red flags that signal telling rather than showing:

- **Using too many adverbs.** Less is usually more; it's always more effective to show actions rather than relying on adverbs to do the work for you. Sometimes you will have no choice but to use adverbs, but they are often a sign of taking the easy way out.

Weaker: "I hate you!" she screamed angrily.

Stronger: "I hate you!" she screamed as she slammed the door behind her.

Or even: "I hate you!" She yanked the door open and slammed it behind her, leaving a wake of anger in the room.

◆ **Using inactive verbs. Example:** *to be.* Using *to be* or any of its variations (*am, is, are,* etc.), deadens the action and indicates that you are telling, not showing. Your writing will grow stronger by eliminating passive verbs.

Weaker: He was running away down the crooked sidewalk. She began to follow.

Stronger: He raced down the crooked sidewalk. She followed.

Or even: He raced down the crooked sidewalk. She sprinted after him.

◆ **Using *look* or *feel*.** Almost as bad as the inactive verb, these words signal that you're taking the easy way out. You may need them occasionally, but in general, they're the sign of a lazy writer.

Weaker: Amanda was sad. She felt tired and lonely as she sat on the park bench. Then she rose and headed toward her apartment.

Stronger: Amanda's sadness overwhelmed her. Tired to the bone, she pushed away from the park bench and headed toward her now-empty apartment.

Or even: Amanda's sadness was like a burden she was too weak to carry. With an effort, she pushed away from the park bench and headed toward her now-empty apartment.

Pen Pal _____

One major difference between fiction and nonfiction is that fiction, in general, features much more in the way of descriptions and details that really help paint a picture for the reader.

◆ **Using clichés.** Experienced writers avoid stale, tired phrases such as "steely blue eyes," or "flaming red hair." If blue eyes or red hair are necessary character details, find more creative ways to describe them. But first consider digging deeper: what really matters about those blue eyes? Is it the way they lure you in, charmed by the unusual color, only to find yourself scrutinized with unbearable intensity? And maybe that red hair is a dead giveaway that Uncle Bill is not her father. Otherwise, why do we really care?

◆ **Using too many adjectives.** Sure, it's easy to write descriptions with adjectives–but try replacing some "easy" adjectives with descriptive language and actions:

Weaker: My old bedroom was large and yellow and bright. It made me feel better to be there. It had wallpaper sprinkled with cheerful sunflowers.

Stronger: My old bedroom was large and yellow and bright. I felt better there, looking at the wallpaper sprinkled with its cheerful sunflowers.

Or even: Sunlight streaming over the window sills warmed the familiar coverlet, lifting my spirits. I couldn't help feeling cheerful, even optimistic. "It's the sunflowers," Mom always said. "I love that wallpaper."

Tips for Showing, Not Telling

Here are some tips for helping to develop your "showing skills:"

◆ **Use specific details.** The more specific, the better. Instead of saying something is blue, use "sky blue" or "the shade of blueberries, bursting with juice." Using specific names also helps readers visualize your scene: "the green car" vs. "the dynamic Mazerati, racing car green." "A big dog." "A dog big as a Shetland pony."

◆ **Use sensory images.** Besides visual descriptions, sensory information such as smells, textures, sounds, warmth or cold will add power to your descriptions. "It was hot and sticky" vs. "A thin film of moisture coated everything I touched. I yearned for a cool breeze."

◆ **Use specific actions to make your point.** Instead of telling us a character is careless, show him dropping important papers, breaking his girlfriend's favorite vase, or dropping his car keys into his pocket, then changing his jeans and leaving without the keys, etc.

◆ **Use dialogue to provide descriptive information.** Adding descriptive details into a conversation between characters is a great way to convey information to the reader.

Uses of Description

Description tells us how people, places, and things look, sound, smell, or taste. It gives important character information by reflecting inner qualities in outward appearances. It creates critical contrasts between characters, settings, and historical periods. The key to successful description is to use it without going overboard and bombarding your readers with too many details.

Adding Information

Sometimes an author uses description as an easy way to convey information to the reader. For example, describing a home as having "piles of unread newspapers on the front porch, and a mailbox jammed with uncollected mail" tells the reader that this is a home where the occupants have not been around for a while.

Enriching Characters

Description is commonly used to bring characters to life—to give readers a much better mental image of who this person is, what he or she is like, and why the person does the things he or she does.

Let's say you describe a character as "a weary, slow-moving man whose hands were covered with large calluses, well-earned from decades of long days at the factory." It will be immediately clear to readers that this character is a hard worker, probably at least middle-aged, and we can also assume he was a blue-collar employee.

Or if another character is said to be "decked out from head to toe in Prada, Gucci, and other designer labels," we can assume that character has a lot of money (or at least a lot of credit cards).

Descriptive details can also provide us with a deeper glimpse into the character. If you describe someone as "glancing with disgust at the homeless man on the street corner," we will assume this is a character who doesn't have much compassion for other people.

Less Is More

When in doubt, it's usually better to err on the side of spare description. In my experience, editors complain more about overly written material than about bare bones writing. Any readers would lose patience with intrusive and unnecessary information.

Adding too many adjectives and adverbs inadvertently makes readers feel as if they don't have minds of their own. Good description strikes a balance, including the necessary details while still leaving something to the reader's imagination.

Striking the right balance comes with experience—and good editing. If you're lucky enough to get feedback on your writing, or—even better—if a professional edits your work, pay special attention to what they take out. Then model future descriptive writing after the edited version.

Here's an example containing some common descriptive errors. See how many you can spot:

Rick ignored the 'closed' sign hanging on the old, wooden door, looking tired and worn, like an old piece of furniture that had been left out in the rain a lot. Throwing his filtered cigarette onto the pavement, he brushed back strands of his overly long and slightly greasy-looking hair, the color of dishwater.

Lazily, he tossed the yellowed, unfinished cigarette into the street, where it landed in a puddle of stagnant rainwater mixed with some kind of sludge and the end of someone's discarded granola bar.

How many errors are there?

Let's look at the opening line:

Rick ignored the 'closed' sign hanging on the old, wooden door, looking tired and worn, like an old piece of furniture that had been left out in the rain a lot.

Errors:

◆ Sentence length: it's easier to read several short, focused sentences than one long complicated one.

◆ Awkward sentence construction: who is tired and worn, Rick or the old wooden door?

- Too much description/unnecessary detail: "… like an old piece of furniture that had been left out in the rain a lot." Besides the fact that it's not clear who or what this phrase describes, it just feels like the author is trying too hard. Adding the phrase "a lot" is unnecessary, and it doesn't fit the tone or voice of the rest of the sentence.

Instead, try:

Rick ignored the 'closed' sign hanging on the weathered wooden door.

Let's move on to the second sentence, which is actually a trick sentence, because the same information is given in the third sentence. But since the passage is taken out of context, there's no way to judge whether we need information about Rick's hair or the fact that he smokes. Were it important, the passage could still be edited for clarity and focus:

Throwing his cigarette onto the pavement, he brushed back hair the color of dishwater.

The final sentence is riddled with errors (see how many you spot):

Lazily, he tossed the yellowed, unfinished cigarette into the street, where it landed in a puddle of stagnant rainwater mixed with some kind of sludge and the end of someone's discarded granola bar.

While I can easily imagine this sentence as a scene in a movie—the camera moving from Rick's face to a close-up of that disgusting puddle—it's exactly the kind of scene that really annoys me. Why focus attention on the puddle unless it plays an important part in the scene? Are we supposed to start wondering about the granola bar and its significance? If not, then don't draw attention to it. Leave it out. There are many opportunities to show that the street is seedy or Rick's hair unwashed, but only if we need to know this information. Extraneous details mislead readers and destroy their confidence in the writer.

Setting a Scene

Frequently, description is used to help set a scene. For example, if you describe a character driving down a tree-lined street, past driveways filled with Humvees, BMWs, and an occasional Lexus or two, the reader will be able to get the idea that this is an affluent neighborhood.

Setting is one of those oft-neglected facets of good storytelling in that it's not often "taught" as an element of writing. But if you look carefully at effective stories, you'll find that it's often hard—even impossible—to separate the setting from the story.

The impact of a place and time on events is immeasurable. Certainly the way characters react to events is deeply impacted by the era in which the events occur and the community or place where events occur.

The setting for *Chinese Handcuffs* is far less important than the events; the same story could happen in any community.

Setting and Pacing

Descriptions are frequently used when a writer needs to establish a setting—whether that means a place, a time period, or a combination of both. This is especially important when your setting involves a time and/or place readers may not be familiar with: an imaginary galaxy in outer space, for example, or a historical period from centuries ago.

Time combines with setting to create atmosphere. Think of two friends meeting in Central Park at two in the afternoon. Now make it two in the morning, and the atmosphere of their meeting becomes furtive or sinister.

Time has another, less literal function in stories. In fiction, time becomes elastic. Think about the sensation of "time stands still," at moments of crisis. Have you ever experienced that feeling, like when you're in an accident, or about to fall, and you're conscious of each fraction of a second that passes by?

In moments of hyper-awareness, you're suddenly alert to every sound, or the lack of it; you feel as if you're moving in slow motion.

Pacing descriptive passages calls for that same kind of elasticity: important events get more attention to detail than nonimportant events.

I always tell students to dramatize important events and summarize noncrucial ones. Similarly, you should take your time spelling out the details of an important scene, but gloss over transitional scenes that lack conflict, drama, or resolution.

Let's take an imaginary scene: a confrontation between two former best friends. We might take only three or four sentences to set it up:

Dean hadn't spoken to Neil in two years. Not since Neil made the softball team, the team Dean dreamed of joining.

Those few lines set the scene, explain the history, give the necessary backstory. But in the next scene, where we will see Neil and Dean meet unexpectedly at the local mall, we would take the time to dramatize exactly what happens between them during this chance meeting.

It might take 2, 4, or even 10 pages, replete with dialogue, description, and narrative, to recreate this pivotal event, as the two boys begin to work out their differences and mend their broken friendship.

No, I'm not going to write it here. (You can do that on your own, as an exercise.) But it's an example of the kind of pacing we've come to expect in fiction, from years of reading, and viewing plays, movies, and TV. There's a sense of pacing we intuitively gain, knowing that a monotonous pace, with each scene as important as the one before, could kill even a fantastic plot.

The key point is to write pivotal moments with full description, getting into the characters' minds to hear what they say, what they think, how they feel, etc.

Pen Pal

Pacing is the art of allowing time to slow down as we minutely examine crucial moments, describing every nuance; moments of lesser importance can be omitted altogether, or sped up with the briefest mention and minimal detail.

Lights, Camera, Keyboard!

When teaching pacing in terms of description, the talk naturally turns (again!) to movies. Think about it: imagine if, a few moments into *Jaws*, Steven Spielberg had suddenly appeared on screen and said, "Now, see this fin sticking out of the water? That's a shark, and he is very dangerous and scary."

Kind of ruins the moment, don't you think? Obviously, that would never happen. Instead, Spielberg uses images of the menacing shark—plus some ominous music, and dialogue between characters discussing this dangerous creature—to convey the idea that this moment is important.

Fiction imitates movies through descriptive pacing, indicating lapses in time when necessary. For example:

… Julie refused to give up her place in the 50 yard dash to Isabel. She'd worked too hard too long to ever give up!

The starter's pistol fired once. The shot rang out. Julie looked up in shock. She'd missed the race!

We have no real idea of how much time elapsed between those two paragraphs, but experienced readers understand that time has passed, partly from the visual cue of extra space between the end of the first passage and the beginning of the second, partly because they can infer that things have happened in the interim.

Easing Into Descriptive Writing: Screenplay Form

When I'm faced with writing description, I often write my ideas in screenplay format; imagining the scene, I jot down what I "see" in my imagination. This not only helps me focus on the visual aspects of a scene, it also eliminates my fear of writing narrative description: I'm not writing prose, I'm merely taking notes. The technique may work for you, too.

Here's a passage I wrote in screenplay form, which dictates that you specify the basic components of a scene: time, place, characters, and actions:

Int. Store. Day. The last of the Mom & Pop stores: attempts at updating mix with vintage '50s gems; that stops short of being trendy and hip. Would feel cozy, but it's a gloomy day and the slowly spinning ceiling fans and half-drawn blinds contribute to the dolorous atmosphere.

Behind the aged wooden counter, "Pop," 50ish, bends over a vintage cash register. A pile of cash rests at his elbow. He seems anguished; if he's not yet defeated, he's certainly in despair; altogether, a man in trouble. Balding, with bags under his eyes, we sense Pop is more exhausted than anything; underneath, he seems fit and in decent shape.

Enter Rick. 18. Exudes an attractive nervous energy; we sense he'd be a formidable foe; he's clearly needy, hungry for something. We hope he's on the side of good, not evil. He seems startled to find Pop inside. Was he expecting someone else?

Pop looks up, taken aback, but not alarmed.

> Pop
>
> We're closed, son. Sorry.

Reworking the scene as narrative description feels less daunting now that the basics are already there. However, a few things must change; most notably, the need to establish a point of view. I'll use Rick's POV, with a third person voice:

Rick hesitated, then entered Pop's—the last Mom & Pop store in the neighborhood. The half-drawn blinds made it hard to see. Vaguely aware of the gentle hum from the slowly spinning fans overhead, he composed a suitable face: mouth relaxed, but ready to flash a disarming grin when she spotted him. He imagined the surprise on her face.

But to his surprise, Pop himself stood behind the chrome and vinyl counter—two relics from another time. A pile of cash rested at Pop's elbow, ignored.

I'll leave the rest of the transformation to you, as a writing exercise.

Descriptions for the YA Reader

Most of the information I have given you in this chapter would apply to any kind of fiction writing, whether for a young adult readership or an adult group. However, there are some specific tips and pitfalls when writing for a younger readership.

Pop-Culture References

Most kids and teens today live, breathe, and eat pop culture. They know all the A-list celebrities, every popular rock band, and all the top TV shows. So pop-culture references can immediately grab YA readers' attention. But you must tread carefully here. For one thing, as I mentioned previously, this can cause your book to become outdated quickly. Also your opinion on which bands or TV shows are hot probably isn't the same as what a YA reader would think. If you do use pop-culture references, enlist the help of some teens who can guide you in this area. Other reference details that will catch YA readers' attention are sports-related items (mainly for male readers) and brand names of clothing, electronics, and other high-ticket items.

Mature References

You also want to use caution when you include details that may be more appropriate for an older, more mature readership. For example, you would probably steer away from graphic details about a female character's figure, unless it is necessary for the story—and your publisher allows it. Be sure to ask your editor(s) for guidelines on which details they may not want you to include.

Improving Your Descriptive Skills

Like many areas of writing, description is something that doesn't necessarily come naturally to many people. It is one of those skills that you can improve (often substantially) with some practice and a few pointers.

The Least You Need to Know

♦ Description is a vital part of any novel and really brings stories and characters to life.

♦ Authors use description to establish a setting, develop characters more fully, set a scene, or convey information.

♦ Be careful not to overdue it. If you start including many long paragraphs of descriptive details in a row, with no action in between, you have probably gone too far.

10

Where Do Ideas Come From?

In This Chapter

- ◆ Brainstorming ideas
- ◆ Adaptation: how it works and why
- ◆ Exercises to generate story ideas
- ◆ Writers talk about getting ideas

Very rarely do professional writers sit around waiting for an idea to come to them. Most keep lists of possible projects on hand; in fact, they probably have lists of stories they can't wait to write next. There's no reason you can't do the same thing. This chapter will try to smooth your road by offering tips and techniques to generate story ideas.

What to Do When the Pump Runs Dry

Basically, ideas come from everywhere. The important thing is to stay open to them and recognize possibilities when they appear. It doesn't hurt to keep in mind that the creative process works differently for different people.

For some writers, brainstorming techniques get the creative juices flowing, and they'll come up with the idea for their next best-seller. For others, writing exercises are a fun way to drum up ideas for other projects, or to improve the story they've already begun. You may find that writing exercises or brainstorming sessions pull together bits and pieces of several ideas into one great story concept.

Of course, you can't expect all your ideas to come when you need them. That's why many writers take part in ongoing writer's groups, take writing classes, and attend readings or book discussion groups.

Generating Ideas

Who knows what makes an idea come to you? The truth is, you can't plan on having ideas when you need them. But you can get in the habit of valuing those fleeting thoughts that aren't yet fully formed premises, but have great potential to become working story ideas.

The What If ...

Here are some examples of coming up with ideas using the "what if's":

◆ What if your boyfriend asks you to write his college application essays for him? Without your help, he'll never get in where you've applied. And you desperately want to be with him.

◆ What if an aspiring artist goes blind? Or a rock guitarist loses an arm? A star football player loses his legs?

◆ What if a girl stumbles across a suicide note—and it's from her best friend? What if the note says where and when she's going to kill herself—and there's only a few minutes to find her before it's too late?

Pen Pal _____

Writer's block ... it's every writer's nightmare, and it comes in many guises: drawing a blank, feeling as if everything's already been written, realizing your plot doesn't work or you hate your characters ... the possibilities are endless. Creativity and self-doubt often go hand-in-hand, and almost every writer is afflicted at one time or another. Although there's no magic cure, you can work through many a creative crisis by getting up and getting out. Take a walk, jump rope, make up limericks or sing silly songs to your canary—the sillier the better. Laughter and physical activity restore energy and dissipate self-doubt.

Plot Seeds

Plot seeds are ideas that come to you as a partial plot, or a loose series of events that can become a plot. For example:

- Bullet train's brakes go out; a boy and girl get all the passengers to safety, but then only one of them can be saved.

- During a media-hyped jury trial, teenaged Alex stumbles across evidence that proves the accused (his older brother? a stepparent?) is innocent. When Alex presents the evidence, he finds the tables turned—now he's accused of the crime, and his brother/stepparent does nothing to help.

Imaginary Conflicts

Perhaps a conflict jump-starts your imagination. Here are some examples:

- Elsa desperately wants to join a secret club. But the members not only reject Elsa's best friend, they make the friend their target. Should Elsa quit?

- Jenny helps Bart win Lucretia, the girl of his dreams. Trouble is, Jenny's learning that Lu's a two-faced phony. Even worse, Jenny's fallen for Bart herself. Will he believe her if she tells him Lu's a loser? And can she ever win him for herself?

- Megan loves Chad. Megan's father hates Chad and forbids her to see him. Dad gets a terrific job assignment—in Europe. He arranges for Megan to go to boarding school. Megan pretends to go, but after Dad flies off, she returns home. To friends, neighbors, and teachers, Megan pretends Dad is still home. To Dad, she pretends she's at school, sending off phony letters from boarding school every week. Can she carry it off? What will happen to her if she's found out? Is Chad worth it?

On Creating Characters

Often plot ideas are developed to suit a particular character that catches your fancy—someone you know, someone you read about, someone you bumped into buying milk at the convenience store, someone you work with.

I'm not saying that you'll use this person as an entire character, intact, but that some aspect of their appearance or their personality might stay with you long enough for you to get some mileage out of it. Maybe you'll take the outward appearance of the train conductor who punched your ticket that morning and combine his looks with the character traits of your boss to create a hybrid character who fits your story ideas.

You might begin with character first, stumbling across someone who begs to be written about. Or you begin with a plot or conflict and set about creating characters to fit the requirements of your story.

Brainstorming Ideas

There are endless ways to start the creative juices flowing. Set aside some time each week or each month and work on one of the brainstorming techniques that follow. Try to clear your mind; begin with no particular expectations and see where your imagination takes you.

Work in a specific genre: mystery, romance, horror, teen problems, etc.

- Choose two characters: from your list of everyone you ever met; friends or relatives; historical figures.

- Give yourself 15 minutes to come up with a basic plot idea using any 2 characters.

- Take the same plot idea and revise it to suit three other genres.

- Skim local and major newspapers for possible story ideas: pay special attention to local news, the engagement announcements, the sports section, the travel section—don't rule anything out.

- Make a list of incidents from your own life that you've never forgotten.

- Think about people who've made you angry—no incident is too small!

- Recall situations when you were frustrated, embarrassed, or ashamed—and couldn't do anything about it. Construct a three-act scene that resolves the conflict in your favor.

- Be an instant critic. The next time you catch yourself tearing apart the plot of a movie or a book, stop and listen. You may be on to something. Loosely outline the story, fixing major plot holes. You may come up with an entirely new take on the basic idea.

Believe it or not, published authors—successful ones—keep files and folders full of story ideas created in all these different ways. If you haven't already started your own

"Ideas" file, now is a great time to begin. Then, whenever you're feeling stuck or need to come up with a story in a hurry, you'll have your own instant idea bank to help you on your way.

Exercises in Adaptation

Adapting a story from venerable sources is a time-honored practice. I'm not suggesting you copy someone else's idea or that you plagiarize word for word. Rather, take a classic prototype and use it for inspiration, imitating the basic setup to get you started. You might, for instance, rework a story by following a similar plot but giving a new spin to the central conflict or a new set of character types. Often, updating a classic story to modern times changes so much in the details that the source story becomes unrecognizable—and you find yourself with a brand-new story.

Slush Pile!

Adapting or reworking classic stories is a great way to learn more about your craft—and possibly come up with a brand-new idea! But if you intend to submit a story based on another work, beware of some very real dangers, like plagiarism. To avoid legal problems when adapting stories from published works, look for properties that are no longer protected by copyright. Works that have been out of print for many years or whose copyrights have expired may be in the public domain, which means you don't need to pay for and obtain formal permission from the author or the author's estate. Ask your librarian for examples of novels or plays in the public domain—and don't forget to review Chapter 25 in this book for more information.

Variations on a Theme

There are so many versions of the Cinderella story out there that it's hard to name them all. *Ella Enchanted* by Gail Carson Levine and *Just Ella* by Margaret Peterson Haddix are two especially popular YA titles that approach the story from unusual angles. And it's possible to create even more variations:

- Cinderella as a boy.

- 1920s Chicago: evil Stepmom is a mob lord, evil stepsisters are petty mobsters. Cinderella is a teenaged newspaper stringer, hoping for her first byline.

- Malibu in the 1950s: Cinderella works in a surf shop and dreams of competing in Hawaii.

- The Virginia colonies: Cinderella is an indentured servant yearning for freedom.

Many successful books (and current teen movies!) are updated versions of Shakespearean dramas, Restoration comedies, or even folktales.

You might use an existing story (a fairy tale or one of your old plot ideas) as a jumping-off point for a totally new story. Adapting a story is an invaluable exercise for learning to build ideas—it's a great way to practice your story-writing skills. Why? Because using an intact structure makes your job much easier. And it can be invigorating to adapt a story. Working on a project that you haven't been mulling over for days or weeks or years, you can surprise yourself. Ideas spring to you and you're amazed at where the story goes.

Benefits of Adapting

The following are the benefits of adapting a story:

♦ The structure is already in place.

♦ The original is a proven entity.

♦ If things go wrong, it wasn't your pet project that's ruined.

Remember back to Chapter 2, in which we adapted *Ferdinand the Bull* from a children's picture book into a YA novel? Why not try a variation of your own? Choose a favorite story or movie plot and create YA characters faced with similar conflicts.

If you've never tried adapting before, you might want to choose from the methods that follow. Find a style that appeals to you.

Parallel Plots: Constructing Outlines Directly from the Source

In this method, you stay close to your source material by creating a thorough outline of the most important people and events in the source story. When you're done, you'll have a complete road map of the story's structure from start to finish—a great way to learn how and when things happen, and how many plot events it takes to move a story forward.

Developing a careful plot outline from the original story will not only show you how to pace developments in the main plot, but also how to construct successful subplots: when they begin, how often they appear, who's involved, how they resolve, etc.

Constructing outlines from source material is especially helpful if you're working in genres in which plot construction plays a major role in building suspense (e.g., mysteries, thrillers, or romance).

Developing an outline from the finished story will show you when and how often to use *foreshadowing* and *misleads* and when to insert clues, as well as how to pull together multiple plot lines at the conclusion.

With this kind of road map you gain a first-hand look at successful pacing—creating tension, pausing for lulls in the action, picking up the tension again, etc. Outlining from a source should answer many of the "technical" questions that plague new writers, and, even better, can provide you with lots of new ideas of your own.

def•i•ni•tion

Foreshadowing is information that lays the groundwork for upcoming plot developments; details that hint at future events. **Misleads** are false clues or any kind of deliberately false information. In mysteries, they are also known as red herrings.

Giving It a Twist

Most people find it hard to step back from their own writing and be truly objective about it. More often, we get caught up in familiar patterns of thinking, and that can make the whole writing process feel stale. That's why I give students a series of "shake up your brain" exercises designed to loosen up their imaginations and help them step outside their own boxes.

One exercise asks them to take the characters from the story they're writing and place them into specific, extreme situations (that have nothing to do with their story) and imagine their reactions in a short scene:

- A long trip in a car that keeps breaking down—in the desert with no air conditioning.
- The family vacation from hell—on a small cruise ship, with no way to get off.
- At a wedding, funeral, bar mitzvah, or graduation ceremony where all goes wrong.
- At a school under attack by a crazed former student.
- Under the guillotine, facing execution.
- On a spaceship with malfunctioning re-entry engines.

As an alternative to this exercise, take a scene from a story you're writing and turn one character into a duck. Or an alien. Or twins.

If you're writing a tragedy, take a scene and play it for laughs. Or vice versa.

As crazy as it sounds, students often say they had breakthrough moments writing something completely outside their usual boundaries. The idea isn't to write an instant classic, just to shock your brain into traveling a different path. You don't have to use the end result, but you may discover that there are more ways to approach your story than you thought.

Try automatic writing, by following these guidelines:

♦ Set your timer for 10 minutes and write anything that comes to mind; don't lift your pen from the paper or your fingers from the keyboard.

♦ Don't worry about punctuation, grammar, or spelling.

♦ Don't censor yourself.

♦ Don't expect anything brilliant to emerge; just keep going.

Start a dream journal, as follows:

♦ Keep a notebook on a bedside table and write down dreams as soon as you wake up.

♦ Write quickly and use the whole page.

♦ Don't make it linear; draw boxes or circles for each detail you remember. If things don't make sense, write it anyway.

♦ Write down your emotions; try to capture the feeling behind the dream. Note how you felt when you were in the dream.

Keep the journal for about a week, then review your notes and see if any common themes emerge. Over time, the themes will change.

Since dreams often work in symbols or visual images, you may need to do some interpreting to capture the essence of the dream in words. It's worth the effort; however, your own subconscious may have more story ideas than you realize!

Stop believing that good stories spring only from divine inspiration and start believing that you can practice writing—the same as you'd practice the piano, or perfect your tennis serve. You can flex your writing muscles the same as you'd stretch and warm up before a run or a swim meet.

Be diligent about developing your creativity. Tend it the way you'd tend a living creature: nourish it and give it exercise.

Here are examples of ways to keep your writing muscles in shape:

- Make it your goal to always have at least three story ideas on hand.

- Save anything that catches your writer's eye: a line, a paragraph, a piece of dialogue, a snippet of scene description—whatever appeals to you.

- Schedule brainstorming time. Sit down every other week, every month, or whenever you think of it, and have fun coming up with story ideas. Save the best ones so that you'll never feel as if the creative pot is empty.

Make lists of possible characters and situations on small slips of paper. Keeping them in separate boxes, mix them up, and draw out two characters and one situation and make up an instant story idea:

- A princess, a homeless teen, time travel (hmm—a variation on the prince and the pauper?)

- A rabbi, a high school basketball star, a traffic accident

- A drug addict, a talking cat, a stalled subway

Be outlandish. Be outrageous. See what happens. And don't worry: another idea is always waiting to happen!

The Least You Need to Know

- Stories can be created from both plots and characters; the best stories place characters in extreme situations.

- Inspiration will strike; in the meantime, learn brainstorming techniques so that you'll have a backlog of project ideas.

- Adaptation is a legitimate, time-honored way to develop fresh ideas.

- Be an idea pack rat: keep a dream journal; fill folders or envelopes with scraps of dialogue, settings, and character descriptions—and use them to keep your imagination working.

Chapter 11

Effective Endings

In This Chapter

- ◆ The difference between pat endings and satisfying resolutions
- ◆ The influence of subplots and underlying themes
- ◆ Tying up multiple story lines
- ◆ Subplot and resolution in popular fiction

Endings … the big moment that everything has been leading up to.

Sound important?

It is.

Sound daunting?

It doesn't have to be.

Everything you've learned so far about constructing a sound story has prepared you for the ending. You've learned how to make the ending an integral part of the plot, setting it up (or at least hinting at the possibilities) from the premise, to a working chapter outline, to building character and conflict—everything that's come before leads directly to this final step. And that's what this chapter is about.

Creating a Satisfying Ending

Here's a question I was asked in one of my classes: "I get the idea of using the four Cs to a satisfying ending (crisis, climax, consequences, conclusion) but I'm bothered by the idea of tying everything up with a pat ending. Could you explain dénouement in the context of a book for older kids—or even adults?"

First of all, let's make a distinction between a "pat" ending and a resolution.

Having things resolve in a satisfactory way doesn't necessarily mean that you're writing a clichéd happy ending. It simply means that you're tying up loose ends to answer the questions posed throughout the story. It's important to leave readers feeling satisfied—and that means addressing all the unspoken questions.

Don't feel like you need to create an artificial happy ending—rather, your focus should be on wrapping things up and resolving the larger issues, happily or not. Then use the "consequences" to hint at what is yet to come.

If you pay attention to your premise and your setup, you'll be able to create endings that resonate throughout the story. For instance, *The Wizard of Oz* (the movie version) opens with young Dorothy expressing boredom and frustration with her humdrum life. She's knocked on the head, visits Oz, and becomes entirely focused on getting back home, realizing that it wasn't as bad as it seemed. In fact, her adventures in Oz satisfy her cravings for the wild life, making her appreciate the very things she'd recently scorned.

Pen Pal

Stories with endings that come out of nowhere leave readers hanging and feeling betrayed. Authors have a responsibility to their readers to deliver what they promise: a story that ends where readers expect it to end. If your setup implies a romance between friends, it had better end with that romance—or offer a reasonable explanation for why the romance never happened.

The opening setup asks if there isn't a better life somewhere; the development of the story shows Dorothy getting more adventure than she bargained for, and the conclusion answers the original question: Is there a better place? No; happiness is in your own backyard and there's no place like home. But suppose the story ended with Dorothy chased from Oz by a wicked witch, or leaving Oz reluctantly, wishing she could come back soon? That ending would not resolve the original conflict. To see Dorothy expressing regret at leaving Oz would violate the unspoken pact implicit in the reader-writer relationship: readers trust the writer to answer all questions, wrap up loose ends, and deliver a satisfying conclusion.

I'll use *Peter Pan* as an example because we're all familiar with the story—I hope! (If you don't know it, briefly, Peter Pan appears to Wendy Darling and whisks her and her brothers off to Neverland, where they have exciting adventures and never grow up—and don't die, despite many bloody encounters). Thematically, *Peter Pan* asks the underlying question, "Do we really have to grow up?"

In any case, the ending of the story begins when Wendy must choose between staying forever young or returning to London and real life and growing up. How the climax plays out depends entirely on the answer: in this case, Wendy (and the boys) decide to return.

Resolution begins from that point on: not only are Wendy and her brothers downright eager to go home, but some of the Lost Boys choose to go with them!

This action effectively answers the question about growing up. Wendy's decision implies that rational girls and boys choose a normal life and the idea of growing up, embracing their future roles as men and women, husbands and wives, fathers and mothers. Even the Lost Boys, who've been in Neverland far longer than Wendy and her brothers, opt for home and mother.

The final resolution in the original book (as opposed to various retellings) neatly brings the story full circle, beginning with the information that, in fact, Peter visited Wendy's mother when she was a girl.

At the end of Wendy's adventure in Neverland, Peter sincerely promises to fetch her back in time for spring cleaning. (Some things never change.) In fact, he does come the next spring, though Wendy's visit is less satisfying this time. Peter forgets to come the year after that, comes again, and then forgets for so many years that when he does return he finds Wendy a grown woman with children of her own.

Then Wendy's daughter, Jane, happily leaves for Neverland, and there's even a final word about Jane's daughter, Margaret, who continues the pattern of accompanying Peter to Neverland each spring—whenever Peter remembers to fetch her, that is.

Thus, the author not only ties up the original plot and subplots, but also neatly resolves the bigger question of whether or not to choose eternal youth. His answer mixes disappointment and sorrow with a kind of wistful happiness: the folly (and privilege) of youth, as represented by Peter, is to not remember. However you look at it, the pleasures and freedom of Neverland are fleeting.

Return to Your Roots

Peter Pan is an enduring example of constructing a full, satisfying ending that can be predicted from the outset; yet the bittersweet resolution is satisfying rather than pat.

Does every story need to come full circle? No.

But in order to end satisfactorily, every story does need to remember where it began.

For instance, if *Homecoming's* Dicey Tellerman is motivated by her need to find a home for her siblings, we expect to see a resolution, one way or the other, that answers the question asked right from the start: will they find a home? They do, but the resolution could be satisfying even if they didn't; happy or not, the ending would still answer the original question.

Resolving Unspoken Questions

The other big question the story *Homecoming* asks (though not directly) is how could their mother leave them? Why did she disappear? And what happened to her after she disappeared?

You might be surprised to see how little writing time is spent on Mama's story in the book as a whole—even though her absence permeates the entire story. Again, the author addresses all the disturbing questions about Mama, though the answers are not happy ones: Mama, whose mental health was always questionable, suffered a break-down so severe that she's withdrawn to the point of being catatonic. Hospitalized, it's clear that she won't be returning to her family.

It so happens that the Tillermans' story doesn't end with this original book. Author Cynthia Voigt follows family and friends through seven more novels—proof that, even if a story comes to an entirely satisfying conclusion, there is always the possibility of more to come.

The Big Picture

If you look closely, you'll see that all our sample books share this basic structure, posing an overall question that's explored throughout the story, resonating within the subplots and minor storylines, and answered by the ending.

Paul Zindel's story *The Pigman,* widely credited with being one of the novels that began the YA revolution, is part of many high-school curricula. Part of the reason for its ongoing appeal is its especially powerful resolution. When the Pigman dies, John and Lorraine face a critical moment in their personal development—dealing with the same question asked of all teens on their way to adulthood: who runs your life?

Should they accept at least partial responsibility for the Pigman's death? It's not a clear-cut situation—John correctly points out that the Pigman would have died anyway; his heart was weak, plus he was already living a half-life, aching with the burden of isolation and loneliness.

Would it have been better for him to die a sad, old man or to have briefly relived the pleasures of youth, enjoyed the sweetness of his imagined family, and then endured the crushing disappointment of betrayal? Does the high price he paid outweigh the pleasures he enjoyed?

Almost as soon as John and Lorraine get involved with Mr. Pignati, the story begins wondering whether they're doing him harm—and vice versa. As John later puts it, "He had no right going backward. When you grow up, you're not supposed to go back." (Shades of *Peter Pan?*)

The power of *The Pigman* lies in the universal complexity of both its questions and its answers. Despite his rationalizations, John understands that he and Lorraine were wrong to pull Mr. Pignati into their fantasy family. With unwanted maturity, John faces the fundamental question of adolescence: who's responsible for my life? Because of his involvement with the Pigman, John progresses from angry teen blaming his parents, his teachers, and the world—all hypocritical—for his problems, to a grounded young man well on the road to adulthood: "… our life would be what we made of it—nothing more, nothing less."

Subplots: The Inside Story

We've examined the big, overall question asked by *The Pigman*'s plot. But what about all those other questions raised by each subplot? You may not have noticed, but this story has multiple subplots—all of them beautifully executed so that they feed into the main story. To end the story successfully, every plot line needs to be addressed.

Subplots support and reinforce a story's theme by echoing the main plot. If novels were musical compositions, the main plot would carry the melody while subplots and minor storylines supplied depth and nuance; at times blending in perfect harmony, other times crashing and grating against the melody with preplanned dissonance. Subplots exist to provide variations on the theme, dancing around the melody, providing contrast and shadings. Even though subplots resolve at their own pace—usually well before story's end—their impact has lasting effect.

Subplot Breakdown

It takes five subplots within *The Pigman* to bring the main plot to resolution. Each serves a double function: first, contributing to the main plot by moving it forward; second, instigating character growth.

Here's how subplots contribute to resolution:

1. John's subplot. Blaming his family for his troubles, John takes refuge in self-destructive behavior: drinking, smoking, and acting out. Will he stop?

Pen Pal

Notice how the subplots involving John and Lorraine also establish their need to seek acceptance elsewhere and set up the central question: do their problems at home justify their growing involvement with the Pigman?

2. Lorraine's subplot. Repressed by a mom who's obsessed with the notion that "men only want one thing," Lorraine is inhibited and burdened by the pull between love for her mother and the resentment and guilt she suffers from constantly lying to her. Will Lorraine ever tell her mother the truth?

3. Norton's subplot. Norton represents what John (or Lorraine) might become without a positive influence in their lives.

Norton also functions as the main antagonist: the bad seed whose appearance foreshadows trouble. Norton provokes the ultimate crisis by trashing the Pigman's house, indirectly causing the Pigman's death.

4. Conchetta's subplot. A mini-mystery within the overall story: the Pigman first pretends she's only away on a visit; in Chapter 8, John learns she's dead; in Chapter 10, the Pigman admits it.

Conchetta also functions as a symbol of all the Pigman has lost in life, emphasizing his insignificance (retired, he has no outside purpose) and his loneliness.

5. Bobo's subplot. Bobo the gorilla functions as a pitiful replacement for Conchetta, further emphasizing the Pigman's emptiness and loss.

Ironically, Bobo also represents the Pigman's reason for living; thus linked, Bobo's death precipitates the Pigman's death.

Beginning as very separate events, the subplots draw closer and closer until they mesh to bring about the inevitable conclusion.

Each subplot contributes to overall character growth:

1. John complains (accurately) about his parents, but learns that ultimately, the way he reacts to them and the choices he makes will determine the course of his life. In a nutshell, what he does is more important than what they say.

2. Lorraine accepts her mother's very real imperfections and finds the courage to talk honestly with her; finds self-confidence through managing their fantasy household, evoking John's admiration; discovers hope for her future.

3. Norton's lack of growth indirectly inspires John and Lorraine to grow.

4. Conchetta's death serves as a reminder of life's fragility, indirectly motivating all the characters to seize the moment.

5. Bobo, by contrast to Conchetta, serves as a reminder to value love and friendship.

It's probably no surprise that literary novels such as *The Pigman*, *I Am the Cheese*, *Holes*, and *Homecoming*, all of which have achieved the status of modern classics, exhibit complex story lines. But they're not the only ones.

Subplots for the People!

The best popular fiction titles, although written in a lighter vein, share the same complexity of structure as their heavyweight counterparts.

For instance, *The Princess Diaries*, volume one in Meg Cabot's wildly successful series, has multiple subplots and an overall plot line that asks the question, "Why would a normal 14-year-old want to be a princess?"

In fact, becoming a princess and trying to hide it because she's dying to be "normal" may provide the overall story line for this title, but the book gets its energy, charm, and action from its many ongoing subplots.

While main character Mia Thermopolous decides how to handle the unwelcome news, she's juggling multiple subplots:

♦ Adjusting to her new bodyguard

♦ Dealing with a lifelong crush on her best friend's brother

♦ Deciding what to do about her first boyfriend—who she really doesn't like

♦ Pursuing heartthrob Josh Richter while avoiding his possessive girlfriend

- Accepting her algebra teacher, Mr. Giannini, as her mother's new boyfriend

- Adjusting to her best friend's involvement with her new boyfriend

- Enduring weekly princess lessons with Grandmere, who represents the conflict over Mia's accepting her new responsibilities as opposed to pursuing her own interests: animal rights and the environment

All of this takes place in a rarified setting—a Manhattan private school, her mother's artist's loft, her grandmother's swank suite in the Plaza Hotel—while a full rostrum of supporting characters pursue story lines of their own.

Cabot handily ties it all together in a resolution where Mia realizes that her new position presents a chance to affect positive social and political change, proving that being a princess has its benefits.

Resolutions at Chapter Breaks

We've examined main plot endings and subplot endings—but what about chapter endings? Don't they deserve attention, too?

Where you end each chapter contributes to the flow and pacing of your entire manuscript. How do you decide where to make logical story breaks?

- Look for conflict. Within each scene there's some kind of resolution to the particular problem at hand—even if it resolves by not solving the problem.

- Look for moments that introduce an element of suspense, deliver shocking or vital new information, or subtly foreshadow coming events.

Having worked as an editor for several kids' mystery series (Nancy Drew, the Bobbsey Twins, The Linda Craig Adventures, The Adventures of Mary-Kate & Ashley), I'm especially aware of the importance of constructing "cliffhangers": that final sentence in a chapter that leaves the reader breathless and dying to know what happens next. Cliffhangers are also called "page turners" for obvious reasons.

It's a given that mysteries rely on cliffhangers, but endings are just as important in all kinds of fiction—in a sense, every good story is a mystery of some kind. (Will Mia learn to be a princess? Will the Tillermans find their long-lost grandmother? Will Stanley get out of prison camp?)

Every chapter should end with a page turner to lure the reader into reading just a little longer.

If you think in terms of potboilers, you'd probably end each chapter something like this:

"… Barton shuffled down the road, vowing he would never return. And he would never tell Mrs. Colman the truth. But wait! Maybe there was a way he could do both, and still get the reward!"

"… at last, John crouched alone in the darkened room. He spun the combination lock in the pattern he had memorized. The locked clicked, the door released and swung wide. John plunged both hands eagerly inside and touched—Oh, no! Could it be?"

Ending with an unanswered question or a leading remark tricks the reader into turning the page. In some formats, it's perfectly acceptable to end chapters with such a blatant tease. But what about more subtle formats? How do you keep readers turning pages?

Several basic choices include the following:

♦ Interrupt the action before it's completely resolved.

♦ Imply a question and leave it unanswered.

♦ Resolve each chapter as if it's a satisfying short story in itself.

The best way I know to learn about great chapter endings is to re-read your favorite books, paying close attention to the way things resolve. A skill that must be acquired through practice, creating successful chapter endings will get easier with experience, and, as always, the guidance of a talented editor.

The Least You Need to Know

♦ Satisfying conclusions are essential to a well-written story.

♦ In successful novels, popular or literary, subplots make important contributions in resolving the story.

♦ Make sure every meaningful story line is resolved before your final conclusion.

♦ Chapter endings contribute to the effectiveness of your entire story.

Part  2

Work in Progress

What good is being a writer if you don't know how to talk about writing? This part focuses on tricks of the trade, teaching you how to talk, think, and write like a pro. Not sure what a third person omniscient narrator is? You'll soon know how to manipulate point of view with the best of them. You'll learn to choose the narrative voice that works best for your story, and how to dot the i's and cross the t's with perfect punctuation. (Well, near-perfect—we're only human!) You'll get actual forms to copy so that you can create character dossiers and keep your facts straight from start to finish. Plus we discuss the dreaded word that's always lurking about, waiting to confront amateurs and seasoned pros: *revision!*

Chapter 12

Point of View: Whose Story Is It?

In This Chapter

- ◆ First, second, and third person: an overview
- ◆ The effects of different points of view
- ◆ How POV determines your most important character
- ◆ The unique qualities of first person
- ◆ Choosing the best POV for your story

Every story is written from a particular point of view (POV). Before you became a writer, you probably never thought much about it because, in a well-written novel, the POV does its job without drawing attention to itself. Once you begin writing fiction, however, knowing how to identify and manipulate POV becomes critical.

Simply put, POV is determined by who tells the story. This chapter will describe the most effective points of view, give examples of each type, and provide enough information to make you a POV expert.

Are You Talking to Me?

Answering the following questions will help you identify the point of view in any particular story:

- Through whose eyes do we see the action unfold?

- Whose thoughts are we privy to?

- Who's present in every important scene?

Pen Pal _____

POV always seems far more complicated than it is, with a slew of technical terms and variations to learn about. While it's important for you to be familiar with all these POV possibilities, in actual practice, you'll probably find one or two forms that best suit your writing needs.

These questions usually have simple answers. What's not so simple is keeping the POV consistent throughout your story and figuring out which one to use in the first place!

Before we go any further, let's define our terms. Simply put, you identify POV by pronouns:

- If *I* narrates your story, it's in first person POV.

- If *you* narrates, it's in second person POV.

- If a narrator tells the story about someone else (he, she, Aunt Edna, and Uncle Donovan), it's in third person POV.

Most fiction is written in third person. It offers the greatest flexibility and is the easiest POV to maintain. However, first person is especially important to YA books because it is the most intimate—and immediate—point of view. Since YA books are often distinguished by their unflinching intimacy and honesty, first person books predominate.

Watch the pronouns in the examples in the sections that follow.

First Person: I Speak

I watched as the stretch limo rounded the corner. It took a while, so I had plenty of time to figure out if Josslyn was inside. The tinted windows made it hard to see, but then, suddenly, a window rolled down and I caught a glimpse of Josslyn's coppery curls. "Joss"—I called without thinking, but luckily stopped myself before the rest of her name came out. Slowly, the window slid back up.

In this example, the first person POV filters the action through the narrator's eyes. He sees the limo coming, he wonders about Josslyn, he calls out to her and watches the window close. We have no idea who or what Josslyn sees, and no idea what she's thinking.

- ◆ *I* tells the story.

- ◆ *I* watches the limo.

- ◆ *I* wonders about Josslyn.

- ◆ *I* describes the scene.

Second Person: You Speak

Second person is rarely used, except for special effect in limited doses. It's an extreme—and limited—point of view, and it can make for tedious reading.

You watched as the stretch limo rounded the corner. It took a while, so you had plenty of time to figure out if Josslyn was inside. The tinted windows made it hard to see, but then, suddenly, a window rolled down and you caught a glimpse of Josslyn's coppery curls.

"Joss"—you called without thinking, but luckily, you stopped before the rest of her name came out. Slowly, the window slid back up.

Second person is like first person in one important way: nothing can be written unless *you* are in the scene. (See *Bright Lights Big City* by Jay McInerney for the best-known example of this highly stylized form.)

Third Person: He, She, and They Speak

Within third person, there are three choices of POV:

- ◆ Regular

- ◆ Limited

- ◆ Omniscient

Here's an example of regular third person:

"Josslyn was always looking for new challenges. Ryan admired her."

The most popular and widely used POV, this format uses an invisible narrator. Reading this style, you have no reason to ever think about who's telling the story—the author is.

Take a look at the same sentence rewritten in third person limited, from Ryan's POV:

"Ryan admired the way Josslyn was always looking for new challenges."

The limited POV switches the focus to Ryan, even though Josslyn is the true subject of the sentence.

Third person limited POV indicates not only that are you writing in third person (about him or her, not I), but also that you are imitating first person by viewing the entire scene or story limited to one particular character's POV (usually the main character's).

Here's a longer passage in third person limited POV:

He watched as the stretch limo rounded the corner. It took a while, so he had plenty of time to figure out if Josslyn was inside. The tinted windows made it hard to see, but then, suddenly, a window rolled down and he caught a glimpse of Josslyn's coppery curls.

"Joss"—he called without thinking, but luckily stopped himself before the rest of her name came out. Slowly, the window slid back up.

"He" acts as narrator, and therefore, we see the scene from his POV.

Alternatively, third person POV can be unlimited, or omniscient; the narrator is not a character in the story, but a disembodied voice that knows everything that's going on. With omniscient third person, you have the option of telling things from any and all characters' POV, as well as knowing everything they're thinking.

Here's the same passage, redone in third person omniscient POV:

Ryan watched as the stretch limo rounded the corner. It took a while, so he had plenty of time to figure out if Josslyn was inside. The tinted windows made it hard to see, but then, suddenly, a window rolled down and he caught a glimpse of her coppery curls.

Josslyn peered out at Ryan, knowing he couldn't see her. She wasn't supposed to make contact, but she had to let him know she'd made it through. Pretending to need fresh air, she rolled the window down partway, praying Ryan would understand it was a signal.

"Joss"—she heard it faintly, and jumped in shock.

Ryan froze; he'd called out without thinking, but luckily stopped himself before finishing the name. But not before his expression gave him away. He knew his face showed both relief and recognition—and horror at what he'd just done ….

In this version, the narrative voice tells the story about both characters, switching freely between Ryan's and Josslyn's points of view.

Most books are written in third person because it's the most efficient POV. In first person, you're limited to one character's mind or eyes. You must orchestrate each scene so that *I* is always present. In third person omniscient POV, you can speak about all characters, anytime you want, and present things from their individual perspective whenever you need to.

Using Point of View

One of the strongest effects of POV is that it automatically identifies the star of your story. Whoever's POV is used automatically takes over. No matter if the story is in first or third person, one character will dominate and be recognized as having the lead role. That's why it's important to keep your POV consistent: readers like to know who is the most important character in any given scene—and in the entire story.

Let's compare the advantages of various POVs. The following are strengths of first person POV:

♦ **Intimacy.** First person is the most intimate and immediate POV. Reading a story that's written in first person automatically makes you feel as if the story is directed at you, the reader—it lets you inside the head of your main character.

♦ **No middleman.** First person lets you in on the main character's every reaction and all their innermost thoughts. Even better, you never have to resort to tricks such as inventing other characters just because you need someone for your main character to talk to. First person gives you a direct line to your character.

> **Pen Pal**
>
> Your first person character narrates the story, but he or she doesn't have to be part of it. First person narrators can tell an entire story about another character with or without revealing their own identity.

♦ **Believability.** Because first person is written as if it comes directly from a character's mouth, it tends to make you believe every word the character says—something that establishes a strong bond between reader and writer.

◆ **The surprise factor.** Of course, you can take advantage of first person POV and deliberately manipulate the reader. A first person character who lies or deliberately misrepresents the facts can be useful as a surprise factor—as long as you make it clear at some point that the mislead is intentional. Readers tend to feel frustrated by the withholding of information or by being led astray by a character they've grown to trust. Still, it's up to you to decide how to best write your story.

◆ **Creativity.** The strongest advantage of all is that writing in first person can be a remarkably liberating experience. When you begin writing—and thinking—as *I*, you're more likely to let loose and invent details you didn't even know you were thinking about.

First Person Limitations

First person has many important strengths—and some severe limitations. The biggest problem with first person is that your narrator (I) has to be in every scene—and for some stories, that can be an insurmountable problem. Think about it: any action that takes place without your first person narrator has to take place "off camera." That means that someone needs to tell the narrator what happened when he or she wasn't around—and that can become tedious or awkward.

First and Third Person

It's a good idea for any writer to get familiar with the simple, useful, and most direct points of view we've just reviewed—first and third person. If your story has a complex structure or if it needs to follow several characters closely, however, an uncomplicated first or third person may not be enough.

Using first person can be the most intimate. In fact, using *I* as your narrator is so effective that you'll hear teachers, myself included, suggest you write every scene from first person POV as an exercise to get into your characters' heads, even if you're actually writing in third person POV.

Pen Pal

Use third person when you need the flexibility to follow separate characters, when your main character doesn't need to be in every scene, and when you want to keep your options open.

Pen Pal _____

Don't confuse POV with verb tense. Currently, there's a trend to write in present tense—which can work well in both first and third person.

First person POV, present tense: I watch as the stretch limo rounds the corner. I have plenty of time to figure out if Josslyn is inside.

Third person POV, present tense: He watches as the stretch limo rounds the corner. He has plenty of time to figure out if Josslyn is inside.

Present tense is easy to use, but becomes awkward when characters refer to things that happened in the past. The only way to know if it's for you is to try it and see.

How Do I Choose the Correct POV?

Knowing which POV to use is no simple matter. If you're lucky, the structure of your story will make the choice for you. If not, you can only proceed by trial and error. What follows are some ways you can try to find the POV that best suits your story.

♦ Create an outline. Write a complete outline of your story, chapter by chapter, to see when each character appears. When you have a good idea of the events of your plot, you can decide whether your main character should—or can—be in every scene.

♦ Put together some samples. Write sample paragraphs or pages in first and third person and compare the end results—and the experience:

Which POV feels more natural?

Which POV is more fun to write?

Which POV gives you the flexibility you need to tell your story?

♦ Get a consensus. Write first and third person versions of the same few pages— enough for your reader to get a good sense of the two different styles. Poll as many people as you can for their vote: first person or third?

♦ Experiment with a combination of points of view. When properly handled, variations and mixtures of the basic points of view can add interest to a story. So experiment with POV all you want.

As always, there is no right or wrong way to go—choosing POV is a matter of your comfort level combined with a few practical considerations (such as plot demands). Ultimately, you're the one who's going to live with the choice for the length of time it takes to complete your manuscript. There'll be ample opportunity to play around with POV and discover which one works best for each particular story.

♦ Don't worry. Relax, write by instinct, and realize that, in a first draft, you can do anything you like. Eventually, your POV will take care of itself.

Popping Heads: What Not to Do

Head popping! This is when you switch from one person's point of view to another in the same scene. It can be confusing to the reader, and it breaks the cardinal rule of consistency.

New writers are often oblivious to point of view, freely switching from one character's "eyes" to another's. It's crucial that you learn to recognize head popping so you can avoid making this common mistake.

An example of head popping, or inconsistent POV:

… He strained to see through the tinted windows; then the window slid down and Josslyn's coppery curls appeared. She frowned at the worried look on his face, thinking that if he weren't careful, he'd give them away.

We begin in the boy's POV (let's call him Ryan) and then switch to Josslyn's. Telling us what Josslyn thinks violates the original POV by pulling us out of Ryan's POV and putting us into her head, showing us what she sees. If you did want to write the passage in Josslyn's point of view, you'd need to begin in her head and stay there.

Here's the same passage, written from Josslyn's POV:

… She saw him straining to see through the tinted windows; then the window slid down and she knew he'd caught a glimpse of her coppery curls. She frowned at the worried look on his face, thinking that if he wasn't careful, he'd give them away.

When written from her POV, we need Josslyn to give us information about Ryan, replacing his thoughts with her observations of him.

Here's how to approach the same passage from Ryan's point of view, but talking about Josslyn:

… He strained to see through the tinted windows; then the window slid down and he caught a glimpse of her coppery curls. He worried, suddenly—if he wasn't careful, he'd give them away.

Third to first and back again.

Playing with POV can strengthen your writing. One useful exercise is to take a third person scene and rewrite it in first person to get more into your main character's head. Try some stream-of-consciousness writing—using first person and letting your thoughts flow freely. Usually, switching to first person and letting go results in details you wouldn't have thought of while writing in third person.

Here's an example of how to take an existing third person passage, rewrite it in first person to get fresh details, and then return the passage to third person while incorporating some of the first person material:

Version 1. This is the original version of the passage, written in third person POV. For the purposes of this example, assume that the story needs to be written in third person:

He watched as the stretch limo rounded the corner. It took a while, so he had plenty of time to figure out if Josslyn was inside. It made him nervous, not knowing if she were. Joss wouldn't be nervous—danger didn't bother her. That's how he knew she'd find a way to tell him if she were there, in the limo—no matter how risky it might be …

Version 2. This is the same passage, rewritten in first person from Ryan's POV, adding stream-of-consciousness thoughts, freely improvised:

I watched as the stretch limo rounded the corner. It took a while, so I had plenty of time to figure out if Josslyn was inside. It made me nervous, not knowing. Really nervous. I wasn't used to this real-life spy stuff; and I wasn't used to worrying about anyone else. It's almost funny—I finally cared about someone. Cared so much, that I almost forgot that I was in danger, too. Well, I'd just worry about that later—that's what Joss would do …

Version 3. In the final version, we'll take the new first person material and add it to the third person original version, keeping whichever details add to the scene:

He watched as the stretch limo rounded the corner. It took a while, so he had plenty of time to figure out if Josslyn was inside. It made him nervous, not knowing. Really nervous. He wasn't used to this real-life spy stuff; and he wasn't used to worrying about anyone else. It was almost funny—he finally cared about someone. Cared so much, that he almost forgot that he was in danger, too. Well, he'd just worry about it later—that's what Joss would do …

The new material really adds to the intimate, personal feeling in the scene—and it makes the third person version as effective as the first person.

Spontaneous Writing

Using first person is a great way to write more spontaneously and create more in-depth details about your characters. Following the pattern of the previous passages, try switching POVs by reworking a passage from your own writing.

Try taking a scene written in third person and turning it into a first person scene—with lots of stream-of-consciousness writing. Put down anything that pops into your head. Then use your editorial eye to go through your expanded first person scene, looking for material worth keeping. Then put that material back into third person.

The Least You Need to Know

- Point of view is determined by who tells the story
- Pronouns define point of view: I, you, he or she.
- Most novels use third person POV, but YAs make heavy use of first person to create an intimate, personal voice.
- Experimenting with POV will help you decide which one (or how many) will work best for your story.
- Be careful to maintain consistent POV in each scene, section, or chapter.

13

Telling Tales: The Narrative Voice

In This Chapter

- ◆ Defining voice and its primary functions
- ◆ The main types of narratives and narrators
- ◆ Special effects: manipulating voice with POV
- ◆ Mystery game: voice in action

Hold on to your hat, because we're about to meet a lot of tricky-sounding narrative points of view. Don't worry about all the technical terms; when it comes down to actual writing, most of these forms are actually quite instinctive. But you should definitely have an awareness of them so that you can speak about your work in a knowledgeable way—and also because understanding how narrative voice works means you can keep yours consistent, or deliberately manipulate it to create different written effects.

Voice is such an intrinsic part of a story that it's hard to define exactly what it is and what it does. Part of the reason it's so hard to pin down a definition is because a story's voice is made up of many elements. In this chapter, you'll learn the differences between narrative, authorial, and characters' voices. This is crucial information that will bring heightened professionalism to your writing efforts.

What Is Voice?

Voice is an intangible quality that distinguishes your writing from someone else's. For me, this is the most pertinent definition of voice, and it refers to the way your writing sounds. Every writer has a natural voice, affected by multiple factors: how you speak; where you grew up; what kind of language you use; particular phrases, syntax, or rhythms that are intrinsic parts of the way you think, speak, and write.

Although everyone has a fairly distinct written voice, with experience, authors can learn to adopt different voices for different stories and different characters the way an actor adopts cadences and accents to create a persona for a particular role.

But there are other meanings for voice, and in actual practice, these separate voice elements mix and mingle and contribute their influence to the overall voice of a story.

The elements I'm thinking of can be separated into three categories:

- Authorial voice
- Character's voice
- Narrative voice

Let's examine each element separately.

Authorial Voice

Your authorial voice is the way your writing "sounds" to your reader. On one level, it's a completely unconscious thing, because it's really the way you sound just because you're you. It exists without premeditated thought or any effort on your part.

In this sense, voice is your individual way with words; the quality that makes it possible for people to recognize your voice in a letter, e-mail, or writing assignment.

Even if you're striving to write in the voice of a particular character, or to reflect a particular time period or a particular place, your authorial voice will still color the overall sound of your writing.

In other words, you can't escape sounding like yourself. And that's good. That's what makes every book a unique experience, fills the bookstores, and keeps readers coming back for more.

Character's Voice

The easiest element to define, your character's voice is the way a character sounds when he or she speaks. Obviously, dialogue expresses character voice in the most literal way.

Factors that affect a character's voice include the following:

- Time period
- Using slang or jargon
- Age
- Education and/or background
- Accent or dialect (where they're from)

Some character traits can—and should—be reflected in voice for a feeling of authenticity. A few possibilities include:

- Impatience
- Arrogance
- Compassion
- Integrity
- Conceit
- Selfishness

Whether your character's voice is formal, slangy and hip, pedantic, or genteel with an overlay of hostility, these endless variations have an impact on the tone of your story.

The attributes of a believable voice reflect the same kind of traits we've discussed in building believable characters. That's because voice—in all its meanings—is one of the most visible aspects of a character's personality.

 Slush Pile!

If you're writing in a young person's voice, you must be extra vigilant. Of course, you need to watch your vocabulary level. But you must also take care that your young character's voice mirrors their age and experience.

Narrative Voice

Another term that has more than one meaning, the phrase *narrative voice* can refer to at least two distinct aspects of a story's overall voice:

◆ The way your narrator sounds

◆ The overall effect created by your authorial voice plus your character's voice

The trouble with discussing narrative voice is that you have to be specific about which aspect of voice you mean. So let's take the time to define our terms.

Omniscient Narrators and Other Know-It-Alls

When you really get into the idea of narrative voice, it starts to intermingle with point of view. For instance, if your narrator knows anything and everything about your character, your narrator is *omniscient*; which is effectively the same as using an omniscient point of view. Here are the features that distinguish an omniscient narrator:

Slush Pile!

Inconsistent voice is a sure sign of an amateur. A narrative that veers from casual, natural speech into a stiff or formal tone will put readers off. At best they'll be confused; at worst they'll lose interest—and respect for the writer.

◆ They know how all the characters in a scene are feeling.

◆ They can see into the characters' minds and are privy to their innermost thoughts and desires.

◆ They can comment on everyone's emotional state.

◆ They know—and can tell the reader—what each character has done in the past, is doing now, or intends to do in the future.

Third Person POV—Limited or Omniscient?

The limited POV, viewing everything through the main character's eyes, functions as an opposite to the omniscient POV, which pays equal attention to all characters.

Now check out an example of a third person omniscient narration:

"Josslyn hated it when Ryan heaped her with praise. She knew she didn't deserve it. In truth, she was totally queasy; her stomach clenched with nervous tension while she pretended not to feel the pressure. Ironically, Ryan felt no need to hide his unsteady nerves; worse, he'd developed a raging headache that threatened to destroy his concentration ....."

In this passage, someone is telling the story, but that someone has no special presence, no distinctive narrative voice. Instead, the narrator is an invisible contributor, a neutral and detached observer reporting back to the reader.

A narrator can remain unidentified and undistinguished throughout your entire story. Most do, especially in third person. But there is another possibility: creating a narrator with a voice all his own.

The Puppet Master

When an omniscient narrator sets the tone for an entire book, I think of the narrator as a puppet master, pulling the strings of every character in their fictional world.

A narrator can act as a force in your story when one of two things occurs:

◆ The narrator has a noticeable or distinctive way of speaking.

◆ The narrator has a presence so strong that he or she functions almost as a separate character.

> **Pen Pal**
>
> Like a third person omniscient narrator, a first person omniscient narrator can also know everything about your characters—and can therefore comment at will about what they're doing, have done, or are about to do.

Classic books such as *Peter Pan* and *The Secret Garden* have narrators with voices so distinct that they influence the entire tone of the story:

◆ From *Peter Pan* by J. M. Barrie; first person omniscient narrator:

"If he thought at all, but I don't believe he ever thought, it was that he and his shadow, when brought near each other, would join like drops of water; and when they did not he was appalled."

◆ From *The Secret Garden* by Frances Hodgson Burnett; third person omniscient narrator:

"When Mary Lennox was sent to Misselthwaite Manor to live with her uncle, everybody said she was the most disagreeable-looking child ever seen. It was true, too."

How do you recognize this type of narrator?

A narrator is a puppet master if ...

- Occasionally, the narrator is the only character in a scene.

- The narrator talks directly to the reader.

- The narrator expresses strong opinions.

- The narrator has attitude.

How POV Affects Voice

Whatever the narrative voice, the effect it has is greatly influenced by POV; conversely, manipulating the POV can have great influence over the effect of the narrative voice.

In *Chinese Handcuffs*, author Chris Crutcher chooses a variety of different points of view to achieve different narrative effects.

Crutcher switches voices for different purposes. Present-day events are shown by an unobtrusive, neutral third person voice. For flashbacks, he changes to present tense third person, creating an especially detached voice—an effective way to indicate the horror and distaste each character feels for those earlier events.

Finally, he uses the letter format to create the equivalent of a first person narrator. In Dillon's letters, we see him at his most vulnerable; anguishing over the past, airing his conflicted emotions in the present.

What Voice Can Tell You About Story Elements

In my classes, we play a game to determine voice, examining mystery passages to see what voice tells us about the basic elements of a story.

Here are some question suggestions:

- When does the story take place (e.g., present day, historical, 1930s or later)?

- Is the setting urban or rural?

- Is the speaker male or female?

- How soon did you decide the gender? Why? Were you right or wrong?

Is the main character ...

- ◆ Young or old?

- ◆ Caring or callous?

- ◆ Smart or dumb?

- ◆ Educated or uneducated?

Some of the answers will be influenced by content. Some will come from intuiting facts, some from information given in the text. I tell students to be aware of factors such as dialect, tone, and content as they affect the overall voice.

We can duplicate the exercise here (though, of course, I won't know your answers!). Read the following passage and decide how you would answer the above questions.

Secret passage:

I remember there was a long time when I thought modern science wasn't nothing but some jive stuff, and that was because the only thing it ever did for 116th Street was to get everybody in jail. And on 116th Street we could get in jail being downright primitive—we sure didn't need new ways. I wasn't the only one in jail so don't think I'm just getting my thing off my chest either. Butch was in jail, Angel was in jail, Fast Sam, Binky, Light Billy, Dark Billy, and Clyde.

Secret passage identified:

From *Fast Sam, Cool Clyde and Stuff* by Walter Dean Myers; one of his many biting urban tales centered on adolescent boys with too much energy and sass for their own good.

The Least You Need to Know

- ◆ The voice of any piece of writing is created by a combination of character details (background, upbringing, locale), setting details (time and place), technical choices (POV), as well as that indefinable something—the author's voice, which lends every piece of writing its own personality.

- ◆ Omniscient narrators know everything about the characters in a story; a limited POV narration tells the story only from the main character's point of view.

- ◆ Some narrators are so distinct in attitude and opinion that they become characters in their own right. Other narrators are "invisible," playing no special role.

- ◆ Point of view influences the voice of a story and can be manipulated to create a variety of effects, such as making the voice more personal or more detached.

The Important Work of Dialogue: "Can We Talk?"

In This Chapter

- ◆ What is dialogue?

- ◆ Putting the reader into the action

- ◆ Dramatized vs. summarized scenes

- ◆ Using dialogue to inform, build character, and forward the plot

Dialogue consists of any words spoken by the characters in your text. Everything else—descriptions of people, places, and things; a character's inner musings and dreamlike reveries; even vivid accounts of action—is narrative.

"How do you recognize dialogue?" she asked.

"If it's dialogue, it's in quotes," he answered.

"You mean, those little double line things?" she asked.

"Exactly. Dialogue is words followed by attributives enclosed in quotation marks."

"Attributives—you mean, 'he said,' or 'she said'?"

"That's it," he told her, grinning.

You may not be aware of the sneaky ways authors manipulate dialogue—but you're about to learn them! That's because written dialogue is rarely about conversation.

Strong fictional dialogue is designed by you, the writer, to perform several crucial functions:

◆ Dialogue informs.

◆ Dialogue establishes character.

◆ Dialogue forwards the plot.

You'll learn about each of these functions in turn, but for now this chapter focuses on the overall, most critical function of all: dramatization.

How Dialogue Dramatizes

Remember back in Chapter 9, where we talked about using description to "Show, don't tell?" Dialogue accomplishes the same task in a different way. Did you ever have show-and-tell day in kindergarten? You were asked to bring in an object to show to the class, and then tell all about it. Well, fiction is just a written form of show-and-tell—many alternating moments of showing and telling. Dialogue is the show—the equivalent of holding up an object so everyone in the class can see what it is; tell is the story you tell about it—explaining and embellishing.

Pen Pal _____

Variety is the spice of life … and the printed page. Readers are affected by the look of a page: Solid blocks of narration or endless pages of dialogue are intimidating—especially to younger readers. Learn to vary the rhythm of your writing by paying attention to how the page looks. Break up lengthy narrative passages with dialogue, and vice versa. Creating balance makes pages look—and sound—more pleasing.

It may sound contradictory that in fiction, telling is not the words your characters speak; if you think about it, however, it makes sense. The words you use to narrate a story are narrative; the pictures you create by using dialogue show what's happening between the characters.

Semantics aside, if you read any book on writing or take any writing class, "show, don't tell" will be in there somewhere. So let me show you what I mean.

Narrative:

Frank asked Ernest if he wanted to go along. Ernest did.

Dialogue:

"Ernest," Frank said, "want to come along?"

"Sure thing!" Ernest grinned.

That may not be the most brilliant dialogue, but it serves my point: without dialogue, you can only explain what's going on. With dialogue, you create a living moment; the reader experiences the moment as it is happening and becomes part of it.

Remember, everything that isn't dialogue is narrative, and narration, by definition, is the act of telling a story. With dialogue, you're not telling, you're showing. Dialogue puts the reader into the action.

> **Pen Pal**
>
> "Show, don't tell!" No doubt your English teacher hammered you with this old catch-phrase. And she was right. The more active your writing is, the more you show a scene by dramatizing events in dialogue, the more effective it is for the reader.

No matter how scrupulously you describe actions, feelings, or thoughts, scenes without dialogue are just that: descriptions of events. Scenes that lack dialogue will always read like an outline, or a commentary, or a summary of events. Only dialogue can fully dramatize a scene.

Even minimal dialogue, including throwaway words or phrases ("Sure!" "You bet!"), has the power to impart this feeling of immediate action to a fictional moment. That's why you'll often see long passages of exposition or narration broken up by throwaways or short bursts of dialogue.

Scene vs. Summary

As an editor, the most frequent editorial note I add to any manuscript is a big circle around a passage and, scrawled in the margin, one word: *dramatize!*

What makes the difference between a dramatized *scene* and a *summarized* scene? Dialogue!

def•i•ni•tion

> **Scenes** are dramatized narrative passages; they are summaries brought to life through dialogue. **Summaries** are explanations (narrations) of events; they describe people, places, and things, and keep readers at a distance.

Let's use the screenplay analogy. Screenplays (and stage plays) consist of scenes made up of dialogue. The little narrative that appears is minimal, usually giving barebones information like who's in the scene, where they are, what time of day it is, etc.

Pen Pal

Adding dialogue is the simplest, most effective way to bring a scene to life. Adding dialogue puts the reader into the action.

Mostly, the narrative is there to help the producers, directors, and actors capture the writer's intent. The narrative describes crucial information pertaining to the way the scene appears. The dramatic content is conveyed through the actors' dialogue.

Narrative fiction is no different; passages with dialogue are scenes. Narrative passages, without dialogue, may give similar information or describe what's going on, but they are not called scenes unless they include characters speaking to one another.

If you have a completed—or nearly completed—story on hand, you can replicate one of my most effective classroom exercises. Go through the story and mark each important moment as either a "scene" or a "summary."

In my classes, most students are surprised to find so many summarized passages. They're even more surprised when I tell them to choose one of the summarized passages and write two to four additional pages of that scene alone, expanding the length simply by adding dialogue.

Usually, there's lots of moaning and groaning, but before long, they're hard at work and amazed at how much more there was to write in a single scene. That's because adding dialogue opens up the dramatic possibilities of a scene. When your characters start talking, personal details pop up, things that might not have occurred to you if you'd simply explained the situation in narrative form.

Expanding the Action

Dialogue also makes scenes longer because lines of dialogue take up a lot more space on the page than lines of narration—helpful to know if you have a quota of pages to fill!

But dialogue expands scenes in more important ways than line count—it makes scenes more personal. It also forces you to use active verbs and enough description to make the reader feel they're in the moment instead of just hearing about it.

Adding material to a scene presents a challenge: how to flesh them out so that the pacing of the story is improved, not slowed down. Let's take a dramatized scene, remove the dialogue, and see what happens.

From *Holes* by Louis Sachar:

In this passage, Stanley, our protagonist, has just arrived at a detention center for boys after being wrongly convicted of stealing. Mr. Sir, one of the guards, taunts Stanley, indirectly warning him not to try to escape. To see how much the scene "shows" without its original dialogue, I'll rewrite it in narrative form, trying to do it justice:

Stanley assured Mr. Sir that he wasn't going to run away. Mr. Sir approved. Told Stanley that nobody ran away. Told him they didn't need a fence. Told him why, too—because they had the only water for a hundred miles. Told him that if he ran away, he'd be buzzard food in three days. Stanley could see some kids dressed in orange and carrying shovels dragging themselves toward the tents. Mr. Sir asked if he was thirsty. He was, Stanley told him gratefully. Mr. Sir said he'd better get used to it. He was going to be thirsty for the next 18 months.

It's a dramatic passage, and even without the dialogue you get a good feel for the give and take of the scene. But only when you restore the original dialogue do you begin to experience Mr. Sir's dryly sardonic cruelty:

"I'm not going to run away," Stanley said. "Good thinking," said Mr. Sir. "Nobody runs away from here. We don't need a fence. Know why? Because we've got the only water for a hundred miles. You want to run away? You'll be buzzard food in three days." Stanley could see some kids dressed in orange and carrying shovels dragging themselves toward the tents. "You thirsty?" asked Mr. Sir. "Yes, Mr. Sir," Stanley said gratefully. "Well, you better get used to it. You're going to be thirsty for the next eighteen months."

It's easy to see what the dialogue accomplishes.

- It gives important information about conditions at Camp Greenwood:

    The other kids are so tired they drag themselves to their tents.

    There's no water for 100 miles.

    Barren desert surrounds the camp.

    Stanley can expect to be thirsty much of the time.

- ◆ It also gives information about Mr. Sir's character:

  He lacks compassion and sympathy.

  He doesn't coddle or protect campers.

  He puts little value on campers' lives.

- ◆ Lastly, it gives information about Stanley's character:

  He's smart enough to placate Mr. Sir.

  He's wary of being tricked.

  He (mistakenly) expects to be treated with basic kindness.

Besides delivering important information, the dialogue also makes the scene more intimate and it eliminates the need for laborious explanations about the mood of the moment, Mr. Sir's mildly amused and threatening tone of voice, his attitude, and other intangibles that flavor the scene.

While the narrative version outlines the actions as they happen, it's like reading a dis-embodied description; we don't get emotionally involved in the scene. The original passage, with dialogue, is easier to read and more interesting; the dialogue adds variety to the descriptions, makes the scene feel livelier, and really creates a sense of what it's like to be in Stanley's shoes. While the best narrative writing can accomplish similar things, we're used to verbal communication and need to "hear" dialogue to feel as if the action is really happening. In other words, dialogue makes scenes feel authentic.

A Mixture of Scenes and Summary

Good writing is a mixture of scenes and summary. Getting the right mix is a matter of experience.

- ◆ Intuition tells you when your writing is droning on too long—whether narrative or dialogue. No one likes to read endless passages of either.

- ◆ Modeling your story after published stories will get you into a rhythm. Fortu-nately, there is no template or rule that tells authors when to use dialogue to break up narration—or vice versa. However, most narratives benefit from even a sprinkling of dialogue. Learn to "show" dialogue in narratives by using bits of dialogue when you can. For example:

Kelly tried not to yawn as Aunt Martha droned on and on. "That's nice," Kelly murmured when she sensed her aunt was waiting for a response. Aunt Martha looked pleased and rambled on again, not noticing that Kelly's eyes had glazed over completely.

The simple "That's nice," is a small tap on the reader's shoulder, a reminder that you're in the middle of a scene, helping to keep a visualize image of the action in the reader's mind.

♦ Learning to look at your typed or printed page will signal when readers need a break. If your page looks like a dense block of text, chances are the reader would welcome some relief. Give their eyes some white space to look at by loosening up narrative with dialogue.

Conversely, break up too-long dialogues with judicious, but ruthless editing: what information could be summarized instead?

♦ Be diligent: make sure all your dialogue exists for a reason. If it's not giving important plot details or deepening character, rip it out.

Should all scenes be expanded with dialogue? Not at all. That would make for tedious reading. When you recognize the importance of dialogue, you become more aware of its use, and that means you'll soon notice the lack of it. Creating the right mix may be a trial-and-error thing at first, but it gets easier with practice. Until then, remember these tips.

When to use dialogue:

♦ Whenever a crucial action occurs

♦ Whenever a character makes a meaningful choice

♦ Whenever we learn something new that affects the plot

Let's look at another passage from *Holes*, by Louis Sachar.

> **Pen Pal** _____
>
> Slow down important moments by using dialogue. Important moments include scenes where a big question needs to be answered, where conflict arises, where critical information needs to be conveyed, and when you need to drop hints or foreshadow upcoming events.

This dialogue passage is preceded by three full paragraphs of narration. The dialogue begins when Mr. Sir first gives Stanley the details of daily routine at Camp Green Lake:

"You are to dig one hole each day, including Saturdays and Sundays. Each hole must be five feet deep, and five feet across in every direction. Your shovel is your measuring stick. Breakfast is served at 4:30."

Stanley must have looked surprised, because Mr. Sir went on to explain that they started early to avoid the hottest part of the day.

"No one is going to baby-sit you," he added. "The longer it takes you to dig, the longer you will be out in the sun …"

Note that the critical information—having to dig a back-breaking hole—is given in dialogue. The less-important, less-shocking information—starting early to avoid the hot sun—is summarized in the narration, as if pausing to let Stanley (and the reader) stand back and react to the harsh facts he's just heard. When the dialogue resumes, it's as if the action begins again.

The effect duplicates the timing of a scene on film or onstage: Stanley, at first attentive, is stunned at the early hours, only half listens to Mr. Sir's explanation, then snaps back to the present as the dialogue resumes.

Pen Pal _____

Experience and intuition dictate when to dramatize and when to summarize.

Through the dialogue, we get plot and character rolled into one, learning enough about both characters to begin anticipating how they will act and react in the rest of the story.

But enough; let's delve into the other three functions we left behind.

The Work of Dialogue

In real life, we chatter, we gossip, we relay news; we fill in silence with innocuous babbling; we conduct long, complicated debates and recaps; we launch into impromptu monologues and spontaneous lectures. Sometimes we don't even expect to be listened to; sometimes we talk just to stall for time while our minds are working or to fill an awkward silence.

But in fiction—in strong, well-constructed fiction—dialogue is not idle talk. It is rarely conversation for the sake of conversing. And it should never be filler.

Dialogue …

◆ Conveys information.

◆ Forwards the plot.

◆ Illuminates character.

Dialogue in fiction exists to serve a purpose. To perform its functions, written dialogue only imitates spoken speech; it is not a faithful reproduction. If you've ever read a transcript of actual, recorded conversations or even formal interviews, they usually go something like this:

"When you met, were you already …?"

"Um, no. Who? I had no—I mean, not until after."

"Well, so then, uh, do you mean you met first, and then …?"

"No, no. Not like that."

"Okay then. Not at first."

Write a few lines of real-life dialogue and no one would read another word. Instead, authors write dialogue to sound natural, yet accomplish a specific job.

Dialogue Conveys Information

The following dialogue conveys the basic information we need to set up a scene:

"The bomb is set to go off at precisely 2:35," Earnest said.

"A.M. or P.M.?" Frank asked.

"I don't know," Ernest answered.

"We've got to get that bomb back!" Frank exclaimed.

Three basic facts are conveyed:

◆ Frank and Ernest know that a bomb has been set.

◆ They are uncertain when the bomb might go off.

◆ They want to get the bomb back before it explodes.

Dialogue Forwards the Plot

Dialogue aids plot by building suspense, foreshadowing events, or explaining backstory.

Here, the dialogue forwards the plot by building suspense; creating a timeline—in this case, a (literal) ticking clock—that imparts a sense of urgency to the scene, prodding the reader to anticipate what might happen next.

But there's not much character development, or information about Frank and Ernest's relationship.

So let's revise to add more suspense by expanding the information given while at the same time establishing the character traits of both Frank and Ernest. (Any new information is in **bold**.)

"It's two-thirty," Ernest said.

"So?" Frank replied.

"So …," Ernest hesitated, "I set the bomb to go off at precisely 2:35."

"I know that," Frank said impatiently.

"Yeah, but was that A.M. or P.M.?" Ernest asked.

"What?"

"Well, that's the thing," Ernest began. "I can't remember which I used …."

"You moron!" Frank exclaimed. "We've got to get that bomb back!"

Note that the revised dialogue is twice as long as it was before. It differs from the original passage in four specific ways:

- We've added the information that it's 2:30, with five minutes to detonation, which deepens the sense of urgency.

- Having Ernest clarify that he set the bomb ("I set the bomb to go off" vs. "The bomb is set …" implies that he and Frank are in cahoots and clarifies that Ernest himself set the bomb, letting us know that he's got some knowledge of detonation techniques.

- Having Ernest query "A.M. or P.M." instead of Frank makes Ernest seem even dumber when we learn that, although he himself set the bomb, he's not sure which hour he set the bomb for. It also implies that, although Ernest may have the skill to set a bomb, he might not have enough common sense to be trusted with one.

- ◆ Varying the attributives (Ernest hesitated; Frank said impatiently) creates a more specific visual image of how Frank and Ernest might look during the scene.

So, in addition to getting more detailed information about their plan, the reader is also given a glimpse of Frank's and Ernest's relationship (they bicker) and we get a hint about Ernest's character (he lacks common sense).

Dialogue Illuminates Character

Although revising the dialogue has added important factual information to the scene, we're also beginning to understand how Frank and Ernest operate, which in turn gives us some character information. Two men who have set off bombs before yet are still bungling the job, making basic mistakes, become more comical than threatening. What happens if we add still more character information?

"Uh, it's almost two-thirty," Ernest said.

"So?" Frank replied.

"So …," Ernest hesitated, "I set the bomb to go off at precisely 2:35."

"I know that," Frank said impatiently.

"Yeah, but was that A.M. OR P.M.?" Ernest asked.

"What?"

"That's the thing," Ernest began. "I can't remember which I used …."

"Not again!" Frank groaned. "You moron—we've got to get that bomb back!"

"Love to help," Ernest said, "but I've got a root canal at three. See ya!"

This time, we've made only two changes, adding the phrase "Not again!" for Frank and the last line of dialogue for Ernest. Minor additions, yet they accomplish a lot.

The simple addition of "not again" immediately establishes a history—not only telling the reader that these two have worked together before, but emphasizing that Ernest has previously fumbled in the same way: an important piece of backstory.

The addition of Ernest's final line puts the finishing touch on his character portrait.

Pen Pal _____

Backstory is any information about characters or events that occurred in the past. Backstory may contain critical facts that are important to the ongoing story. For instance, a character who lost a leg in a car accident may harbor a grudge against the car's driver; and that grudge may alter the way he acts in the present.

It lets us know that Ernest is a cad, that he's happy to leave Frank holding the bag and feels no remorse about it—even though the mistake is his fault. It also implies something about Frank's character: he's willing to keep working with Ernest despite Ernest's obvious flaws—so either Frank is a loyal and steadfast partner or else he's an idiot. Or both.

Either way, this brief exchange accomplishes a lot in terms of the basic uses of dialogue:

- ◆ It conveys vital information: Frank and Ernest have set off bombs before; this bomb may explode too soon.

- ◆ It forwards the plot by creating suspense: one of them needs to get to the bomb in the next five minutes.

- ◆ It illuminates character: Ernest is feckless and slipshod; Frank is bossy, trusting, and not too bright.

Thus, through the dialogue, readers begin to anticipate what happens next—and anticipation compels readers to keep on reading.

Direct vs. Indirect Information

In dialogue, we learn important facts either directly—by what characters tell us outright—or indirectly, by information that's implied in a character's words.

Direct:

"He's 65."

Indirect:

"He's set to retire this year."

Direct:

"I never even finished grade school."

Indirect:

"Don't act all superior just 'cause I don't have no fancy degrees."

Direct:

"I'm a child genius."

Indirect:

"Does scoring 135 on the IQ test mean I can skip kindergarten?"

Through word choice, patterns of speech, dialects, or even intentional grammatical errors, we can learn if characters are young or old and from an urban, suburban, or rural area; we can also infer likes and dislikes, biases and inclinations, etc.

Internal vs. External Dialogue

Whether the information we get is direct or indirect, all the above kind of information is external; it doesn't tell us much about character or motivation. Dialogue can also convey internal information, illuminating character.

By the things characters say, by how they say them, by the appropriateness or inappropriateness of their comments, by the way their comments are received, we learn whether they're emotionally stable or oddballs; if they're quirky or dangerous; if they're resilient and sensitive or rigid, unyielding, and stubborn as cement.

Pen Pal _____

Dialogue can convey both direct and indirect, internal and external information. Knowing when and how to use it is a skill that comes with practice.

Here's an example of using dialogue to give internal character information:

The basic line of dialogue conveys external information only: "I'll get that book you asked for."

To convey that your character is lazy and unmotivated, you might phrase it this way:

"I'll probably be able to get that book you asked for."

The more you embellish the dialogue, the more character information you convey:

"I'll definitely get that book you asked for. In fact, I typed the request this morning. Here it is."

Or, "I'll probably be able to get that book you asked for. Shouldn't take too long, once I get to it."

Through dialogue we can learn whether a character's mind works logically, methodically, or mathematically; whether the character is inspired with poetic visions, or if his thoughts are a horrible jumble of illogical, garbled, random ideas—and this informs us about the character's inner character.

Pen Pal _____

Dialogue reinforces character by showing individuals reacting to specific circumstances.

And being informed about inner character leads us to certain expectations about how these individuals will act and react in any given situation. Sound familiar? It should, because it all leads back to the basis of fiction: pitting character against circumstance.

Improve Your Dialogue-Writing Skills

The following exercise will hone your dialogue-writing skills: Write a one-page confrontation scene between two characters, of which one must be a young adult. Make the confrontation dramatic. Suggestions:

◆ A teen caught selling drugs

◆ A teen caught cheating

◆ A teen learning that his father is not his biological father

◆ A teen finding out that she has two months to live

Write the scene entirely in dialogue, as shown in the sample exercise as follows:

"You mean I can't use adverbs?"

"Silly boy. You don't need adverbs. Or attributives, either."

"You mean, no 'he said, she said'?"

"Exactly."

"But … how will anyone know who's talking?"

"Aha! You'll make it clear by what they say and how they say it."

"Fat chance."

"Wait—that's not all. You're also going to give important background information, make one major plot point, and expose something tangible about each person's character."

"That's an awful lot to ask."

"It'll be fun. Here—use my best pen."

"Thanks anyway, Gramps, but I'll take the laptop."

Use your dialogue to give backstory and characterization as well as to convey plot information. Try to give dialogue the form of a completed scene, with a beginning, middle, and end.

The Least You Need to Know

♦ Using dialogue is the most effective way to bring scenes to life.

♦ Dialogue makes writing dramatic, giving a feeling of intimacy and immediacy—and really putting the reader into the action.

♦ Learn to break up long narrative passages by injecting short bits of dialogue; a word or two makes all the difference.

♦ With practice, you'll develop an instinct for alternating dialogue and narration to establish a pleasing rhythm in your writing.

♦ Dialogue is never idle conversation—use it to forward the plot, convey important information, and illustrate character.

15

More Dialogue: Nitty-Gritty Mechanics

In This Chapter

♦ Punctuation and formats for the different uses of dialogue

♦ Using dialogue to alter the look of a page

♦ How to use attributives for variety, style, and informing the reader

♦ Dialect—how much and when to use it

Reading is probably the best way to get familiar with the various forms of written dialogue. You can review technicalities in solid reference books, such as the *Chicago Manual of Style*, easily available in any library. Make sure you also look through *The Elements of Style* by William Strunk Jr. and E. B. White—a classic reference, regularly updated, written succinctly yet containing lots of examples.

There's also a current passion for funny, informative books on punctuation that you can ask for in either your library or bookstore. Or you can simply take a close look at the dialogue in any novels you already have around the house. But the quick review of punctuation and dialogue mechanics in this chapter should help get you started.

@*!!&$*$??$! Punctuation and Dialogue

I'm sure you're familiar with the standard dialogue formatting. It can be simply described as follows:

Opening quotation marks, followed by your dialogue text, the first word of which begins with a capital letter, the rest of which is in lowercase letters; then, at the end of your sentence, a comma, period, question mark, exclamation point, ellipses, or long dash; then closing quotation marks, a period if there's no attributive, a comma if there is.

Okay, it's not so simply described! So let's take a look at the common elements that make up dialogue formats.

Opening and Closing Quotation Marks

Your word processing program inserts opening and closing quotation marks when you press the appropriate keys. But mine gets confused when I revise, and sometimes gets it wrong, so keep an eye out for instances where you vary the conventional dialogue formatting:

"Opening quotation marks angle to the right. They're followed by closing quotation marks, which are angled to the left."

Dialogue Text Beginning with a Capital Letter

When you begin dialogue with a new thought or a complete sentence, the first letter of the first word is capitalized:

"Don't forget that you need to wear gloves," Frank warned.

"Do you think I'm an idiot?" Ernest responded.

Continued Thoughts and Interrupted Sentences

Dialogue that continues a thought begins with a three-dot ellipsis and a lowercase letter:

"… and remember, I told you to wear gloves," Frank continued.

Simultaneous dialogue that interrupts a speaker is signified by an opening long dash followed by a lowercase letter:

"Remember, I told you to wear gloves," Frank added.

"—and I forgot my gloves," Ernest said at the same time.

Dialogue that is abruptly cut off ends with a long dash:

"Don't forget to wear—" Frank began.

"I forgot my gloves!" Ernest interrupted.

Format for an interrupted sentence plus an interrupting sentence:

"Don't forget to wear—" Frank began.

"—and I forgot my gloves," Ernest interrupted.

Ellipses vs. Long Dash

Generally speaking, ellipses at the end of sentences signify ongoing thoughts, pauses, or sentences fading away. Ellipses used at the end of a line of dialogue are four dots long:

"But I never used gloves before and my fingerprints …." Ernest's voice trailed off.

Ellipses used within a line of dialogue signify a pause, hesitation, or omitted words, and are three dots long:

"But I never used gloves before … and my fingerprints …." Ernest's voice trailed off.

"You little … all this time, and I … you moron!" Frank exploded.

Dialogue Within Dialogue

Quotes within dialogue referring to a title are put into single quotation marks. A direct quote within dialogue (such as in a reference to a past conversation) is still placed within regular, double quotation marks:

"What if I'm telling a story about something that happened three weeks ago?"

"Like the time you flirted with my brother Rob, until he told you that, technically, he was really 'Brother Rob'?"

"You could have warned me," she snapped bitterly.

He shrugged. "I did warn you, remember? I told you, 'a brown monk's robe is a dead giveaway.'"

About Monologues

Those long, ongoing diatribes by a single speaker—*monologues*—are handled a bit differently. When your speaker has so much to say that their dialogue must be broken into paragraphs, you have a monologue on your hands, and they have a format all their own.

def•i•ni•tion

Monologues are lengthy, ongoing passages of dialogue spoken by a single character.

Monologues use opening quotation marks at the beginning of each new paragraph, but closing quotation marks only when the speaker is completely done speaking.

Example (using very short paragraphs for illustration purposes only):

"I never thought about fingerprints. I never even thought about getting caught—why would I? I'm not a criminal. I don't care about fingerprints. I was never breaking and entering, I was gathering evidence!

"Evidence needed by honest guys. Evidence that was going to put the real criminals in jail. Not me. I don't belong in jail. It's you, Frank—you're always getting me in trouble. Always!

"I was never in trouble until you butted in. You, and your big ideas. Always trying to impress someone. Well, I'm done this time. I'm sick of it. Sick of you. Find yourself another fall guy!"

Attributives

Attributives are those short phrases that punctuate your dialogue to keep track of whoever is speaking: the familiar "he said" and "she said" that alternate throughout a passage.

With practice, you'll learn how to vary attributives to keep your writing flowing, while still making it clear who says what, and when.

Ways to Vary Attributives

Those handy "-ly" words—quickly, tersely, eagerly—make attributes more explicit by indicating a specific attitude, action, or emotion.

Watch out for adverbs that feel awkward or unnatural—words that impart a formal tone or just plain don't sound right. Find more natural ways to say what you mean, or eliminate clunky adverbs altogether and substitute descriptions instead.

Here are examples of attributives plus adverbs:

"No way," she said snappishly.

"No way," he said feverishly.

"No way," she said self-confidently.

Here are examples of attributives, eliminating adverbs:

"No way," she snapped.

"No way," he said in a fevered tone.

"No way," she asserted.

Here are examples of eliminate adverbs and attributives:

Her words came out clipped and impatient. "No way!"

His voice rose, sounding fevered. "No way!"

Arms folded, she stared him down. "No way."

Pen Pal

Vary attributives to keep long dialogue passages lively.

Strictly alternating "he said" with "she said" makes tedious reading. So mix up attributives by using them at the beginning, middle, or end of sentences. And leave them out sometimes, just for variety.

As you may have guessed, there is no right way or wrong way to handle attributives—but there are often ways to make them more productive, more descriptive of your characters, and more graceful.

"So, like, the rules are flexible?" Ernest asked.

"In the extreme," Frank assured him.

"Oh." Ernest frowned, looking confused. "Then how do I know which kind to use when?"

"You decide."

"On my own?" Ernest asked, horrified.

"Sure. You got a problem with that?"

The more you write, and rewrite, the easier it becomes to use attributives effectively, varying placement, style, and content. And sometimes, you can leave them out completely:

"I'm not sure I can write convincing dialogue without using attributives. Your lecture said I can leave them out, but—"

"You don't need them, believe me."

"But—I need to spell out emotions, and reactions, and get across important plot information and …."

"Trust your reader! Less is more. Make every line count. No one wants to read meaningless chatter."

"Sure, but … hey, what's that funny ticking noise? Is it coming from that wrapped box under your desk?"

"Uh, what ticking noise? Listen, kid, you wait right here. I've got to run out for a sec—"

"Well, okay, but …"

Kaboom!

The teacher chortled to herself as she raced through the lobby. "Another pesky student bites the dust!"

Other Uses of Attributives

Attributives do more than identify who is speaking. Used creatively, they can add to the look of the printed page.

I've mentioned that most readers shy away from long, dense blocks of type—including endless lines of dialogue. Attributives can vary the pacing of lengthy dialogues, lending rhythm to the piece.

How Long Is Too Long to Go On in Dialogue?

Take note of your own patience level when reading: how much is too much for you? There's really no right answer; it's a matter of personal style. In general, readers lose patience with more than a page of either solid dialogue or solid narrative. The eye likes to see white space on the printed page; it's restful and less likely to induce stupor.

It's also easy to get confused or irritated by lengthy blocks of dialogue, especially if it becomes a chore to keep track of who is speaking. If you can't avoid lengthy dialogue passages, take advantage of attributives to break up dense blocks of text. You'll perk up the flow of the writing while keeping the speakers clear.

Do I Need a "Good Ear" to Write Good Dialogue?

It doesn't hurt! Students often ask if it's important to *listen* to the dialogue they write—actually read it out loud to a friend, or tape it and play it back.

Written dialogue is vastly different from spoken dialogue: just record an actual conversation, transcribe it, and read it. You'll see broken phrases, incomplete thoughts, ahs and ums, inconclusive thoughts, constant pauses, and interruptions. What torture it would be to read that dialogue!

So you must *imitate* the feeling of real dialogue. You must use the proper vocabulary, syntax, phrasing for your characters. You must also make it sound natural. But remember: written dialogue *isn't* natural. It imitates natural dialogue while pointedly accomplishing set purposes (such as describing character or moving the plot).

The good news is that you can develop a good ear for dialogue, even if you weren't born with one. You can (judiciously) eavesdrop on strangers' conversations and write down speech the way it's really spoken. You can learn to write the way people speak by listening carefully, taking notes, and then imitating their patterns of language. In the end, it's a skill that can be learned, practiced, and perfected.

Writing in Dialect

Having a "good ear" can mean one of two things:

◆ You have a knack for replicating natural speech in written dialogue.

◆ You have a knack for writing in *dialect*.

Writing in dialect can become a nerve-wracking exercise for both writer and reader, but it's been done effectively by authors as diverse as Mark Twain (*The Adventures of Tom Sawyer, Huckleberry Finn*) and J. K. Rowling (any of the best-selling Harry Potter books).

def•i•ni•tion

Dialect is idiosyncratic language belonging to a group of people from a particular area or time period; writing that imitates the pronunciation of distinctive speech or lingo.

There's no denying that spoken dialect is a flavorful and efficient way to convey information (i.e., where a character comes from) and for reinforcing character (i.e., social class). But reading written dialect can be tedious.

So instead of going through the painstaking process of trying to replicate dialect on the page, why not emulate authors who create a tone or rhythm that gives a flavor of a specific place or time without resorting to dialect?

Below is an example from an author who's suggested dialect with a few well-chosen words and phrasings.

From *Catherine, Called Birdy* by Karen Cushman

In this passage, Catherine, a member of the landed gentry in medieval times, uses her wits to discourage a potential suitor:

Corpus bones, I thought. To be wedded to this perfumed prig with his mouth in a knot and a frown always on his face! That is when I had my next very good idea.

"The lady Catherine," I repeated, trying to sound like a villager. "Oh, good fortune to ye, good sir. Ye sorely will need it."

"I will? Is aught amiss with the lady?"

"No, sir. Oh, no. She is a goodly lady, given that her wits are lacking and her back stooped. Mostly she is gentle and quiet, when she is not locked up. And the pits on her face are much better now. Truly. Please, sir, never say I suggested the lady Catherine was lacking. Please, sir."

In this passage, we get a good sense of the era and the characters' social standing by the way the author manipulates language. The closest she comes to duplicating spoken dialect is the word *ye*. In her normal speech, Lady Catherine would use the word *you*. Here Catherine deliberately uses *ye* to indicate a lower social stature.

A medieval atmosphere is also created through the author's choice of words, phrasing, and syntax:

"Corpus bones"

"Is aught amiss?"

"a goodly lady"

"her wits are lacking"

"good fortune to ye, good sir"

Down with Attributives!

Try writing a two-page farewell scene between two characters, entirely in dialogue. At least one of your characters must be a teen. The following are some suggestions.

- Leaving for summer camp

- Leaving for a year-round trip around the world

- Moving cross-country to a new house

- Moving as the result of a divorce

- Saying good-bye to a friend/relative who is dying

For a more challenging exercise, try writing the dialogue entirely without attributives.

Here's an example of what *not* to do:

Jake was furious. He turned red. "Whatta ya mean, I can't go in there?"

"Do you ever listen?" Samantha stamped her foot. "It's a secret, that's why. And you can't keep a secret, Jake."

"Oh yeah?" Jake replied, looking smug. "Then how come you don't know I'm not your real brother? Huh, Samantha, smarty pants …"

Samantha turned pale. She could feel the blood draining from her face.

Jake stared at her. "Why do you look so pale?" he asked excitedly, staring harder. "Are you okay?"

Instead, see how much information you can convey without attributives. And while you're at it, keep the adjectives and adverbs to a minimum, too!

Here's the same dialogue, stripped of all but the essentials:

"Whatta ya mean, I can't go in there?"

"Do you ever listen? It's a secret, that's why. And you can't keep a secret, Jake."

"Then how come you don't know I'm not your real brother? Huh, Samantha, smarty pants …. Hey, why do you look so pale? Are you okay?"

The Least You Need to Know

- ◆ If you read, you're already familiar with the basic format of written dialogue.

- ◆ You can quickly learn proper dialogue punctuation—use a reference book or copy formatting from published novels.

- ◆ Blocks of dialogue can be intimidating, so pay attention to the look of text on the page—keep it reasonably loose and varied.

- ◆ Attributives contribute to the information you give in a scene as well as altering the look of the printed age.

- ◆ You can approximate the sound and feeling of a specific time and place without resorting to complicated dialects.

Chapter 16

The Writer's Bible

In This Chapter

- ◆ What is a writer's bible?
- ◆ Tips for organizing your bible
- ◆ Authors' advice on bibles
- ◆ Keeping character bios

Let's face it: your characters have busy, exciting lives (much busier and more exciting than yours or mine, I'll bet). Keeping all of their lives straight—and keeping track of your settings, scenes, actions, and other important facts—can be a real challenge, especially if your memory isn't the greatest. In this chapter, I show you how to keep track of your characters and their story.

The Writer's Bible Explained

Some authors find it useful to keep a *writer's bible*. And no, that doesn't mean the thing on which you pray for plum assignments or long overdue checks (although that would be helpful, too).

def•i•ni•tion

A **writer's bible** is sometimes called by other names. Some writers refer to it simply as their "master file." Others may call it their "story bible." Still other authors only keep lists of important details regarding each major character. This may then be called a "character profile" or "character biography."

For our purposes, a writer's bible refers to the master file that many fiction writers use to keep track of all the important details about their book: character traits, setting info, etc. When you are writing a long novel with many characters and settings, it can be tough to keep track of everything and everyone in the book.

You might want to keep a separate file for each character. While it's convenient to type notes in a separate file as you work on your computer, you'll also want to print hard copies; it's a lot easier to flip through papers than to constantly scroll through lengthy files looking for details.

What to Keep in Your Bible

Bibles differ greatly from one writer to another. In fact, some writers don't keep a bible at all, whereas others swear by an extremely detailed bible.

Your particular bible can be whatever you want it to be and can include whatever information you think is important. But there are some basic things that I recommend keeping in your bible.

Pen Pal

Keep separate files for each chapter. Note the main incident in each important scene, and who is in it. Note each time a character is introduced, and keep a record of any important descriptions. That way, you won't make the mistake of mentioning a character that has not even been introduced yet.

Character Bios

It is a good idea to keep a biography or profile for each of your characters—or, at the least, the major characters. This would contain details such as physical characteristics, personality traits, occupation, lifestyle, any unique habits or features, and anything else you think is important to your book. Often writers include details about their characters' backstory, such as childhood traumas and other important aspects of their background.

Specifics About Your Settings

You should also include information about the various settings mentioned in your book. This is especially important when your setting is a fictional place/time or a setting that you have not seen firsthand. This way, you will be sure to keep your facts straight and keep your descriptions of this setting consistent. For real-life, modern-day locations, many writers find it helpful to collect magazine articles, promotional materials, or other informative literature about the location.

Pen Pal

You've probably seen books with detailed front matter, such as a list of characters, a family tree, or a map of a book's important locations. The same things should be part of your bible. Many writers also create timelines to keep track of events that could be mentioned out of chronological order. And who knows? Some of this material may end up in your published book.

Scene Cards

Some writers find it helpful to maintain a "scene card" or other reference resource that helps you keep track of what is happening within a specific scene. This is a technique recommended by Jessica Morrell, author of *Between the Lines, Master the Subtle Aspects of Fiction Writing*, published by Writer's Digest Books. Morrell says a typical scene card would look something like this:

SCENE CARD:

Event:

Time:

Day:

Weather:

Cast:

Action:

Protagonist's goal:

Opposition/conflict:

Failure/success:

Realization/decision:

Authors' Takes on Writers' Bibles

As I mentioned, a writer's bible is a very individual thing that can vary widely from one writer to another. I thought it would be helpful to include examples of how a few successful writers approach this.

Shirley Jump

Shirley Jump, who usually writes six to eight novels a year, admits it is a challenge for her. "I'm really not that organized. I have tried to do it a hundred times but by and large, I do not have time to assemble anything like that.

"However, there are some books that demand one because of the sheer volume of information needed to research. I tend to keep one clear flap folder labeled for the current book. I can see what's in there, and it's large enough that I can insert folders and divide information. I recently did a book set in Louisiana and because of the hurricanes, had to cancel my planned research trip. I spent a lot of time at the library and had about a dozen folders on Cajun dialect, mannerisms, foods, indigenous plants, etc. so that my book would be accurate. With something like that, having an organized system that works for you is vital.

> **Pen Pal**
>
> Shirley Jump's most recent comic series includes *The Bachelor Preferred Pastry*, *The Angel Craved Lobster*, and *The Devil Served Tortellini*, available from Zebra books.

"I also keep a running file in my computer on each book that contains relevant character and place details, both for my own good (to make sure I don't change blue eyes to brown) and for the editor's benefit. In this file, I put all the links to sites that feature, say, the truck my hero drives or the type of house my heroine lives in, as well as brief character histories and family links."

Kelly James-Enger

"My version of the 'bible' comes down to three simple documents: a character list that includes some basic info about each one; a timeline so I know how much time has elapsed between chapters, for example, and what time of the year/season it is; and a 'what could happen' brainstorming list. When I'm working on the first draft, I'll refer to the 'what could happen' list when I'm stuck plot-wise.

"I also find it helpful to keep a journal as I'm writing the novel. In it, I might explore potential themes or issues I want to include—e.g., 'Trina's problem is that she doesn't have passion for anything the way everyone around her seems to' or simply write notes about scenes, pivotal moments, or bits of dialogue I want to include.

"I only write a very brief character bio for my main characters, but I learn more about them as I write the novel. Then on my second draft I can take what I've learned about the characters and make sure the book is consistent."

 Pen Pal _____

Kelly James-Enger has written *Read, Aim, Specialize! Create Your Own Specialty and Make More Money*, as well as the popular fiction titles *Did You Get the Vibe?* and *White Bikini Panties*.

Sandra Dark

"If a character trait, such as a facial tic or repetitive figure of speech, needs to be reinforced regularly throughout the story, I jot it on a sticky note and paste it to my computer monitor. It's nice to be able to use all the bells and whistles on your word processing software, but sometimes low tech is a whole lot handier.

"I also sometimes use a 'character board' for novels. Find magazine and ad photos that remind me of my characters and tack them up on a bulletin board so I can refer to their physical appearance at a glance."

Pen Pal _____

Sandra Dark's well-received novels include *Calypso Wind* and *Silent Cathedrals*.

Sample Character Bio

Here is a sample character bio (provided by Jessica Morrell, author of *Between the Lines, Master the Subtle Aspects of Fiction Writing*, published by Writer's Digest Books). Tip: before filling in any information, make several copies of this sample so that you have plenty to use for all of your characters.

Profile for Main Characters

Character's name:_____

Sex:_____ Occupation:_____ City/town/region:_____

Single/Married:_____   Race/Nationality:_____

Economic status:_____   Education:_____

Politics:_____

Values:_____

Attitudes:_____

Prejudices:_____

Passions/drives:_____

Emotionality/Emotional stability:_____

_____

Introvert/Extrovert:_____

Age:_____Hair color:_____ Eye color:_____ Glasses?_____

Weight:_____ Height:_____ Build:_____

Unusual/Exceptional physical characteristics:_____

_____

Mannerisms:_____

_____

How does your character feel about his or her looks? Does he or she like his/her body? Consider himself/herself attractive?

_____

_____

Story goals:_____

_____

Character's background

Where was he or she born? City/Town/Region:_____

Religion:_____ Manners/Social graces:_____

_____

Have any significant people in your character's circle died?_____

How did he or she react? _____

Who was the most significant person in his or her childhood?

_____

_____

_____

Relationships

Present relationship with significant other:_____

_____

Past relationship that most influenced him or her:_____

_____

How did the last relationship end?_____

_____

Does your character fall in love often?_____

Does your character long for a different kind of relationship?_____

_____

Consequences of past sexual relationships:_____

_____

_____

Best friend:_____ Confidant:_____

Antagonist:_____

Children:_____ Age:_____

_____ Age:_____

_____ Age:_____

Siblings/Family members in the story:

A._____

Age:_____

B._____

Age:_____

C._____

Age:_____

D._____

Age:_____

E._____

Age:_____

F._____

Age:_____

Friends/Co-workers in the story:

_____Age:_____ Relationship:_____

_____Age:_____ Relationship:_____

_____Age:_____ Relationship:_____

_____Age:_____ Relationship:_____

_____Age:_____ Relationship:_____

Preferences

Hobbies/Interests/Leisure activities:_____

_____

_____

Does your character exercise?_____

How? _____

Favorite foods:_____

Favorite beverages: _____

Musical tastes?_____

Miscellaneous information

Special gifts, talents:_____

_____

Special knacks, skills:_____

_____

Strengths:_____

_____

Flaws:_____

_____

Main traits:_____

_____

Achievements:_____

Defeats:_____

When does your character feel most vulnerable?_____

_____

Did your character have a major childhood trauma?_____

Describe:_____

_____

_____

What occurrence from his or her past will affect the plot?_____

_____

What kind of first impression does he or she make?_____

_____

How does your character react to adversity?_____

_____

How would your character describe herself/himself in one sentence?_____

_____

Described by enemies or antagonist:_____

_____

_____

What is your character's basic temperament (calm, volatile, placid, etc.)?_____

_____

Worst fear(s):_____

_____

Secret from the past:_____

_____

_____

_____

The Least You Need to Know

- A writer's bible—also sometimes called a master file or story bible—can be a valuable asset in keeping track of your characters and story details.

- A writer's bible can prove especially helpful when your book involves many characters or unusual settings or locations.

- Character bios record important facts and are invaluable for maintaining consistency. No one can remember every detail about every character.

- Each author has his or her own approach to maintaining a writer's bible. The key is to figure out which style works best for you and helps you save time and aggravation.

Chapter 17

Outlines That Work for You

In This Chapter

- ◆ Outlining before, during, and after you write
- ◆ Creating working outlines
- ◆ Using narrative outlines

If you're a believer in outlines, I applaud you. Many new writers are terrified at the thought of planning their work, as if planning and careful thought might destroy their creativity. In this chapter, I hope to convince you that the opposite is true!

To begin, let me assure you that you don't need to worry about fancy formats. Fiction outlines are not written in that complicated system of indentations with headers and subheads and confusing numbering and lettering—something I absolutely cannot manage. Story outlines are really just lists. Fabulous, helpful, creative, practical lists that make your writing life so much easier!

But if the idea of making outlines frightens you, it may help to think of writing as architecture. An architect might begin a project inspired by a vision of an incredible building, but before he or she would dream of starting to build, the architect would translate that vision into carefully planned blueprints.

A piece of creative writing can also be built on the solid foundation of an outline, which is no more than a blueprint that takes your story from start to finish. Using outlines won't interfere with your inspiration or eliminate spontaneity—in fact, the opposite happens: with your story's basic structure and plot points lined up, you'll be free to focus on the actual writing.

As you'll see in this chapter, there are many times when outlines will be your best friend. You may be surprised to find yourself using them in multiple ways, as a creative tool and as a practical tool.

When Are Outlines Helpful?

Before you begin writing, outlines can help you …

- Develop your story's overall structure.
- Map out subplots.
- Track the story lines of individual characters, major and minor.

While you are writing, outlines can help you …

- Develop a bible listing main events, important characters, and factual information such as important locations and settings.
- Check the balance of action vs. dialogue and/or description.
- Make sure you're paying attention to subplots and minor characters (readers easily forget characters who disappear from your story for long periods of time).
- Develop a point-by-point summary, helpful in revising.

After you write, your outlines can help you …

- As a diagnostic tool, to see where problems exist.
- Complete a submission package for an agent or publisher.

Again, outlines are a writer's best friend. Work out your plot structure, subplots, and even individual story lines in a set of outlines, and you'll be free to flood the written page with creativity and energy.

Ink Spot _____

   I definitely plan (stories) in an outline. I'm a big fan of outlining. Here's the theory: If I outline, then I can see the mistakes I'm liable to make. They come out more clearly in the outline than they do in the pages. Sometimes if I've written something and I don't like it, I go back and make an outline. Then I can see where the mistakes are.

—Cynthia Voigt, author of *Homecoming* (from Books.scholastic.com/teachers/authorsandbooks)

Blueprints for Effective Plots

You've already learned how to develop a story according to a classic plot form and seen the method in action by analyzing *Peter Rabbit* and developing an outline of the finished piece.

In my classes, beginning students are asked to submit a sample outline before they start working on a story. We spend a lot of class time going over the outlines, sharing comments about what's missing or what needs to be added. Because we can't do that process in a book, I'll tell you what we're looking for when we critique outlines:

- A conflict big enough to propel the plot

- Compelling characters that fit the story

- An appropriate and believable inciting incident

- Enough ideas for major scenes or plot events to sustain the reader's interest (Remember that *Peter Rabbit*, a simple children's picture book, has 10 major plot events.)

- A sense of pacing and development in the overall story

- A sense of pacing and development within each chapter

- A balance between narrative and dialogue, both chapter by chapter and scene by scene

- Something happening in each chapter

- The sense that something has been accomplished by the end of the story—character change, plot-based change, change by implication

Slush Pile! _____

Inexperienced or clumsy writing can be remedied by a good editor or freelance writer. A poor idea, even if beautifully written, is harder to fix and therefore far less likely to attract positive attention. So do learn to use outlines to identify and fix story problems—they'll help your story get noticed!

Note that nothing in this list pertains to the actual writing or the writing style you might use. That's because writing can be separated from plot, and vice versa. Having a wonderful style is only half the battle—so is having a fantastic, original idea. I've seen manuscripts sold on the basis of a terrific plot, even if the writing itself needs lots of refining or editing help.

Conversely, I've never seen a manuscript sold because the writing style was beautiful, unique, or revolutionary when the basic idea or finished plot was sorely lacking. In rare cases, being an accomplished stylist might get you an invitation to submit other story ideas; but the strength of your story is always the bottom line.

Outlining for Publication

If you're at all interested in publishing your work, you must submit an outline at some point in the editorial process. It's increasingly rare to submit an entire, finished manuscript to drum up interest in your work. Most editors and agents want to see the story in a summary form first so that they can judge the plot, your basic writing skills, and your story's marketability.

Pen Pal _____

It's smart to develop outlines that you can send out to drum up interest in your work. If you have a great idea but haven't finished (or even begun!) your manuscript, you can still submit a basic query or pitch letter and an outline to get feedback and find potential publishers.

For better or worse, the publishing process can sometimes be a lengthy one. It's entirely possible to send a query or pitch letter while you work on an outline and sample chapters. Then when you're asked to send more of your project, you'll be ready with one to three completed chapters (not necessarily the first three) and your complete outline.

Outlining for Yourself

Outlining before you write is a good way to see whether you have a story worth writing. You're going to be spending months (or more) writing, revising, and editing your story. It's a big investment of energy—and ego—and nothing is more devastating than getting bogged down or blocked at the very end of the process.

It can be positively exhilarating to sketch out the major moments of your story in outline form. Characters and events start to interact, new ideas suddenly spring forth, and bits of dialogue create themselves. Best of all, you don't have to worry about your grammar, spelling, continuity, or writing style—it's all about ideas and generating raw material that you can use as you see fit.

Working Outlines

Working outlines can take different forms and be used for multiple purposes. Because they're for you, you don't need to worry about how you write them or what they look like.

Use a working outline to …

- Keep track of events within each chapter.

- Keep track of events chapter by chapter.

- Keep separate track of the main plot and subplots.

- Keep track of major characters' story lines.

Sometimes a complex story structure makes it necessary to use several different outlines at once to keep track of exactly what's going on. Stories that switch from one character's point of view to another, stories with parallel plots, or plots that follow several characters simultaneously make it especially hard to remember what you've done in any particular chapter.

In these situations, you probably want to keep several sets of outlines.

Chapter-by-chapter outlines let you see what you've covered and when, who's been in each scene of the chapter, and which main events took place.

Separate outlines for each plot line can keep track of individual story lines and subplots, show how to pace the story as a whole, and indicate where you need to insert foreshadowing, backstory, or clues.

You can keep one set of outlines that follow each narrator or main character and another outline that keeps track of every chapter in order.

Sample Working Outlines

Here is a sample working outline by chapter:

Chapter 1. Miranda: establish backstory re jail time; introduce idea of mother's secret identity.

Chapter 2. Carlos: He's introduced setting up fox traps in the woods behind the farm. Hears gunshots; finds Charlotte in the barn, bleeding.

Chapter 3. Leo: gas station; Ryan pulls up, skids to a stop. Filling R's tank, Leo overhears R. on phone with Carlos; when Leo hears Charlotte is injured, he drops gas nozzle, runs.

Chapter 4. Hospital: Miranda visits Charlotte. Sees Leo arrive, hides, watches him with Charlotte.

Chapter 5. Carlos hangs up with Ryan. Goes to attic, digs out old photo albums. Finds pic of Charlotte and Miranda with older woman—their mother. Carlos torn about telling Charlotte secret of her birth … takes photo to desk, starts writing letter, Dear Miranda ….

Chapter 6. Flashback: 1952. Minnie, in prom dress, opens door to Cal. He's overwhelmed. "You look beautiful," he says. Minnie smiles, tells him re change of plans after dance. They hurry to school gym.

Chapter 7. Farm: Leo pretends to be lost, tricks Carlos into talking about Charlotte. Miranda pulls up.

Here is a sample working outline, Miranda's story:

Chapter 1. Establish backstory re jail time; introduce idea of mother's secret identity.

Chapter 4. Hospital: Miranda visits Charlotte. Sees Leo arrive, hides, watches him with Charlotte.

Chapter 7. Farm: Leo pretends to be lost, tricks Carlos into talking about Charlotte. Miranda pulls up.

Here is a sample working outline, Carlos's story:

Chapter 2. Carlos: Introduced setting up fox traps in the woods behind the farm. Hears gunshots; finds Charlotte in the barn, bleeding.

Chapter 5. Carlos hangs up with Ryan. Goes to attic, digs out old photo albums. Finds pic of Charlotte and Miranda with older woman—their mother. Carlos torn about telling Charlotte secret of her birth … takes photo to desk, starts writing letter, Dear Miranda ….

Chapter 7. Farm: Leo pretends to be lost, tricks Carlos into talking about Charlotte. Miranda pulls up.

Outline Length

If you're keeping outlines for your own use, they can be as long, short, sketchy, or detailed as you'd like. Outlines for submission are another story.

Depending on what the outline is needed for, you may be asked to submit an outline or summary that ranges from 1 to 3 pages, or up to 10 or 20 pages.

In my classes on preparing for publication, students with finished manuscripts must develop an outline that covers their story from beginning to end. At first, they struggle to keep to the 20-page limit. In the following weeks, they learn how to condense and summarize and delete unnecessary events and characters until they've whittled their original outlines down to 10 pages, and then 4.

In one class, we had just completed four-page outlines when a student's agent called to ask him to fax a two-page outline that same evening. Was he happy that we'd practiced cutting and slashing—he whipped out the two-page version in just a few hours.

 Pen Pal

Unless you're specifically asked to write a chapter-by-chapter breakdown, write your outline in narrative form. Instead of indenting, use extra spacing between paragraph blocks to indicate natural breaks in the story.

Tricks of the Trade

Remember that submitted outlines are used as selling tools for your story. Try to capture a sense of what your book will be like by using a narrative format whenever possible.

Here are some tips to help you write successful outlines:

- ◆ Use active verbs as much as possible.

- ◆ Avoid a detached tone; make the story come alive.

- ◆ Try to pack the most punch into every line.

- ◆ If you're given a required length, stick to it. If not, keep it short and to the point.

- ◆ Try to use the same style that you use in your writing, or to capture the flavor of the story.

- ◆ Pay attention to pacing, building suspense and dramatizing the high points of the story.

- ◆ Make sure something active happens in every scene.

- ◆ Use a rough three-act structure.

- ◆ Take your time when summarizing the ending.

Sample Outline

Based on *The Pigman* by Paul Zindel:

Introductory oath: John and Lorraine vow to tell the whole truth about what happened with the Pigman. (No information yet about who the Pigman is.)

Chapters 1–3. Set up and identify the main characters' wants and needs. Backstory throughout the opening chapters.

1. POV John: John hates school, a troublemaker, prankster. Says Lorraine has been too sad since the Pigman died. Glad writing their confession is making her more lively, opinionated again.

2. POV Lorraine: re John handsome, though drinks and smokes too much, self-destructive acts caused by his dysfunctional family. Lorraine has an analytical mind, is superstitious, believes in signs and omens. Her mom is a private-duty nurse and hypercritical, always telling Lorraine she's not pretty, putting her down.

3. POV John: Explains how they play phone pranks after school. We meet his friend Norton, a social outcast. We get plot hints: "the Pigman would have died anyway." He and Lorraine just "speeded things up."

Inciting incident. The main plot begins.

POV Lorraine: We meet John's parents; Mom placating, Dad intense. Later, with friends, playing phone pranks, Lorraine chooses the name Pignati (the Pigman) and John asks him to donate money to the fictitious J&L Fund.

Chapters 5–7. Development; sad things to come.

Submission Outlines: Narrative Form

There are endless variations of narrative style outlines. They may be written in full, descriptive sentences sticking exactly to the chronological order of events, listed chapter by chapter.

They may be written in three-act form, loosely summarizing events within that format by selectively picking and choosing between plot lines and characters. Though events are freely interpreted, with narrative flow and pacing foremost, they still group events as belonging to the beginning, middle, and end.

They may be written with minimal attention to chronology or chapter content, focusing instead on creating a dramatic summary that leads readers through a very subjective version of the story, freely omitting entire story lines, characters, or subplots.

Narrative Outline, Chronological

Here is an example of a chronological narrative outline:

1. POV John: John hates school. He's a troublemaker, a prankster. But Lorraine has been so sad since the Pigman died—he's glad that writing their confession is making her more lively and opinionated again. Like her old self.

2. POV Lorraine: Lorraine can't deny that John is handsome, though he drinks and smokes way too much. His self-destruction comes from his dysfunctional family. Lorraine has no self-destructive inclinations—except for hanging out with John. She has an analytical mind, but she's also superstitious and believes in signs and omens. Her mom, a private-duty nurse, is hypercritical, always telling Lorraine she's not pretty and putting her down … etc.

Pen Pal

A chronological outline has chapter-by-chapter events described in full sentences. It closely follows the events of the manuscript. The outline is numbered by chapter and is the least labor-intensive.

Narrative Outline, Three-Act Form

Here is an example of a three-act form narrative outline (to keep the length down, this outline covers only a portion of the story):

John and Lorraine couldn't be more different. John, smart aleck, prankster, and aspiring actor, delights in stirring things up and breaking the rules—"Without getting caught," he's always quick to add.

Lorraine, superstitious, analytical, and practical, finds that pulling pranks with John— and lying about it—provides welcome relief from life with her relentlessly critical mom. Plus, John is gorgeous!

And they never intended to hurt the Pigman; it all started with an innocent phone prank: Lorraine picks Mr. Pignati at random from the phone book, surprised that he readily agrees to donate to the fictitious J&L Fund. Arriving at his modest house, John and Lorraine are soon caught up in the Pigman's sadness and his eagerness to befriend them.

Agreeing to meet Pignati at the zoo, John and Lorraine have no idea their friendship will lead to tragedy. Soon they're meeting daily at the Pigman's house, playing games, sharing meals, and uncovering truths: though the Pigman insists his wife is away, visiting, they soon discover that she's dead.

Before they know it, John and Lorraine are either pretending to be the Pigman's children—or he's pretending to be one of them!

This outline presents events in general chronological order, loosely incorporating backstory with descriptions of events. Because it's more important to create drama in the narrative than to pay strict attention to when things happen, this style relies more on the cumulative effect of events rather than the individual steps leading to events.

Pen Pal

A three-act form outline has events grouped in loose chronological order, roughly falling into beginning, middle, and end sections. The narrative drive is more important than including every detail. There is no numbering, and it is more labor-intensive.

Notice that some subplots and minor characters (Norton, the parents) are completely omitted and would be mentioned only when and if they became crucial to the story events at hand.

Since this type of outline tries to convey a sense of narrative flow, you should pay attention to sentence structure: make sure you vary sentence length and structure and intersperse bits of dialogue to make things more lively. Compare a very short sample of chronological version to the narrative form of this outline.

Chronological:

1. POV John: John hates school. He's a troublemaker, a prankster.

Narrative:

John and Lorraine couldn't be more different. John, smart aleck, prankster, and aspiring actor, delights in stirring things up and breaking the rules—"Without getting caught," he's always quick to add.

Experience in writing narrative outlines comes in handy when you need to submit a story summary. Here is an example of our narrative outline reworked into a dramatic summary that tells the entire story, playing fast and loose with chronology:

John and Lorraine couldn't be more different. John, smart aleck, prankster, and aspiring actor, delights in stirring things up and breaking the rules— "Without getting caught." Lorraine, superstitious, analytical, and practical, finds that pulling pranks with John—and lying about it—provides welcome relief from life with her relentlessly critical mom. Plus, John is gorgeous!

No one is supposed to get hurt. Not when it all starts with a crank call to Mr. Angelo Pignati, retired engineer. To John and Lorraine, the Pigman is like a big, old kid, always eager to join the fun—the sillier, the better—like the time they roller-skate through stuffy Beekman's Department Store.

But even the Pigman can't keep them safe from all their troubles, and when an impromptu party escalates into vandalism and violence, John and Lorraine realize they've finally gone too far. Are they responsible for the Pigman's death?

Pen Pal

A dramatic summary outline is free form, striving to convey a sense of the story using descriptive language and dramatic pacing. It may be in nonchronological order. There is no numbering and it is the most labor-intensive.

Step Sheet Outlines

A step sheet is the sketchiest kind of outline—one that indicates the main events in each step of the story. It may be arranged according to chapter, randomly numbered by the sequence of events, or not numbered at all.

You might be asked to send a step sheet with a submission package; more likely, you'll use them as a quick way to show editors or agents where your story is heading, before your manuscript is complete. Or you might keep one for your own reference.

Step sheets are useful in keeping track of story events without having to worry about the writing—which is why they're the least labor-intensive of all the outline forms.

Here is an example of a step sheet outline:

Intro = oath

1. John intro. Re writing confessional makes Lorraine more herself again.

2. Lorraine intro. Re John self-destructive from dysfunctional family. Lorraine analytical, superstitious. Mom always says Lorraine not pretty.

3. John re phone pranks. Meet Norton, social outcast.

4. Lorraine; meet John's parents. Lorraine chooses Pignati, John asks him to donate money to J&L Fund.

Etc.

No matter which type of outline you end up needing, you must prepare a narrative outline of your story at some point. So why not get ahead of the game? Practice writing outlines of different styles and lengths as you work on writing projects. You won't be sorry!

The Least You Need to Know

◆ There are numerous types of outlines for different purposes—some for your own use, some for submitting.

◆ Both editors and agents will ask to see an outline at some point.

◆ Outlining before, during, or after you write can help in revising your story—and in creating a submission package.

◆ Step sheets, narrative summaries, chronological outlines, and outlines of individual story lines all have unique benefits in the writing process.

18

Revise, Revise, Revise

In This Chapter

- ◆ When to make revisions
- ◆ How to look for problems
- ◆ Asking the right questions
- ◆ Revising by chapter, by scene, by paragraph, and by sentence

It's been said before and I'll say it again—most of writing is revision. You should expect to write draft after draft of a project, sometimes even after you think it has reached a state of utter perfection. Why?

Because no one can see his or her own work objectively.

Because editors and agents have their own ideas of what they want from your story.

Because you may not know what's actually on the page.

This chapter will help you focus on typical—and recurrent—revisions that all authors need to make.

Reality Check

Before you can become a professional writer, you need to accept one hard truth: until the day it's published, your beloved manuscript is very much a work in progress. You might labor for years on your story, but when you finally submit it to an agent or editor, they may ask for changes you never even thought of—a good reason not to obsess about details. If you can embrace the idea that your writing is fair game, you'll have taken a big step toward your first writing contract.

The Objective Eye

Every writer must learn to be his or her own editor. But it's tough to learn on your own work. Reading someone else's writing is a completely different experience from reading your own, because few writers can respond objectively to something they've been dreaming about, planning, and writing for weeks, months, or years. That's why it's so helpful to take a writing class or join a writer's group.

The experience you'll gain by reading and analyzing other people's work is invaluable. Spotting weak areas and giving constructive comments about possible ways to fix them is a skill that will help you in two important ways:

- You'll learn practical ways to improve your own writing craft and technique.

- Giving constructive criticism will help you receive constructive criticism without resentment or defensiveness—and teach you to improve your writing.

The Cardinal Rule of Revision: Get a Second Opinion!

Not only are most writers too close to their own beloved projects to see the flaws clearly, they're also less likely to see its strengths. After a few drafts, it's easy to lose sight of what's important and unique in a piece of writing.

After reading a few drafts of your story, it's easy to memorize your own words—to the point that you're no longer able to see it objectively. Knowing your work too well can blind you to the fact that it might be better written another way. Do yourself a favor and learn that your words aren't necessarily precious—it'll help you be more flexible and open to improvement.

Another danger is writer's fatigue—the state of mind where you're so over-familiar with what you've written that you start to throw out your best lines. Knowing when to stop revising is a skill that develops over time. Until then, don't rely on your own opinion—ask for help!

Question Your Second Opinion Readers

Let's say you've spent the time and effort to find or form a writer's group, or you've decided to approach a trusted family member or friend to solicit their advice and opinions. You may even decide to pay a professional editor to review your work. No matter who you go to, of all the questions you might ask, there's one question that is the most important of all: what story did I write?

It's happened to all of us. What we think is on the page is actually still in our minds; it hasn't been effectively communicated to the reader. Don't be afraid to find out what your readers think you've written about. If this draft missed the mark, don't lose heart. That's what revising is for. You might need to set your manuscript aside and take a breather for a while, but be a pro: when you're ready, rewrite.

 Slush Pile!

I've seen writers overwork manuscripts until they've unwittingly removed the best parts. Even if your writing is brilliant, after reading the same passages over and over, it's easy to get sick of your own words. Get a second opinion.

Guidelines for Second Opinion Readers

Because most people you'll ask to read your work in progress won't be publishing professionals, it will help if you follow a few guidelines:

- Begin with questions that ensure a positive response—that will break the ice and make your reader feel that you really want to hear their opinions. For example, "I hope there was something you really liked. Was there?" "What do you think really worked?" "I hope you think there's an audience for my story. Do you?"

- Don't ask loaded questions. Starting with questions such as "Was it good?" just puts your reader on the spot. Worse, the answer won't help you revise!

- Don't argue. Don't even answer back. Of course, you have the right to disagree, but it's best to keep your opinions to yourself. Even if you get answers that seem harsh or completely miss the point, always thank readers for taking the time and trouble to help you out.

◆ Above all, avoid the general. Prepare questions that focus your readers on what works and what needs help.

If you want your readers to be honest with you, start by being honest with yourself. What aspects of writing make you insecure? Do you hate writing description? Is creating dialogue sheer torture?

Focus on your weaknesses; maybe they're not as bad as you think. Or if they are, knowing ahead of time will give you a chance to revise those areas before submitting your work to an editor or agent.

Pen Pal

If you're reluctant to ask for this kind of commitment from friends, family, or fellow writers, or don't know anyone qualified to be your reader, then it might be worth your while to pay for an editorial consultation. You'll find lists of consultants in the *Literary Market Place,* the yearly *Writer's Guide,* and in writing magazines. Check out online directories; visit publisher's websites, or websites of writers associations such as the Author's Guild. You might try calling or visiting local colleges and universities, including their continuing education programs, to ask for recommendations. Any reputable consultant will have a list of services offered and rates of pay. They should also give you an idea of what you'll receive in return. Expect to choose between anything from 1 to 2 hour phone consultations to brief checklists of story elements to lengthy written reports.

Second-Opinion Sample Questions

Here are some questions to ask about content:

1. What was your favorite moment in the story?

2. Did you need to know more about any of the characters?

3. Did you get a clear vision of the characters in your mind?

4. What's the best thing about the story?

Here are some questions to ask about perceptions:

1. Do you think the story makes a point?

2. Who felt like the most important character?

3. Who felt like the least important character?

4. Do you think teenagers would enjoy this story?

And here are some valuable questions to ask about craft:

1. Was my language clear?

2. Was the dialogue realistic? Suited to the characters?

3. Did the beginning grab your attention?

4. Did the ending answer all your questions?

5. What confused you about the plot?

6. Did the descriptions work for you?

Now that you've prepared the questions, prepare yourself for the answers. Don't be surprised if the responses you get aren't what you expected. That's why you're asking!

Question Yourself

As you begin revising, keep an open mind. Although other people will comment on what's on the page, you, as the author, need to assess what isn't on the page: how close is your draft to the story you intended to write in the first place? Realistically, can you accomplish what you set out to do?

Remember—until you complete a first draft, you won't really know your story or your characters. So don't be afraid to make major changes. Perhaps you'll decide to alter the plot, get rid of characters that aren't working, or even scrap the first draft and set out in a whole new direction.

> **Ink Spot**
>
> I love to re-write. First drafts are usually painful. But a good re-write morning is bliss. Teachers love to hear me say this, but I must hasten to add that when I was in elementary school I didn't even know what a revision was.
>
> —Katherine Paterson (from Terabithia.com)

Circles of Revision

You've elicited comments on your work. You've gotten a rough idea of its successes and, painful as it may be, its shortcomings. Now it's time to bite the bullet, admit to the flaws, and fix them. But where do you start?

I've always envisioned the revision process as a series of concentric circles. The outermost circle, surrounding all the other elements, is the idea that inspired you in the first place. It's at once the most elusive layer, and the most important.

Circle One: Overall Concept

Now go back and ask yourself the following questions about your book's overall concept:

- Is the story you wrote the one you first envisioned?

- Does the finished story support your underlying theme?

- Are you happy with the story or is something missing?

- What do you wish you had done instead; what would you change?

Circle Two: Characters

Then ask yourself the following questions about your book's characters:

- Did your main character change or grow during the course of the story?

- How about other major characters—do they learn from the events in your story?

- Does your main character carry the story, or does a secondary character take over? If so, should your secondary character become the main character?

- Does growth illustrate your main point or underlying theme?

- Would you want to spend time with your characters? Who? Why?

Circle Three: Plot

Go back to the basic plot formula and answer the questions again:

- Did you create a strong enough need for your main character?

- Did you create a worthy opponent?

- Is the question you asked at the beginning of the story answered by the events of the ending?

- Do the events you devised adequately support your character's journey?

Pen Pal _____

Things change. Whether you let your stories evolve through multiple drafts, like Louis Sachar, or carefully outline major events, like Katherine Patterson, you can expect your finished draft to be at least slightly different from your original idea. Chances are, you'll need to do some sizeable rewrites. Train yourself to embrace the revision process. Keep your expectations small: view your first draft as a jumping-off point. Instead of asking "Was it any good?" try asking "Was it a good start?" Above all, applaud your efforts. Writers know how hard writing is. A finished draft is cause for celebration, so celebrate!

Circle Four: Craft

At the core of the circles are the components that comprise the writing itself, in descending order: chapter, scene, paragraph, sentence, word.

Chapter by chapter:

Outlining after the fact is a great way to organize a revision. Listing story events as they appear quickly gives you an overview of the story's pacing; is there a sense of rising tension leading to the final resolution? Your outline will show if the action bogs down anywhere.

Check each chapter to ensure that some main event occurs: look for big emotional moments or turning points that forward the plot.

Scene by scene:

Within each chapter you'll have several scenes. Heed the same warning: make sure something happens in each scene.

The event needn't be earthshaking; it may be that we get a crucial piece of information; it may be that a character reveals some trait for the first time. Your goal is to improve the pacing by eliminating empty moments.

Paragraph, sentence, and word:

Every writer works differently. Some like to revise language almost immediately, rereading and tightening each chapter as it's finished. Others prefer to write an entire first draft without paying much attention to details and then go back and polish the language later.

Either way, you'll want to pay attention to paragraphs, sentences, and word choice at some point, following these basic guidelines:

- ◆ Check dialogue. Replace empty chatter with information that forwards the plot or illustrates character.

- ◆ Check descriptions. Replace vague words or tired adjectives with fresher language.

- ◆ Replace passive verbs with active verbs.

- ◆ Streamline sentences by eliminating extra words or phrases.

- ◆ Rearrange sentences by moving the most important words or phrases to the end.

Revision in Action

Here are some examples of student work and suggestions for their revision.

Example 1. The dialogue in this passage sounded stiff and not very kidlike:

"Maybe we will get lucky and find a Yugo," said Nick, referring to the small car produced in Yugoslavia in the 1980s.

Adding more dialogue lets you give the same information with a more casual feeling:

"Maybe we'll get lucky and find a Yugo," Nick said.

Jim look puzzled.

"Yugos," Greg repeated. "Aren't they those old, boxy things from Yugoslavia?"

"Vintage, not old," Nick corrected. "From the '80s. They're totally hot!"

"With our luck, we'll probably find SUVs," Jim joked.

They all laughed …

Example 2. Watch out for repeated sentence construction, such as "he clutched," "he rode," "he pumped."

Instead, use variations, such as "Clutching a newspaper, he …," "His legs moved faster, pumping the pedals, as he …."

Example 3. Replace passive verbs with active ones.

This:

"Nick saw that his friends Jim and Greg were already there."

Could be:

"Jim and Greg were already there, crouching behind the fence ...."

This:

"He started jogging up his driveway and then started running toward the white brick house at the end of the block to meet up with his friends."

Could be:

"He jogged up the driveway, heading toward the white brick house at the end of the block where Greg and John were already waiting."

Or even:

"He jogged up the driveway, heading toward the white brick house at the end of the block. He hoped Greg and John were there already; he couldn't wait to pull their next prank."

Pen Pal

Inevitably, something you revised, changed, or eliminated altogether will come back to haunt you. Lost passages can attain Pulitzer-winning status in your memory. To avoid future regret, save copies of your project at various stages. And try this exercise: pretend that your computer swallowed your favorite chapter. Rewrite the chapter from memory or outline notes. It can be done! Will your rewrite be the same as your original? No. It might be better. Writing is flexible and forgiving, and any story can survive the loss of one or two brilliant passages.

Example 4. Watch out for adult-sounding narration.

This:

"Afraid that any type of explanation would only direct more attention her way, she decided to keep her mouth shut."

Could be:

"Everyone stared. She decided to keep her mouth shut."

Or even:

"She decided to keep her mouth shut. Give them another reason to stare? No way."

Above all, never be afraid to tear your work apart or to begin all over again—whatever it takes to get the best story. That's the true meaning of revision. We've all read about some first-time wonder that dashes off a novel, and six weeks later has a best-seller on his or her hands. May this happen to each and every one of us! Until then, remember that nothing beats the experience you gain when you revise, revise, revise.

The Least You Need to Know

- ◆ Writing pros realize that no draft is final until it's published; don't obsess over details that may be changed.

- ◆ Most writers can't be objective about their own work, so find trusted readers to give you feedback.

- ◆ Asking focused questions of your second opinion readers will help you revise more effectively.

- ◆ Begin by comparing your original idea to your completed first draft; then revise by chapter, by scene, by paragraph, and by sentence.

Part

Advanced Class

So much to learn, so little time … wait! You're not on deadline yet. So why not take time now to dip into meaty subjects that are usually reserved for advanced students? Understanding the unspoken laws of your story will put you head and shoulders above the crowd. Then take your story to the next level by learning how to infuse each moment with meaning—using emotions and underlying themes to take a "good read" and turn it into an enduring classic.

19

The World of the Story: Continuity, Please!

In This Chapter

♦ Understanding the rules of your universe

♦ When to design your own conventions

♦ Creating authenticity

♦ How to handle details

♦ Manipulating time and place

You are about to enter a different world …

Sound like the intro to a sci-fi fantasy? Not necessarily. Every piece of fiction takes us into a different world; isn't that much of the appeal of reading—to lose yourself in someone else's life?

In this chapter, we talk about "the world" of stories—the universe we enter when we read.

Unspoken Laws

It may be a fantasy world, where you, the author, create the rules from start to finish, as in Narnia or Oz. Or it may be a prehistoric or historical world, based in fact, but as foreign to our modern sensibilities as any imagined world. It could be a place where animals act like humans. Or it could be a reality-based world where the community observes conventions that we may not comprehend or be able to imagine. Whatever it is, you need to be aware of the universe you're writing about so that you can keep your facts straight.

If you express any inconsistencies in the ground rules of your story milieu, you'll lose credibility with your readers. And you may hear from them, too; readers love to let authors know when they find flaws in facts or logic.

Think of the conventions in Oz—a world that demands we accept disappearing witches, humanoid beasts, constant tension between good and evil, and a sly undercurrent of "don't believe everything you see."

We accept that, in Oz, men can be made of tin and straw, and timid lions can come to life, speak American English, and act according to our own familiar standards and norms; indeed, according to contemporary American conventions of morality, propriety, etc.

We accept that some beings are evil and work for evil witches, but are willing to follow good witches if given the chance. There are probably other rules that apply, if you stop to think more closely about the story. Some of the rules are subtle, some not so subtle. We don't usually stop to analyze the fact that there are rules, but there are. And they are consistent. (Unless you can think of some that aren't. Please let me know!)

Man vs. Rabbit: Human Characteristics

A completely different world exists in my old standby, the world of Peter Rabbit. Beatrix Potter gives her rabbits humanlike thoughts and feelings, but it's possible to accept or believe that when there is dialogue between the bunnies it's actually "rabbit talk" and we just read it as English.

If you look closely, one basic rule of this world is that rabbits don't speak to humans, only to other animals. Peter speaks to the little mouse, for instance, but not to Mr. Macgregor. Whereas, by another set of rules, he might taunt or tease Mr. M: "Nyah, nyah, you can't catch me!" or something like that. But as it is, bunny speaking to human would violate the rules of Peter's universe. Humans and animals simply don't mix.

The rabbits have humanlike traits only in the context of their own world, among their own kind. It's a tricky rule, but consistent. The line of their reality is never crossed.

We get the whimsy that rabbits speak, wear proper little outfits, snack on currant buns and sip afternoon tea, yet their rabbitness doesn't cross the line to speak with humans or to interact with them as equals. Thus the rules of their world remain consistent throughout the book.

When you're dealing with fantasy of any kind, you've got to be aware of the rules that govern the world. Do your characters have all the basic human qualities? What about characters who are mutants, or aliens, or androids? Can humans understand their speech? Do they wear clothes? What's considered proper, polite, or expected among them?

Create Your Own Conventions

What do you do if your characters are nonhuman but you need readers to know what they're saying? Invent your own convention.

Suppose your omniscient narrator acts as translator:

Norex needed the humans to understand that their clothing irritated his mineral-secreting glands. Guessing they were earthlings, he searched his language banks for English: "Terribly sorry, old man, but I fear your garmenture offends my metallic-spewing facilities."

In other words, know what you need and make it work for you. After you've established the unspoken rules within the world of your story, run to your bible and record every single one. And then be careful not to violate them.

Find the Conventions!

Maybe you're having trouble identifying the conventions of your particular world. Maybe you think there aren't any special rules. This exercise helps to rattle your brain, shaking up preconceived notions and allowing you to see rules so familiar that they've become invisible.

Take one of your own characters and devise a scene where they meet an incongruous character from a completely different world. Write a dialogue for them centered on a simple conflict.

For instance, what if your main character, or, say, Princess Mia, clicks on her iPod and inexplicably finds herself transported to the Planet of the Apes—where she tries to convince the commoners to lead a rebellion against their leaders, demanding electronic devices? What could Mia say to convince the apes that iPods are the best thing since sliced bread and that Earth life is preferable? Or maybe she starts a sustainable agriculture movement, disrupting their usual practices. What would happen? Who would win?

Whatever you choose, try to be outrageous enough to force your brain into unexpected ways of thinking. You may generate fantastic story ideas. But hopefully, comparing our world to an unfamiliar one is a great way to expose the strange rules and conventions we follow without giving it a second thought.

Use Your Bible

At some point in the writing process, you'll want—and need—to start making those lists that will turn into your bible—the official guide to the world of your manuscript.

Keep it fluid, adding categories and content as they come to mind. You can use the general format of the regular writer's bible to generate ideas for the kinds of things you'll need to know about a fantasy, futuristic, or any type of imaginary world. Get used to keeping notebooks on hand, or open windows on your computer, so that you can switch between files as ideas come to you.

Slush Pile!

It's happened to everyone—you forget to save your file, you lose your precious notebook, whatever. Everyone loses material sometime, somehow. Make it part of your routine to keep close tabs on notes and bursts of inspiration; just assume you won't remember that brilliant insight you had in the middle of Chapter 13 that you just knew you'd never forget. You will forget.

Authenticity = Truth

Some stories ring true; some don't. There really isn't any logic to what people will believe. That's why books and movies come with this proud announcement: based on a true story. People will scoff at a tall tale; but if you tell them it really happened, suddenly you've got the story stamp of approval plastered across your forehead.

Whatever the world you're writing about, readers expect the feeling of authenticity. Far-fetched or fantastical, readers accept any possibility as long as you create a believable atmosphere.

Remember what we learned about writing dialogue? You don't try to duplicate actual speech because the real thing is usually a jumbled, illogical mess. You want to approximate the feeling of real speech, but make it better—give it a focus and a purpose while still sounding spontaneous and believable.

The same rule applies to constructing a believable world. If you duplicate reality, you'll bore readers to death. In some ways, your written world is more real than reality, even though it's actually a representation of the real world. To create a world that looks, feels, and sounds authentic, you've got to imitate real life, but without all the extraneous details.

Be Selective with Details

New writers often ask how much detail to include in a scene. They've yet to acquire the skill of sifting through real-life moments to flush out unnecessary trimmings. Have you ever read a piece of writing that tells you things you just don't need—or want—to know? The sections that follow will give you examples of unnecessary and necessary details.

Unnecessary Details

… Louisa leaned across the table and lifted the heavy pitcher. She slowly poured herself a glass of water and put it down.

Jason sat across from her, tucking a snowy napkin into his yellow shirt. Louisa hesitated, and then took a dainty taste of her soup. It was still hot so she picked up her water glass and took a delicate sip to cool her mouth.

Jason lifted an eyebrow … etc.

When did you start to lose interest? Some of this description may be necessary to set up the scene—but only if it really needs to be there. Readers expect to know where they're being led within a sentence or two. Including more than we need to know makes us wait too long for the payoff—a sure sign of an amateur at work, and a good way to irritate readers.

Necessary Details

… Louisa leaned across the table and lifted the pitcher. She poured herself a glass of water and put it down.

"Stop stalling," Jason complained, tucking a napkin into his shirt.

Louisa hesitated, and then tasted her soup. "Hot!" she exclaimed, grabbing her glass. "But ... good," she managed to add.

Jason lifted an eyebrow.

"Very good," she added, more enthusiastically. Jason brightened...."

The revised scene begins to draw us in as soon as Jason's line conveys some action and emotion:

"Stop stalling," Jason complained, tucking a napkin into his shirt.

Now we understand that Louisa poured the water for a reason; or rather, that the author showed her pouring it for a reason—she was stalling.

We don't yet know why she's stalling, but we're willing to read a bit further:

Louisa hesitated, and then tasted her soup.

In this line we guess that Louisa was trying to avoid tasting her soup—which would justify her earlier action of pouring the water. We still don't know exactly where the scene is headed, or why Jason is impatient, but we get the sense that the author is being fair and only telling us what we need to know. So we'll put up with him a little longer.

"Hot!" she exclaimed, grabbing her glass. "But ... good," she managed to say.

Aha! At last we know that Jason's goal was to get Louisa's opinion on the soup. Hmm ... is he a chef? Did he prepare the soup? Is it a special recipe, does he usually cook, or is this a rare, special event ...?

This kind of curiosity—questions that flit through our mind in an instant, barely noticed—is what hooks readers, keeps them plugged into a scene, and creates an atmosphere of trust. Because it has a point, the scene feels authentic.

By the way, I'm not suggesting that you think this hard about every single sentence you write! After you get the idea, you won't need to monitor yourself this closely—or at all.

Time and Place

Think of two friends meeting in Central Park at two in the afternoon. Now make it two in the morning, and you've got a completely different atmosphere.

Manipulating place can add to your story, creating tension or comfort, relaxation or threat. Look carefully at effective stories, and you'll find that it's often impossible to separate the setting from the plot. When we step into a story, it's important to know where we are, when we are there, and what particular details affect the community. The impact of a place and time on events is immeasurable. Certainly the way characters react to events is deeply impacted by the era in which the events occur and the community or place where events occur.

Walter Dean Myers, the notable African American YA author, sets his stories in city ghettos. His characters are formed by the harsh rules of their surroundings, by the crime rate, drop-out rate, and poverty level in their neighborhoods.

The tough, fast-paced city setting of Myers's *Miracles of Modern Science*, a comic masterpiece, works by contrasting the harsh setting to the acts of individual courage (and inner beauty) that take place there.

Thus his characters' stories revolve around their setting. The language, style, and culture portrayed in his books are a unique product of the surroundings of his characters, and therefore the setting hugely influences the plots he constructs.

Fish out of Water: Setting Your World

For lots of mileage from a simple idea, just take a character from one world and set him into a completely different world.

Think of the familiar "fish out of water" scenario. How many books and movies rely on that contrast between settings to create a plot? Here are some examples:

- Airhead Valley Girl plunked into an elite intellectual eastern setting (*Legally Blonde*)

- Blue-collar woman plunked into the world of high finance (*Working Girl*)

- Rube who conquers the sophisticated city (*Crocodile Dundee*)

The list goes on and on.

Suspending Disbelief

Remember back in Chapter 6, where we discussed suspension of disbelief? That concept really comes into play when you're creating a believable world. As always, consistency is more important than basing your details on reality.

If you stop to think about it, conventions that we all accept so readily in stories truly strain credibility:

- **Filling in the blanks.** As you saw in the previous soup scene, listing every move a character makes would be unbearably tedious. It's possible to set the scene with only a few specifics because readers are conditioned to supply the missing details on their own.

- **Omniscient narrators.** Do we really believe there are people walking around who know every thought in everyone else's head?

- **Incongruities.** Remember Nana the dog, the children's nursemaid in *Peter Pan?* Aside from the crocodile (who remains totally true to his reptilian nature), no other animal in the story interacts with humans that way. Yet readers accept Nana without question.

  Why?

  Because the author creates the rules that in this world, it's perfectly all right for a dog to be a nanny ... and for elfin boys to fly, and drop their shadows in someone's house, and a lot of other things that are rationally ridiculous.

More important, we accept these conventions because they separate fiction from fact—and make it more fun than real life. Do your job well, and readers will do their jobs, too.

The Least You Need to Know

- Every story is set in a world with rules and conventions of its own.

- Fantasy and science fiction writers create worlds from scratch; writers of historical novels create worlds based on research; fiction writers shape the world to suit their needs.

- Consistency is crucial in creating any world.

- Create a bible to record the rules of your world—never trust your memory!

- You're in charge of your world, so make the rules work for your story.

Chapter 20

The Emotional Outline: Infusing Each Moment with Meaning

In This Chapter

◆ Adding emotions to your story

◆ Visualizing your scene

◆ Giving your work an emotional checkup

One night, tired after hours of reviewing student homework, I realized that some stories still caught and held my interest. When I looked more closely, I realized that the stories I was drawn to used emotion as an essential element of the plot.

So I researched some of my favorite books and decided that the secret lay in creating an emotional core for each important scene. Placing emotions at the core of a scene energizes your writing and gives scenes more dramatic impact.

Scenes built around specific emotional events also have more focus as events build up to an emotional high point. When structured around strong emotion, a single scene can set the tone for an entire chapter.

Even better, nothing hooks readers faster than engaging their emotions; and nothing makes a character more appealing than uncovering their emotional vulnerabilities. In this chapter, you'll learn how to use emotions to enliven your writing and grab your readers' attention.

Emotion in Opening Scenes

Openings are notoriously hard. I always tell students to worry about their "real" opening later; for a first draft, getting started is what matters most. Openings are tough to write because they must accomplish so much, for example:

- Engage the reader
- Hint at main ideas
- Introduce main characters
- Establish a conflict
- Establish the setting

That's a lot to ask of a few pages of writing. It's easy to overload openings with too much information, forgetting that drawing the reader in is more important than anything else at this point. That's where emotion comes in. You need to communicate only the most necessary facts in your opening. That way you make room for the feelings.

Emotions First

Check any writing book and you'll probably read that you should begin a story in active mode—either a line, paragraph, or scene that plunges us right into the story, or that establishes an immediate mood. I'll add a third possibility: open a story with emotion.

A classic trick to create effective openings is to search your first draft for an especially active, engaging, emotional scene and move it to the very beginning of your story. You can usually take your original opening material and use it elsewhere—often as back-story right after your *new* initial scene.

Setting the Stage

Emotions not only engage your reader, they also create conflict and build drama. Start thinking now about specifying characters' emotions at every crucial moment—but especially in major scenes such as the opening or at a point of rising conflict.

Think about your characters as actors you've placed onstage. They're going to be up there for the entire scene. What are they going to do? What emotion will drive them? What will their attitude be?

Actors take cues from the *emotional subtext* of a scene in order to shape their presentation.

Let's say the scene involves giving some needed information—perhaps a train schedule. More dramatically, the scene also reveals the fact that one of the characters has a twin—a secret up until this moment. In essence, the scene is pure *exposition*.

def•i•ni•tion

Emotional subtext is the underlying emotions in a dramatic scene; emotions that are not explained in dialogue. The emotional subtext often contradicts spoken lines.

Exposition is narrative or dialogue that explains facts or gives background information necessary to understand the plot. Exposition does not create dramatic tension or convey emotion.

How does an actor act out pure exposition? He doesn't. A scene would be pretty dull if an actor just stood there and recited facts:

Joe

(to Jenny)

"The train leaves at eight."

"But before you go—you have a twin."

But color the scene with an emotional subtext and you'll make up for the playwright's lack of imagination. Depending on what's happened before this moment, you already have emotional possibilities to draw on to bring life to the scene.

For instance, Joe might be caught off-guard and blurt out the train schedule, then be so flustered that he also spills the secret that Jenny has a twin:

Joe

(flustered)

"The train? … Uh, eight, it leaves at eight. But … before you go …"

(blurting it out)

"You have a twin!"

Or Joe might toss the train schedule out in a challenging manner, then taunt Jenny with the fact that only he knew all along that she has a twin:

Joe

"The train leaves at eight."

"But before you go …"

(meaningful pause)

"You have a twin."

Without specific emotion, a potentially dramatic scene falls flat. Of course, a stage actor has the benefit of using body language, tone of voice, and inflection to convey his emotional attitude. Writers must work a little harder, but they can convey the same emotional information.

Visualize the Emotional Impact

One way to check a scene for emotional impact is to imagine the written scene as if it were a scene from a play. Visualize the characters on the page as characters on the stage and ask yourself whether you've given them enough emotional subtext to work with:

- Is there a clear attitude beneath their words?

- Could physical gestures convey their underlying emotion?

- Does your dialogue reflect a specific emotional state?

Ask yourself these questions about each important character and each important moment. Go through your story paragraph by paragraph or scene by scene and identify the underlying (or blatant) emotions.

Constantly ask how each major character feels at important moments. Remember that how they feel should influence the way they say something as well as what they say. Most important, check to see that your characters' actions spring believably from a specific emotion.

Here is an example in an instant story:

Initial premise = Two brothers fight over a legacy of land.

One brother is willing to accept any portion of land as his half. The other wants to hold out for just the right portion of the land.

Pen Pal _____

At important moments, characters should convey specific emotions. Actions that spring from emotions are more believable to your readers.

This premise creates a good conflict (and an active want!) on the part of both brothers. But watch how adding their emotional attitudes makes the scene more specific, and more dramatic.

Version 1: Jack is impatient, happy-go-lucky. He hates chaos and just wants the legacy settled. Ambrose is methodical and calculating. He's also seething with inner resentment: Jack is not his equal! Jack will mismanage his half of the land. Ambrose schemes to rob Jack of his inheritance.

Version 2: Jack is disgruntled. But it's better to get the deal over with than to drag their heels. Ambrose is thrilled with the legacy. He's willing to wait and select the best parcel for himself; mostly, he's grateful that Dad's hard work made the legacy possible.

Either version takes the same premise but uses emotions to strengthen the core conflict. No matter which specific emotions you choose for your scene, your reader will be able to use those emotions to identify characters and to experience what's at stake for them.

Pen Pal _____

Emotionally specific subtext personalizes conflicts while heightening dramatic tension.

The Emotional Checkup

As an editor, a common editorial note I make is "reaction?"

Meaning that at each significant moment in your story, we need to know not only what happened, but how the important characters feel about what happened—which leads to how they will react.

When I worked as editor of The New Nancy Drew mystery series, the supervising editor was notorious for asking minute, picky, detailed questions. My personal favorite was always when, in the middle of the action—say, when Nancy and friends were tracking a dangerous suspect—the editor's usual query was, "But when do they eat lunch?"

Maybe we don't need to know exactly when everyone eats lunch, but it doesn't hurt to know how they feel about eating lunch. Are they starving but so intent that they forget about eating? Or do they casually stop for lunch because they're not going to nail the suspect anyway?

Doing an emotional checkup on important scenes ensures that you don't miss an opportunity to maximize your story's impact.

Updated Emotions

I often ask students to take a familiar story and, using the same plot steps, rewrite it as something completely different.

It's a three-part exercise:

- ◆ Part 1: Identify the important steps of a classic plot.

- ◆ Part 2: Rewrite the steps for a completely different story.

- ◆ Part 3: Specify emotions for each plot step.

Here's how one student transformed a fairy tale into a modern cautionary fable: Little Red Riding Hood Joins the Internet era.

Plot steps for *Little Red Riding Hood:*

Step 1. Little Red needs to bring food to Grandma's house.

Step 2. On her way, she meets a wolf. Engaging her in conversation, the wolf learns where she's going and gets there first, eating Grandma and disguising himself in her clothes.

Step 3. When Red Riding Hood arrives she becomes suspicious. Just as the wolf is about to pounce, a noble woodsman leaps into the cottage and saves the day.

Plot steps for *Julie Goes Internet:*

Step 1. Julie joins a teen chat room for girls interested in modeling careers.

Step 2. E-mailing her photo puts Julie in touch with Wanda, a modeling agent who invites Julie to her studio.

Step 3. When Julie arrives she finds Wolfgang, Wanda's "assistant." Julie becomes suspicious when Wolfgang orders her to pose for indecent photos. An undercover policeman bursts in and arrests Wolfgang for running an Internet pornography ring. Julie is rescued at the last moment and learns an important lesson: beware of wolves in sheep's clothing! (And don't arrange meetings with strangers you meet on the Internet.)

Adding Emotions to the Plot

I love that *Little Red Riding Hood* is unrecognizable in the adapted story, although the plot steps are close variations of the original. The plot survives the transitions, but something is lacking.

Although the motives, conflict, and resolution are clear, the adaptation gives us a plot without emotion. Adding Julie's emotions will enrich the story, changing it from generic to specific …

Step 1. Julie desperately wants to realize her dream of becoming a model. Her self-esteem is shaky (her parents, abusive cocaine addicts, constantly complain that she's the bane of their existence), so Julie is thrilled, nervous, tense, and hopeful as she chats online with Wanda.

Step 2. Excited, but with some misgivings, Julie e-mails her photo to Wanda, who promises to make Julie's dream come true. Julie agrees to meet Wanda at her studio.

Step 3. Hopes high, Julie arrives to find only Wolfgang, Wanda's smarmy "assistant." Julie's excited expectation gives way to uneasiness as Wolfgang has her pose for photos. As Wolfgang asks for increasingly explicit poses, Julie's discomfort gives way to fear and revulsion. Just as fear turns to terror, an undercover policeman bursts in and arrests Wolfgang for running an Internet pornography ring.

Julie's relief and gratitude give way to uncertainty; has she ruined her future? With powerful resolve, Julie vows to contact legitimate modeling agencies. Her self-esteem renewed, Julie vows never to be taken advantage of again.

A torrid example, but you can see how the plot springs to life as soon as emotion is introduced. And the emotions themselves follow a structure as they establish the character's need, reflect her various conflicts, and resolve into a new beginning …

Step 1. Desire; hope; lack of confidence; excitement; nervousness; tension; hope.

Step 2. Excitement; trepidation; anticipation.

Step 3. Hope; expectation; discomfort; revulsion; fear; terror; relief; gratitude; uncertainty; despair; confidence, excited anticipation.

Julie takes quite a journey, traveling from hopefulness to despair and back to renewed hope and faith in her future. Notice also how much her emotions change in each stage of her journey; never static, she experiences buildup, letdown, reversals, and restoration of her original hope.

Pen Pal

If you want to try this yourself, choose a favorite children's story or fairy tale and break it into simple plot steps. Revise the plot steps to create a YA story. Then add specific emotions into each plot step, list the emotions for each step, and check to see whether your character takes an active emotional journey, with ups and downs, reversals, and resolution.

As you write, do an emotional checkup on your story. You can examine your outline, individual chapters, scenes within the chapters, and/or the story as a whole.

Make sure each scene has an emotional core and that your main character goes through some kind of emotional change throughout the scene. Your scenes will feel more dramatic, more human, and never static.

The Least You Need to Know

- Emotions are so much a part of a story's soul that it's easy to overlook the fact that they can be treated like any other craft element.

- Outlining the emotions in a scene lets you judge whether it has the movement and drama it needs to succeed.

- Adaptation exercises show how you can manipulate emotions to improve the pacing and impact of any scene.

21

Themes: The Underlying Message

In This Chapter

- ◆ Discovering themes from finished stories
- ◆ How simple themes generate endless plot ideas
- ◆ Using underlying messages for universal appeal

"Everything happens for a reason."

How many times have you heard someone use that phrase?

After recounting a minor mishap, major mistake, or colossal misfortune, people are apt to cap off the tale with "It must have happened for a reason."

Have you said it yourself? If so, you're blessed with the basic human desire to find meaning in everyday events, large or small, temporary or permanent. The literary equivalent is when you finish reading a book, close the cover, and think, "Nice story. But what was it all *about?*"

Finding a story's underlying meaning—or theme—fulfills that same desire to make sense of events. Reading a book from start to finish is a commitment of time and energy, and no one likes feeling that either one has been wasted. In this chapter, you'll learn how to identify and create underlying themes that will enrich your stories and satisfy your readers' craving for meaningful experience.

Find the Theme!

For some reason or other, it's entirely possible to write an entire book, revise it, revise it again, polish it from beginning to end, and, only then, discover what it's been about all along. Suddenly, you see past the actions and motivations, the clever and surprising plot twists you labored over, the spontaneous bursts of genius, and realize that it's really about ...

♦ Learning to trust your instincts.

♦ Discovering the path to redemption.

♦ Seeing that everyone deserves a second chance.

♦ Learning to stand on your own two feet.

♦ Breaking free to discover your own identity.

Whatever message you discover in your particular story, you may be startled that it's even there. But maybe, when you start thinking about it, you'll discover similar themes in your other writing pieces. Don't be surprised, you're not alone.

Chances are, your writing will reflect several personal themes of deep meaning to you: a child's need for a strong mother or father, the meaning of friendship, the pain of betrayal.

Countless writers discover the themes underlying their fiction after the writing is done. This happens for two reasons:

♦ **Writing is personal.** The experiences that mold your personality and character are bound to show through in something as personal as writing. Aware of it or not, your experiences influence your words. Individual fears, foibles, and favorites become recurring motifs even when you don't realize they're there.

♦ **Themes can be separate from plot.** It's true: because themes can emerge on their own, you can create a perfectly good plot without purposely constructing it around an underlying theme. But considering that themes will appear, why not take your writing up a notch and strengthen the connection between the plot and your personal themes?

If you can't already identify your themes, try answering the following questions:

◆ What motifs repeat in your writing?

◆ What traits do your characters share?

◆ What do most of your characters want?

◆ What obstacles do they need to overcome?

◆ Who—or what—gets in their way?

◆ Who helps them out of trouble?

◆ Who do they confide in?

◆ Who do they trust?

◆ What makes them happy/sad/nervous/afraid/comfortable?

Remember our study of *Little Red Riding Hood* in the previous chapter? Themes running through this fairy tale include "don't believe everything you see," or, more pointedly, "don't trust a wolf in sheep's (Grandma's) clothing."

The story illustrates this theme through the familiar plot events where Little Red avoids the big bad wolf only to be duped when he dresses up in Grandma's nightie and swallows her whole.

Pen Pal _____

Remember, a story using the same theme and basic plot steps can bear no resemblance to its source. In this way, themes can be recycled in endless variations, and the resulting stories will still be fresh and engrossing.

Using Themes to Strengthen Your Writing

Knowing how to make the most of a theme strengthens your writing in two important ways:

◆ Identifying a theme focuses your plot.

◆ A conscious theme gives your story added depth.

When you purposely incorporate a theme into your story, you give it a chance to transcend the plot events and attain deeper meaning—often on a more universal level.

And that means readers all over the world will enjoy your story, and, on some level, will recognize and feel comfortable with your message.

Practice Finding Themes

Think about the stories we've studied in this book. What themes do they illustrate? What lessons do they teach?

Ferdinand the Bull: Teaches a lesson about character through its theme of "to thine own self be true." Approached from a different angle, the underlying message is "a tiger doesn't change its stripes."

Homecoming: Teaches that "blood is thicker than water."

The Tellerman children's troubles arise when family members (Mom, a cousin) let them down, and resolve when other family members (Dicey, Gram) support them. Both of the Tellerman kids' journeys—the literal one and the metaphorical one—take place because of Dicey's unwavering vow to keep her siblings together.

Dicey's persistence pays off when Gram reluctantly opens heart and home to them. Eventually, Gram becomes Dicey's partner, making up for her own past mistakes by keeping her grandchildren together.

The Pigman: Teaches that "individuals are responsible for shaping their own lives."

Another theme that runs through most of Zindel's books might be "you can learn to make the best of a bad situation." Coming from families that are all dysfunctional in one way or another, his teen characters are motivated by more than the usual quest for independence. These teens must create separate identities in order to escape the poisonous atmospheres that surround them.

A similar theme pervaded *Chinese Handcuffs.* The protagonist rises above various dysfunctional backgrounds, leaving self-imposed isolation by learning to seek and accept help from others. Theme: "No man is an island."

Holes: How about "Am I not my bother's keeper?" Or even "virtue is its own reward."

Stanley takes the road of virtuous action by befriending Zero and teaching him to read. Later, when the boys escape Camp Greenwood and it turns out that their fates are linked, Stanley's unselfish actions break their shared curse, and both boys regain unclouded futures.

And don't forget the mother of all stories with the same underlying theme of "virtue is its own reward": *Cinderella.*

Like Stanley (or vice versa) Cinderella is dutiful to her tormentors while befriending the downtrodden. Maintaining her kind, loving nature despite daily abuse, when Cinderella finally finds herself pushed beyond endurance she musters the courage to reclaim what's rightfully hers: the right to attend the ball, which leads to reclaiming her station in life.

Stanley's path may be completely different in the details but, like Cinderella, Stanley remains true to his basic nature—honest and kind, despite the abuse of his evil keepers, the Warden and Mr. Sir. For his efforts, Stanley earns loyal friendship (Zero's) and regains his own family, who, successful for the first time in their lives, find their own station in life elevated.

Digging Deeper

Still having trouble finding themes in your own writing? Try asking these questions:

- What is the overall point of my story(s)?

- What do my main characters learn?

- How do my main characters change at the end of their journey?

Theme First, Story to Follow

Want to try something different? Shift focus to the opposite approach: make a list of sayings or adages and construct bare-bone, four-step plots (remember the formula?) based on their underlying themes:

- Don't judge a book by its cover.

- Don't count your chickens before they're hatched.

- Act in haste, repent at leisure.

- The sins of the fathers are visited upon the children.

- It takes courage to break out of a destructive cycle.

- The best lessons learned are the hardest.

- The best-laid plans often go awry.

After you've identified an appealing message and brainstormed some plot ideas, it's time to shape plot and message into a contemporary YA story. Whether you create new characters or recycle them from one of your existing stories, reshaping your story to reflect its underlying theme should spark important changes—and maybe inspire some fresh ideas.

Pen Pal

A story that lacks an underlying theme can end up formless, meandering aimlessly from beginning to end. If you're not sure what kind of theme to work with, or aren't yet sure what an underlying message is, you might look up Aesop's fables, or African folktales, or any stories springing from the oral storytelling tradition; all of these feature plots that illustrate an underlying moral or theme.

Children's book librarians can steer you to picture books based on such tales. Think of picture books as story outlines, and you'll find them a rich source of inspiration.

Last-Ditch Efforts

If all else fails and you still can't identify your personal themes, share your written stories or story ideas with friends and fellow writers and ask them to help you identify the underlying messages.

Transforming Your Source: Beauty and the Beast

Your goal in all of these steps is to identify a theme that gives your story added resonance and universal appeal. Let's take a sample story through the process and see how it works.

A classic fairy tale that's been interpreted and transformed into movies, stage plays, musical theatre and animated films, Beauty and the Beast can be taken literally or as an allegory. Whatever your take, it obviously has elements with powerful, lasting appeal. (If you only know the story from the animated versions, run to your nearest video store for Jean Cocteau's groundbreaking 1946 film.)

Here is the story as a three-part plot:

1. Protagonist, usually a fair young maid, is forced by circumstance to take shelter at the home of the antagonist—the beast.

2. Initially repelled, the maiden slowly discovers the beast's admirable character.

3. His inner beauty revealed, the maid falls in love with him, which breaks the evil spell he's under, miraculously restoring him to his true identity as a handsome prince.

Several possible themes immediately spring to my mind:

◆ Beauty is in the eye of the beholder.

◆ Don't judge a book by its cover.

And possibly:

◆ Virtue is its own reward.

Heavenly Inspiration

Similar themes underlie the plot of the 1976 movie *Heaven Can Wait*, a remake of 1941's *Here Comes Mr. Jordan*.

Heaven Can Wait begins with loveable quarterback Joe Pendleton on his way to the Super Bowl. Hit by an oncoming train, Joe is "rescued" by a bungling angel who snatches him before his time. The mistake is fixed by installing Joe's soul into the body of wealthy, self-absorbed tycoon Bruce Farnsworth, whose business interests include the tuna industry.

Enter environmentalist Bette Logan, come to plead the cause of innocent dolphins trapped in tuna nets. Joe is instantly smitten. To please Bette he institutes environmentally correct company policies, confusing Farnsworth's wife and his accountant, who are happily plotting Farnsworth's murder. When Farnsworth is killed, Joe is out of a body and promptly demands another one. It happens that a fellow football player is due for an early demise. Joe is thrilled to reclaim his old life and permanently takes over his new body, losing all memory of his former identity. When Joe meets Bette again, they're strangely drawn to each other. The film ends with the promise that the incompatible pair will discover that, deep down, they're soul mates.

Besides succeeding as entertaining romantic comedy, both versions of the story exploit the human desire to find a soul mate who sees past our beastly side to accept and love us for who we are.

To Bette, Farnsworth's odious beliefs and practices make him beastly. Inhabited by Joe, evil Farnsworth assumes Joe's childlike simplicity and openhearted generosity, traits that Bette finds irresistible.

Now let's transfer this plot to the four basic plot steps:

1. Hero's need: Joe needs a body. He gets Farnsworth's.

2. Villain's need: Mrs. Farnsworth and cohort need to kill Farnsworth.

3. Conflicts erupt when: Joe, as Farnsworth, falls for soul mate Bette. Joe/Farnsworth is killed; needs to return to Bette.

4. Conflicts resolve when: Joe, in his new identity, reconnects with Bette, and despite outward differences, each recognizes their soul mate.

Let's examine both stories, broken into three acts, to see exactly how much they share:

- ♦ Initially judging Joe/Beast by appearances, Bette/Beauty is put off.

- ♦ Learning to see Joe's/Beast's inner beauty, Bette/Beauty comes to love him.

- ♦ The restorative power of love returns Beast/Joe to his original, desirable form.

No one would immediately recognize Beauty and the Beast in *Heaven Can Wait*, but the two share the same three-act form.

Where a Theme Can Lead You

Let's see how we could rephrase the Beauty and the Beast theme as an active premise in order to originate story ideas.

Seeing beauty through your own eyes leads to …

- ♦ *Literally*, a beautiful girl falling for a disfigured boy.

- ♦ *Figuratively*, a beautiful girl falling for a boy that no one else likes, leading her to fight with her best friend, drop her group of friends, drop after-school activities, get in trouble with parents, etc.

Clearly the figurative story leads to more possible plot events; the extra action implied by the fact that no one else likes the boy creates conflict, which leads to plot.

In the first story idea, the fact that the boy is disfigured doesn't say anything about his character, and although liking a boy who's disfigured might create gossip, it does nothing to create or imply conflict.

Keep in mind that these techniques are story-generating methods. You'll need to add subplots, twists and turns, and, above all, character growth to create truly meaningful stories.

The Least You Need to Know

◆ Most likely, your stories or story ideas share similar themes—even if you're not aware of them.

◆ The same theme can generate countless different plots and stories.

◆ It's okay to find your theme after a story is finished.

◆ Underlying themes and great plot ideas will fall flat unless they're accompanied by character growth.

Part

The Business of Writing

I never met a student who wasn't dying to know whether he or she needed an agent—or exactly how to get that manuscript off the desk and into the bookstore. So this part covers the information you need to turn works in progress into submissions and send them out into the publishing world. And as if that isn't enough, you'll also find an illuminating chapter on writing nonfiction for YA readers—which, surprisingly, may actually help your fiction-writing career!

Wrapping It Up: The Submission Package

In This Chapter

- ◆ What really matters to agents and publishers
- ◆ Why books get rejected
- ◆ How to remedy the most common mistakes new writers make

Let's begin talking about the submission package by reviewing what *not* to say in your submission letter. Here are some common examples:

"Although you publish nautical adventures, I've enclosed sample chapters from my YA novel, *My Life in Rodeo*, because Todd, the main character, goes sailing in Chapter 16."

"Although I don't have an agent yet, I thought you wouldn't mind looking at this unsolicited manuscript …"

"The enclosed story, *Montana Beeswax*, is a beautifully crafted coming-of-age novel bursting with passion and adventure and …

"My family and friends loved my novel, and I know you will, too …"

"I was born in Alabama and won the English medal every year of grade school. Then I moved to Milwaukee, and attended community college, then transferred to U Wisconsin, and started writing more creative fiction when I …."

The road from story idea to published book is littered with manuscripts that died before they reached that hallowed destination. This chapter takes a look at the process of traveling that road, with tips for avoiding potholes, detours, and fatal crashes along the way.

Throughout this book we've covered many of the basic skills you need to write your YA novel and given you an idea of what's involved in creating the story from start to finish. At this point in the process, most writers are chomping at the bit to get started—and filled with questions.

For most of them, the biggest question of all is: how do I get published?

Why Books Get Rejected

The number-one reason a book gets rejected is because it just doesn't work.

Your manuscript may have a lovely style, an interesting, compelling, or even thrilling story idea, and you may know exactly what you hope to accomplish, but it's not on the page.

Or your story idea is fresh, funny, and compelling, but the writing is so excruciatingly bad that even the most revered editor in all the land can't save it.

In either case, no amount of edits, rewrites, and revisions will help. Before you start cursing that first pile of rejection letters, take a step back and try to be objective. Remember that agents and publishers want to find the next great writer. Their livelihood depends on it.

If your manuscript has even a glimmer of potential success, editors will leap at it; they'll go out of their way to get it into publishable shape. So be a pro:

- Accept that you'll probably need to revise a lot more than you thought. Be open to it. Expect it.

- Remember that the story sells the manuscript. If you can write a beginning, middle, and end, you're head and shoulders above the competition.

- There are no shortcuts.

Like everyone else, you'll have to learn by making mistakes—and then improving.

And the Point Is ...?

It's my experience from editing, teaching, and consulting that beginning writers all make the same mistakes. And the number-one common mistake is: there is no point to the story. Overall, there is no sense of progressing through the story to get somewhere.

Here's how to recognize a story with no point:

◆ It's impossible to write a blurb for.

◆ It's impossible to summarize in a few lines.

◆ It's hard to pin down exactly what it's about.

◆ It's impossible to say what the main character learned or how he or she changed.

How to remedy the mistake (do yourself a favor and believe the advice you get from the pros):

◆ Pay attention to all the lessons on craft, on plot, character, and narration in all those books and classes and workshops. They're remarkably similar for a reason. Listen and learn.

◆ Relax. Be yourself. Try to remember that writing is fun. If you've lost your energy, your drive, or your enthusiasm, do anything it takes to get it back. Sometimes you need to take a break. Sometimes you need to work through the doldrums. Follow your instincts.

◆ Ease the pressure. Keep in mind that not every writer is strong in every area. Some can't write dialogue. Some use too much narration, others not enough. Some have a terrible sense of pacing, or write weak characterizations. Those things can be fixed by careful editing, rewrites, or revisions.

◆ Remember that experience is the best teacher: don't give up—write more.

Slush Pile!

By the time the average manuscript has been through the editorial process, as much as 90 percent of the language may come from various editors—the unsung heroes of the industry, who earn a living getting your novel onto the shelves.

Ready to Submit?

Newcomers: leave your egos behind. I can't tell you how many writer-wannabes submit inappropriate manuscripts, accompanied by letters justifying themselves. Remember the following:

◆ Be open to change.

◆ Be ready to accept criticism and suggestions.

◆ Listen to the pros.

◆ Be reasonable.

◆ Don't think your project is the exception to the rule—whatever the rule is.

◆ Follow submission guidelines for publishers and agents.

◆ Keep within suggested page counts. Use the requested typeface and font size. Submit only the requested materials; no more, no less.

To sum up, don't make excuses for not following the guidelines. Just follow them.

Way before you submit your YA manuscript, you really should know whether you're writing suspense, romance, mystery, horror, fantasy, or sci-fi. You should know if your story is geared toward older or younger teens, and be confident that it wouldn't appeal more to kids or adults. Respect the process, put in the time and effort to learn your craft, and be realistic about your project's marketability.

You'll know you're ready to submit when:

◆ Your manuscript is complete or nearly so.

◆ Your outline and sample chapters are ready for submission.

◆ You're prepared with pitch letters and story summaries.

◆ You've researched publishers and/or agents to learn which are appropriate for your story.

Barring some remarkable stroke of great good fortune, the process of becoming a published author can be difficult and time-consuming, without many shortcuts. Yet, as with any worthwhile pursuit, the rewards are immense.

Exceptions to the Rule

First of all, it's bound to happen that for every "rule" I give you, you can cite two exceptions to that rule. ("Believable characters are full of contradictions." "But (insert name of best-selling book's main character) isn't contradictor at all!") That's true with every creative field, isn't it? That's why there are hundreds of books and magazines and classes and workshops on writing, playwriting, screenwriting, etc. And you usually find something valuable in each one.

Sometimes it seems as if some people are just lucky and they get published with no effort; but it may take many, many rejections before striking pay dirt.

So keep reality in mind:

- Finding an agent or publisher is a combination of talent, hard work, persistence, and luck.

- You can't know what a publisher's next list will be.

- You can't know whether a particular editor will like your submission on any given day.

- Write what you know, because you can't escape your own voice, which was formed by your own unique experience. Be yourself. It's the only surefire way to be an original.

If you have a solid idea, strong characters, a good conflict, and you can get it all on paper, imperfections in your dialogue, description, or narrative skills or grammar will be forgiven. And edited. And revised. And then your wonderful idea will be published, and believe me, you'll have learned a lot along the way.

Slush Pile!

Writing what you know only means that fiction should feel real, believable, and true—not that every book you write is your autobiography.

Common Questions and Answers

Question 1: On the subject of pacing, what happens in a novel if you have a dead chapter—one that doesn't seem to go anywhere but is needed to carry the plot? Should it be cut and the plot carried elsewhere if possible? Or do all books have one of those chapters lurking somewhere?

Answer: You have to work to not have that kind of chapter. It's time to get creative and find a way to use the information you need in a way that does forward the plot—as a conversation, as a purely descriptive scene (if it's an action that takes place). Can you give a specific example? Is this happening in your own work? It's tough to be general about this question, but you do need to think of something clever to do to keep the book active. It's great that you can see you have a dead space. Then you can do something about it!

Question 2: How deliberate do you think writers should be in writing books?

Answer: I have written several chapter books and have not planned out the plot, but have let it emerge. A plot is going to be tighter and have more appeal to a reader if you plan out your plot. Think about the "wants" issue (from Chapter 4), which is a real teaser to your reader and makes them want to read on.

Question 3: But what about the magic? When I don't plan, there's magic that comes; my story surprises even me as it emerges. Do I just have to give up on that and enjoy the smaller surprises along the way as my planned plot falls into place?

Answer: As to planning or finding magic, of course I vote for magic! That's not to say that you should guess at the theme or meaning of your story, or your character's main want and conflict. Those things should be in place as you begin to write. Then yes, surprises do pop up, which is what makes writing fun. You can't stick completely to your planned idea if your characters become real to you. I know it's a cliché, but it actually does happen that characters dictate plot as a story develops. You just know that so-and-so wouldn't do or say what you had planned for them. So I would say to have those basic elements in mind as you begin, and give as much planning as you can to your story, but always be open to those wonderful surprises.

Pen Pal

I read an interview with J. K. Rowling, who is an incredible planner, having planned all seven books at one time, and she said that even with all the planning, she is still able to enjoy surprises as she writes.

I find it crucial to know the ending to a story, and that's often my starting point. Then things fall into place, and you can always change the details if you don't like them. There's so much writing process, and then revising, that it's really best to just get the basics down, then plunge in. You will also hear writers say that they didn't know what their book was about until they'd finished it, or finished a first draft. This is true! So don't worry too much, because you learn so much about your story, and writing in general, from revising a first draft! Get anything down on paper—then you have raw material to work with. And you'll find yourself "planning" as you work deeper into the story, because you'll be asking, what happens next? How can I make it more exciting, fun, believable? That process never stops!

Question 4: I'm worried about coming up with an original idea. How do you find a story that hasn't been done before? And how do I know someone won't steal it if I do find it?

Answer: First, don't worry. Second, be specific. For instance, let's say you want to write about 14-year-old Dorka, who needs to find a way to join his family in America. Create the details, unique to Dorka, that are specifically related to that goal.

Maybe he first stows away on a ship and gets discovered. And thrown in jail. And meets some shady character who turns out to be his best friend, and teaches him to steal so he steals enough money for a steerage ticket, but then the person he stole the money from turns up on the same ship. Maybe it's a kid Dorka's age—maybe they become friends, or partners, or maybe they trade identities in America, and Dorka thinks he'll be better off as the other kid, but he finds out the other is a criminal wanted by the police.

Or maybe the victim is a girl—who Dorka thought was a wealthy young lady of fine breeding—but she's just like him, only better at social climbing. And she gives him English lessons and helps him with manners, so when they get to America they can become ... wealthy? educated? con artists?

Or maybe he meets a cobbler who teaches him the trade, and he eventually earns enough to pay back the money he stole, and the victim is so impressed that he ... adopts him? Makes him an apprentice in his ... furrier business? tire company? family-owned newspaper?

Details are what make a story. Your choices should be as specific as possible. You could take the same idea and make Dorka a mouse—then you'd have a picture book. You could turn Dorka into a mystic-in-training—then you'd have a fantasy combined with historical. The structure and even some or most of the events could be almost the same (though vocabulary and setting and cast would need modification.)

Plots are not unique.

Details are unique.

How you get from beginning to end is unique. That's why it's important to identify the underlying structure of a story. How you treat the story is entirely personal because it's unique to your voice, writing style, and the sum of your life experiences, which all influence the way you see your story unfolding. (Back to the list of everyone you've ever known.)

Pen Pal

In accordance with copyright law, ideas are not protected because people come up with the same ideas all the time. That's why you can only protect the execution of that idea.

Three people may write about an immigrant boy reuniting with his family or about the Charles Manson murders. But if one person writes about an immigrant boy in third person, and one writes from an independent narrator's POV, those two stories will immediately be distinct.

If one writer covers the Manson murders as a realistic, day-by-day, timeline-dependent pseudo-journalistic piece, it will feel totally different from someone who invents a complex series of imaginary letters from Manson's cult followers—even though both tell basically the same story.

Sometimes I think YA fantasy or science fiction stories feel more "real" than some reality-based novels because the author had to construct an entire universe, and this made him or her take the time to create the details we crave. When readers and writers inhabit the same world, it's easier for the author to be a little lax with detail.

That's why your main job as a writer is not so much to find a unique plot (though that wouldn't hurt, obviously) as to find a unique and specific way to tell the story. When the writing begins, your basic idea becomes almost an afterthought: "Boy wants ship's passage; boy encounters obstacles; boy overcomes obstacles, earns passage; boy is reunited with family."

The real work begins after the idea (and maybe your plot outline?) is in place. So, as always, spend time on the basics and create solid conflicts and wants and underlying themes so that you can dispense with them and let your creativity take over.

Question 5: How do I avoid a really predictable ending?

Answer: If you review your favorite stories or films, I'll bet you find that the endings themselves are fairly predictable. And fairly simple. In fact, you could probably guess the ending (the general idea of the ending, anyway) before you finish reading a book or seeing a movie. I think people in general like "predictable" endings. It's the stuff that comes right before the ending that can provide the real surprise.

Question 6: Does a first-time writer have a better chance at being accepted by a smaller publishing house or would a bigger publishing company consider that writer?

Answer: Try both. You can't know what anyone is looking for at any given time.

Question 7: The website I checked asks for a summary of the story. Do I write an outline, or do they mean a narrative that tells the story?

Answer: If you can, call and clarify; but you may hear "Send whatever you like." Anything you send is a sales tool, and you want them to buy your book; so if they don't specify summary, outline, or step sheet, send whichever best shows off your story and your writing style.

Outlines are usually used as a tool to see whether you can plot a story from start to finish. At this point, it's more important to sell your story idea than to include every character or every subplot. So if given a choice, I'd send a well-written summary over an outline because summaries can have narrative passion, excitement, and suspense.

I've taught classes on getting ready for publication, and I can't stress enough that the major stumbling block for most students was being able to summarize the story in the required number of pages.

> **Pen Pal**
>
> A step sheet is, literally, a step-by-step list of scenes in your book, even sketchier than an outline. An outline includes minor characters and events, chapter by chapter. A step sheet is more of a rough outline, a guide that can leave out the details. Refer to Chapter 17 for more information on step sheets.

I'll never forget how we were working on cutting 10- to 12-page summaries down to 4 pages when one student got an agent interested in his project. The agent asked him to e-mail a two-page summary that evening; he spent a few hours revising, sent it off, and was grateful we'd been pounding away at summaries and outlines for weeks!

Question 8: Are pitch letters supposed to resemble blurbs or are they meant to be more no-nonsense? Just how much room for creativity is allowed in pitch letter writing? As I write my pitch letter, I'm catching myself being too cute, too blurby.

Answer: There are two schools of thought. One says be clever and stand out; the other says just tell the story. I say let the story tell itself. You can make your pitch more enticing by showing a bit of your writing style or letting your "voice" show. If you ask me, "cutesy" should always be avoided.

Pen Pal _____

The usual conversion ratio from an 8½-by-11 double-spaced typewritten page to the average book-size page yields about 250 words per page. Production departments calculate specs on your soon-to-be-published manuscript. They tell the editor how long the printed book will be according to the font size and design and the amount of spacing between words and spacing between lines (leading).

Editors may need to cut your text to fit the number of folios (sets of eight-page bundles) allotted to your printed book. Conversely, books can be made longer by increasing the font size or leading or adding extra space to chapter openers or between chapters.

The Least You Need to Know

◆ Most stories get rejected for the same reasons: no story or a story with no point.

◆ Hundreds of books, articles, classes, and workshops teach fairly similar writing techniques. Believe them.

◆ There's no shortcut to success. Talent, hard work, and perseverance (and a little luck!) lead to success.

Finding the Perfect Agent and Publisher

In This Chapter

◆ Finding agents

◆ Agreements with agents

◆ Crafting the perfect pitch

◆ Finding publishers

You've written the next great American YA novel—or you've at least got the idea. How do you go about finding the best agent and publisher to bring your work to market? This chapter has the 411 on getting your book in print.

Selling Your Stuff

The first step in selling your book is almost always finding an agent to represent you. Many of the bigger publishing houses do not consider work unless it's represented by an agent. An agent who is actively placing work in the genre in which you write can help you more easily find a good home for your book. In addition, a good agent can help you negotiate a bigger advance and navigate any potential pitfalls in your contract, ensuring that you get the best possible deal.

Some authors choose to represent themselves and have had success. However, publishers are often concerned about litigation related to idea theft, and working with reputable agents provides another safeguard against allegations of such practices. Therefore, many publishers return unsolicited manuscripts unopened if they do not come from an agent.

Pen Pal _____

The initial fee that an agent negotiates is an "advance," which is usually an amount of money that is drawn against the potential royalties the book will earn. Depending on the contract you sign, you may begin earning additional royalties when the book "earns out" the advance—that is, the book has earned more than the royalties that were given to you in the initial advance.

In exchange for representing your work, the agent usually collects somewhere in the neighborhood of 15 percent of any money you earn on the book. That's usually a now-and-forever proposition. In other words, if your book sells for a $10,000 advance, the agent gets $1,500 of that, leaving you with $8,500.

If your book earns out, the agent also collects a percentage of any royalties that the book earns for the amount of time that it's in print, even if you sever your ties with the agent. Usually, the publisher sends payment for advances and royalties to the agent, who deducts his or her cut and forwards the rest of the money along to you. Because this is a long-term relationship, it's important that you find an agent who is experienced and trustworthy.

Finding the Right Agent

So how do you find the right agent? First, you need to figure out who the pool of potential candidates are. Nothing screams "amateur" more than sending an agent a pitch or proposal for a genre that he or she doesn't represent. If Big Name Agent only represents business or health books, and you send a pitch for a YA novel, your proposal, query, or manuscript will go in the garbage faster than yesterday's tuna sandwich.

There are a number of ways to find agents who specialize in a particular genre:

♦ Check out Jeff Herman's annual *Guide to Book Publishers, Editors & Literary Agents: Who they are! What they want! How to win them over!* This book has sections on various agents and the type of work they represent, as well as contact information and the agent's preferences for being pitched.

♦ Surf the web. Google "young adult literary agents" or other variations of those words and see who pops up.

♦ Check with the Association of Author Representatives (www.aar-online.org). Many reputable agents belong to this association, which also has a list of agent screening questions on the website.

♦ Read *Literary Market Place*, an industry directory, which is available at www. literarymarketplace.com or at your local library.

♦ Check out the acknowledgments pages of books in your genre. Authors often thank their agents, and that will give you some leads.

♦ Ask colleagues who write in this genre.

♦ Read trade publications such as *Publisher's Weekly* and *Publisher's Marketplace* to see who's selling titles in this genre.

You'll want to be sure that these agents have experience selling YA novels or nonfiction, because those are the agents who are most likely to have the greatest knowledge of the market and of what publishers are looking for.

Checking Out the Agent

After you've compiled a list of agents, you'll want to be sure that they are reputable in their field. Most professional agents will have a website that details their current and former clients and sales. In addition, you can look for them on www.PublishersMarketplace.com, which is fast becoming the premier place for industry watching. Here, you can see which publishers have scored which deals and often get a general idea of the advances they are negotiating.

Other ways to check out agents include contacting their clients, asking for recommendations from people in the industry, and reading industry publications and websites.

Pen Pal

Like most things in life, there are good agents and there are bad agents. Having a bad agent can be worse than having no agent at all, leaving a bad impression with publishers and failing to protect your rights during the negotiating process. For some insight about good agents and bad agents, check out www.PublishersMarketplace.com and www.predatorsandeditors.com.

The Perfect Pitch

After you've compiled an agent wish list, it's time to craft the perfect pitch letter. A pitch letter is a one-page summary of the book and why it's the greatest thing since sliced bread. Your pitch letter should be pithy and compelling—if the agent isn't wowed in the first paragraph, you can pretty much kiss your chances of representation "good-bye."

Generally, a pitch letter follows a specific sequence.

Start with a salutation. Obviously, address your letter to the proper agent and address him or her in an appropriate manner.

Get to the point. Think of your first paragraph as the be-all and end-all of your letter. This is the text that needs to grab the agent by the collar and keep those agent eyes glued to the page. "This is a story about rivalry between friends," or "this is about how divorce affects a 15-year-old girl," etc. Then describe it a little more: "The story centers on John's efforts to run the family farm by himself after his dad dies."

Give a brief synopsis of the book, including major plot details. Include anything that distinguishes the book from the competition, or that will make it particularly interesting to audiences. Then describe the resolution and anything that further distinguishes the book:

"With the help of a crusty caretaker, John learns he can accomplish the work of an adult. But his dream of leaving the farm for a city career never quite dies, and John ultimately abandons his family to pursue his long-dormant dream. The story is written in first person, with diary excerpts."

Next comes a paragraph of any credentials that make you the perfect person to write the book. Don't include a resumé, but do include the top four to six credentials, especially if you've been previously published or have experience that gives you particular insight into the topic.

Watch out for writing that sounds like a book review. The following example, written as student homework, pitches the children's classic *Where the Wild Things Are* by Maurice Sendak. It begins beautifully, with a brisk summary that lists important story points, and also captures the irreverent flavor of the writing:

"It's hard to miss Max. He's the one in a wolf suit, howling at the moon. But when rude Max goes too far, Mom sends him to bed without dinner. So Max's imagination cooks up a better place to live—a jungle crawling with scary monsters. They don't behave either! Max has found his new home—or has he? In the end, Max returns to his room, choosing to be boy rather than beast. Wouldn't you know it—Mom has saved him dinner!"

This description captures the tone and spirit of the story, and tells the tale from start to finish without bogging down once. But watch what happens next:

"You'll love the story's lively, playful writing, which captures the allure of monsters in all their glory. Max's adventure will bring a smile to kids and adults alike. Don't miss this fun book."

Unfortunately, that final paragraph, although well written, is too close to both a review and a sales pitch. It makes the mistake of telling the reader how they should feel after reading the book, and then warns the reader not to pass it by. No agent or editor needs to be told what he or she is looking for. If they didn't know, they wouldn't be in business!

Above all, avoid being overly effusive when describing your work. The following example illustrates the problem with grandiose language:

"You know Harry Potter. You know Olivia the Pig. But have you met Max? The only way you will is by flipping through the next children's book to take kids by storm—*Where the Wild Things Are*. This delightful creation is the perfect read for any kid who dreams of escaping punishment after stirring up trouble."

Instead, stick to the facts and let your story speak for itself:

"You know Harry Potter. You know Olivia the Pig. But you've got to meet Max! Irrepressible Max goes Where the Wild Things Are to escape punishment after behaving badly."

The Windup to the Pitch

Your pitch is professional and fun to read. But before you mail your letter or proposal package to an agent or publisher, make sure it's also letter-perfect:

❏ Proof your pitch letter for spelling, grammatical errors, and typos.

❏ Double-check the spelling of the agent's name, as well as the address and zip code of the recipient. Incorrect spelling is a pet peeve of many agents.

❏ Be sure your contact information is on both the letter and, if you're sending one, on the cover page of the proposal.

❏ Make sure the package is neat and free of marks or coffee stains.

❏ When requested, send SASE: Self-addressed stamped envelope. It's acceptable to omit the SASE as long as you note that you don't want the manuscript returned to you.

❏ Take a deep breath, seal the package, affix the proper postage, and send!

The Sample Pitch Letter

The following pitch letter is an example of how a pitch letter is generally constructed. This is not an actual pitch but was written as an example.

Date

Ms. Sally Bigwig
Massively Successful Literary Agency
000 Park Avenue
New York, New York 12345
Dear Ms. Bigwig:

When John Blanchard's parents are killed in a horrible car accident, the devastated 15-year-old is sent to live with his crusty grandfather. He believes that his arrival at the dilapidated Three Chances Farm—once an institution in the world of horse racing—marks the beginning of a dark period in his life.

Young John tries to make the most of his situation and is befriended by Spud, the farm's only remaining stable hand. To stay out of his bitter grandfather's way, John spends his summer days helping Spud with the farm's few remaining horses and begins to learn about Three Chances' illustrious past. One day, while the two are working in the stable, the mysterious delivery of a fiery thoroughbred changes the course of the three men's lives forever.

Three Chances Farm is the story of the human spirit triumphing over the most hopeless and tragic circumstances. Against the backdrop of the thrilling sport of horse racing, three men find that their shattered lives are reconstructed, thanks to the fierce, independent spirit of a mysterious horse. Targeted to readers age 13 to 16, the book's messages of hope and persistence, as seen through the eyes of John Blanchard, will resonate with young audiences.

I have been a horse-racing fan since my childhood and can bring the dynamic world of this popular sport alive on the pages of *Three Chances Farm*. My work has been published in *Dallas Horseracing Daily* and in the *Four Star Penny Saver*.

Thank you for your consideration. Please contact me at (123) 456-7890 or at imayawriter@imayawriter.com if you would like to review the manuscript.

I look forward to your response.

Sincerely,

Ima Y.A. Writer

Not-So-Secret Agent

Courting agents can be tricky, and there are rules. Send material only as it is requested—don't deluge the agent with a full manuscript at the first contact. It's usually better to contact agents by postal service; many do *not* accept faxed or even e-mailed queries. It's also a good idea to call the agency first to find out whether they are accepting new authors and to find out the name of the person (and its correct spelling) to whom you should address your query.

So you've sent your pitch letter and your wildest dreams are starting to come true: the agent is interested and wants to see your submission package. You've already learned about creating your submission package in Chapter 22, so you send it off for a look. Then, wonder of wonders, the agent wants to see the full manuscript (or proposal, which is usually the case with nonfiction books).

If all goes well, the agent will want to "sign" you, which means that he or she wants to represent your work. Then it's time to negotiate your agreement. This is great news and confirmation that the agent believes your work is worthy of representation.

Slush Pile!

Sometimes an agent will request exclusive review of a project for a period of time. In this case, be sure to put a limit on the amount of time you're willing to offer an exclusive look—usually no more than a few weeks. Otherwise, the agent could keep your manuscript tied up for months before deciding that she doesn't want to represent it, leaving you back at square one.

A Few Questions

When an agent offers representation, you may be willing to agree to just about anything. However, before you agree to anything, ask a few questions to be sure that this agent is the best possible fit for you. A full list of questions is available on the Association of Author Representatives website, but some of the key points you want to ask are:

- How familiar are you with the young adult market?

- What other works in this genre have you sold? To which publishers?

- Will you be the person representing my book?

- How do you intend to market the book to get publishers interested?

- How will you report the submissions you've made and the feedback you've gotten?

- What are the provisions of your agency agreement? May I review this agreement?

Pen Pal

As you're interviewing agents, look for someone who is truly enthusiastic about your work. Someone who is excited about what you've written is going to sell it better than someone who is lukewarm.

There are many other questions you should ask, so do visit the AAR website and review them. Don't be afraid to decline an offer of representation if you feel it's not the right fit for you. There are many agents out there, and if one liked your book enough to represent it, chances are that others—who may be a better fit for you—will, too.

Agreeing with Your Agent

When you've found an agent with whom you're comfortable and who wants to represent you, you'll likely be asked to sign an agent agreement. Agent agreements are simpler documents than full-blown publication contracts. The agreement with the agent protects both of you by outlining the provisions of your relationship.

For the agent, the agreement ensures that you won't try to work with multiple agents and see who can sell your work first. Your agreement will require that you exclusively allow the agent in question to represent this work. It will outline the agency commissions, fees, and expenses and what you're responsible for paying. Sometimes agencies require that you pay expenses related to the marketing of the book—photocopying, postage, etc.—out of your own pocket. Others simply absorb that cost or deduct it out of any potential sales.

For you, the agreement ensures you that the agent represents your interests on behalf of publishers. As your representative, the agent will be responsible for marketing your work with the intention of selling it for the best possible deal. Your editor may review your manuscript or proposal and offer you suggestions to make them better. And he or she will bring insight into the marketplace to bear on the marketing of your work.

Read the agency agreement carefully and question any clauses or provisions with which you are not comfortable. These agreements are often negotiable, and if there is a provision that's causing you concern, you may find that it can be taken out.

> **Slush Pile!**
>
> Some agents try to work sneaky verbiage into their agreements that gives them the right to represent all of your work. It's usually not a good idea to agree to such sweeping exclusivity. See how well your agent does on your first project together before signing on for the long haul.

Targeting Publishers

Your agent usually makes the determination of which publishers to target, using his or her knowledge of the marketplace. However, you can help; don't be afraid to share your knowledge or preferences with the agent.

As someone who specializes in a genre, chances are that you know something about who's publishing what. Feel free to share that with your agent. If you sense that your agent isn't open to collaboration, that could be a warning sign and is probably something that you need to address. Your agent is your representative to the publishing world and should be open to your ideas.

That said, after you've signed on with an agent and he or she is working on your behalf, you need to let the agent do his or her job. Frantic status calls and angst-ridden e-mails do nothing but take the agent's attention away from selling your book. You should establish clear communication parameters with your agent—for example, in the beginning you may want to plan biweekly update calls. Find out whether the agent will be sharing publisher feedback with you directly and how that will happen. But if you become too much of a pain, the agent may lose interest and enthusiasm for your work. Selling a work for publication takes time. So if you've done your due diligence and picked a good representative, you should give her the latitude to work on your behalf.

Finding the right agent is a thrilling experience, and it's even better when your agent successfully sells your work to a good publishing house. When a publisher makes an offer on your work, it's usually done through your agent. The advance will usually be split into segments based on the work that needs to be done.

After the sale has happened, you will be assigned to an editor who will help you shape your work into an acceptable format for publication. If you've sold your work based on a proposal, you'll work with the editor to create your manuscript. Either way, it's the next phase of work on your book—and the most exciting because at the end of this road will be a published work with your name on the cover!

The Least You Need to Know

- Most publishers prefer authors who are represented by agents.

- It's important to find an agent who has experience selling the type of work you write.

- Keep your pitches pithy and fact-based. Long-winded sales proposals are almost never a good idea.

- Send prospective agents material only as it's requested. Deluging agents with unrequested proposals or manuscripts is frowned upon.

- Share your feedback with your agent. He or she should view the relationship as a collaboration.

Chapter 24

Just the Facts: Nonfiction for YA Readers

In This Chapter

◆ Nonfiction topics

◆ Finding nonfiction projects

◆ Using the right voice for young readers

Nonfiction is as popular as ever (maybe even more so) with young adult readers. From biographies of hot celebrities to a detailed account of some major historical event, young people never seem to lose interest in learning about interesting true people, places, and happenings. And, as they say, truth is often stranger than fiction, so in many cases you will find that real-life material is just as good as anything your imagination could dream up.

This chapter will help you decide if nonfiction is right for you, offer pointers on breaking into this exciting market, and explain how writing nonfiction may help your fiction career!

Fiction vs. Nonfiction

As a writer (or aspiring writer) of YA books, are you better off pursuing fiction or nonfiction projects? That depends. There is no one right answer to that question because it involves factors such as your writing experience/background, interests, goals, and lots of other things.

If you have a vivid imagination and an uncontrollable urge to flex your creative muscles, then fiction might be your calling. That's not to say that you can't be imaginative or creative when writing nonfiction, but these traits often play a lesser part when doing a nonfiction book.

On the other hand, if you enjoy dealing with real-life topics such as science, history, or interesting people and places, then you would probably enjoy writing nonfiction.

There are other factors to consider, though. For the most part, it is easier to earn a (relatively) steady income in the nonfiction market. The fiction market, by contrast, tends to be highly speculative and unpredictable—at least, from the standpoint of a writer trying to make a living. So if finances are a major concern, you might want to focus on nonfiction for the bulk of your income.

It can also sometimes be easier to break into nonfiction markets, especially if you have any kind of special expertise. As a result, if you are a new writer seeking your first book credit, the nonfiction route may be your better choice.

 Slush Pile!

Kids today are way more savvy than they were even a few years ago. Even young children seem to be wise beyond their years. And if they don't know something, they know how to easily find out, thanks to modern technology. (There's almost no fact that can't be verified via a quick Internet search, it seems.) Bottom line: don't think you can slack off on your research simply because you are writing for younger readers. If anything, these readers are even more perceptive than adults; so if they spot something that is incorrect, they will call you on it.

Using Magazines as a Springboard

If you have never written a book before, you need to prove to publishers that you have the writing skills they want. Most authors do this by assembling an assortment of magazine articles they have written. (If you haven't even written a magazine article yet, I strongly advise you to consider doing this first, to establish yourself as a writer and develop the writing techniques and work skills you need to write an entire book.)

After you have assembled this packet of magazine articles—known as "clips" in the writing business—you then send them to the appropriate editors at publishers, to demonstrate your writing ability and experience.

Your magazine articles can prove helpful to you in another way when you are pursuing book projects. When writers do articles for the adult market, they often find themselves with much more material than they need or can use within the confines of a magazine article. In that case, sometimes the writer decides to use the extra material and research as the foundation for a book project on that topic. Or the writer might get such a strong positive reaction to the article that he realizes there is a hunger among readers for more information on the topic. However it happens, the writer uses the magazine article as a springboard for what make eventually become a really good book.

The same is true in the YA sector. If you write magazine articles for a teen readership, you may gain valuable insight as to what topics have good book potential. You will also be able to gauge readers' feelings on a particular topic.

> **Pen Pal**
>
> Here's a relatively new trend in the YA book market: authors of adult books (or their publishers) edit their books and release a revised, more teen-friendly version as a YA book. This allows them to tap into a whole new market with relatively little extra work.

New Nonfiction Topics

Fortunately (or unfortunately, depending on how you look at it), a lot of real-life issues and topics play a major role in young people's lives these days. Of course, there are the old standbys such as dating, parents, teachers, etc., but there are also new worries, including school violence, online predators, and modern security issues.

Today's teens are very aware of the world around them, so politics and current events can be good possibilities. There is also a renewed interest among young people in things historical, such as U.S. presidents of the past and world history.

It is pretty easy to figure out what other topics interest young people today. Spend a little time watching TV shows or channels that target teens or preteens. For example, you will see a ton of reality adventure and extreme sports shows targeting teens, so biographies of extreme athletes might make for a good YA nonfiction series.

Check out the popular teen magazines. If you are brave enough, hang out at the mall on a Friday night, when teens are usually out in droves, and eavesdrop on the hot topics of conversation. (Fortunately, teens have a knack for talking loudly, so it's easy to overhear them without skulking around like a criminal.)

Pen Pal

With YA nonfiction, many publishers like to include extra elements that will make the books more fun—and thus more attractive to teen readers or younger readers with short attention spans. For example, a book about colonial history might include fun quizzes on Ben Franklin's inventions or projects where readers can make their own colonial-type creations. When proposing a nonfiction idea to a publisher, suggesting a few fun extras just may help you seal the deal.

Finding Markets

When you decide you want to write a nonfiction YA book, you need to find a publisher that is interested in giving you an opportunity. Fortunately, it is fairly easy to locate these markets. Simply doing an online search for "young adult" and "publisher" will give you a good start.

Writer's Market publishes an annual guide to publishers, and you can look for ones that specialize in books for kids or teens. For more up-to-date listings, consider subscribing to the Writer's Market online service, which only costs a few dollars a month.

You can also join writers' organizations, where you can network with veteran YA authors who may be willing to share leads and market information.

Then there's old-fashioned detective work. Ask the young people you know for ideas as to what books are "hot" with kids their age. Or head to a bookstore and see which YA titles are prominently displayed. If you encounter chatty employees, perhaps they'd be willing to tell you which YA titles sell the best, or which publishers produce the most YA titles. After you have gotten some names, do an online search for the contact information, call the publisher, and ask to speak with someone in the editorial department. If you get a friendly employee on the phone, she may give you the scoop as to whether they are seeking authors at the moment. At the very least, she can probably tell you where to submit your samples and letter of interest.

Pen Pal

Have an idea for a nonfiction series that would interest YA readers? Do some research and try and pinpoint a publisher for which this might be a good fit (but which they—or, ideally, their competitors—have not already done). Put together a persuasive proposal and send it to the publisher's editorial director. Be sure to stress the reasons why you would be the best candidate to write some or all of the books in this series. With any luck, they will like your idea—and you will have secured a multi-book project for yourself.

Work on Demand

Unlike fiction—where publishers may just have a general vague idea of what they are looking for (such as "historical coming-of-age novels")—with nonfiction, the needs are often much more specific. In fact, publishers may plot out their agenda, complete with detailed planned titles—a year in advance or more. This is especially true if the titles are part of an ongoing series. For example, if a publisher is doing a series on biographies of U.S. presidents, they may know that within the next year they want to do books on Abraham Lincoln, George Washington, and John F. Kennedy. They will then seek out writers to do those specific projects. Those writers, in essence, are doing work on demand.

Advantages for Writers

There are some advantages to writers in doing these types of work-on-demand projects. For one thing, the publisher already knows exactly what it wants, so the writer doesn't have to come up with an idea. As a result, the writer does not need to do any proposal or query letter. Generally, the writer would simply need to submit a resumé/bio and sample of his previous work, if the publisher is not already familiar with the writer. If the publisher does not already have an outline in place, the writer may also need to prepare one of those. Also, if the publisher has an ongoing need for more books and they are pleased with the writer's work, this can lead to a steady work stream for the writer.

Pen Pal

It can be very helpful to recruit a few smart teens—your kids, siblings, neighbors, etc.—to serve as your "test panel." Have them read your manuscript or work in progress and give their critiques or comments. This way, you'll be sure the material passes the "teen test" before your editor lays eyes on it.

Disadvantages for Writers

There are also some negative points (from a writer's perspective) with these kinds of projects. There are often strict, specific guidelines and format procedures, which some writers may find time-consuming and annoying. Also, because the publisher often has a detailed idea of exactly what they want, writers may be forced to stifle much of their creativity and individual style to conform with the publisher's formulaic approach. In other words, this is not a situation in which writers are likely to get the chance to show off their individual style or express their offbeat personality.

More important, works such as these are often assigned on a work-for-hire basis, meaning the writer gets only a flat fee, with no royalties, and gives the publisher all rights to the work. Because YA nonfiction tends to be shorter than adult books, the fees to writers for these projects are often relatively small.

Slush Pile!

YA nonfiction projects are notorious for including not-so-great contact terms, such as work-for-hire clauses and no royalties. Be sure to read your contract closely and ask for clarification of any points you don't understand. If possible, have an agent look at the contract to spot any potentially problematic terms.

Finding On-Demand Projects

As previously mentioned, writers usually do not need to query for these kind of "on-demand" projects. So how do you nab these assignments? In these situations, publishers usually take the easiest route, going with the first qualified writer they can find. So it is a good idea to stay on their radar screen. Do some research at the bookstore or library to identify publishers who do a lot of YA nonfiction books—especially those who do a lot of series works. Then prepare a professional-looking package composed of your resumé/bio, some samples of your work, and any other relevant items that demonstrate your writing ability. You usually send this to the editorial director or senior editor, but it's a good idea to call the publisher and ask, just to make sure your materials reach the right person.

Sometimes publishers enlist the help of an agent to match writers to these projects, so it is also a good idea to make contacts with agents who handle YA nonfiction works. Check *Writer's Market* or other writers' reference sources for clues as to which agents deal with these types of books.

Pen Pal

A writer's conference can be a great place to connect with editors, as well as experienced YA writers who can share valuable tips and advice. Check out writers' magazines and websites for leads on upcoming conferences.

Occasionally publishers also recruit writers by means of online classifieds such as CraigsList, so it may be worthwhile to scan those ads regularly, too.

Mine Your Expertise

When it comes to nonfiction, the old adage "write what you know" definitely rings true. This is especially important for YA writers. Young people these days are very perceptive and intelligent, and their "bluffing detectors" tend to be pretty advanced, so they can often quickly recognize an author who doesn't quite know what he's talking about.

The good news? Writers who have any kind of special expertise or experience will immediately become much more attractive to a publisher. Have you worked as a veterinary assistant? A publisher doing a series on dog breeds would probably love to hear from you. Crime and criminal investigations are hot topics right now, so if you have any kind of law-enforcement background, be sure to play that up when contacting publishers. Same thing goes with anything related to technology or high-tech gadgets.

Pen Pal

Young people spell big profits for publishers. Most major publishing houses now have entire divisions handling books for younger readers. Random House, for example, has a large book division consisting of about a dozen different book lines targeting kids and teens. This division alone cranks out about 400 books of all types each year. Translation: lots of opportunities for writers!

From Author to Expert

A funny thing happens when you write a nonfiction book. Suddenly, as if someone has waved a magic wand, the world now sees you as an expert on that particular topic. This can be a really good thing.

Each writer has his or her own agenda and motivation for writing books. Obviously, most enjoy the writing itself—and many would write just for the simple joy they get from it. But usually there are also other, more practical reasons for writing. For many, it is the need to keep a roof over their head and put food on the table.

For some writers, books are just one step toward their larger career goals. Perhaps they want to be a public speaker. Maybe they'd like to do presentations at schools, libraries, or other organizations. Now that the world sees you as an expert, this goal can be much closer to becoming a reality.

Let's say you have an interest in exotic wild animals and would love to do presentations on the topic for elementary schools. But first you write a YA book (or several) on exotic animals—a book which, hopefully, received good feedback from critics and, more important, from young readers. It is now much more likely that schools would take you seriously as an expert in the field—better yet, an expert who has proven he can connect with that challenging YA age group.

Slush Pile!

Each publisher has their own particular guidelines and style when it comes to content. Whereas some may be fine with using slang and casual language in nonfiction books, for example, others may find this unacceptable. To avoid starting off on the wrong foot with a publisher, be sure to get clear details on their particular style before you start your manuscript. For added insight, check out some of their existing books and pay close attention to the style and tone.

Finding the Right Voice

As a writer, it is critical to find the right "voice" for your readers—meaning, speaking (writing) in a way that won't be distracting or off-putting to them, and avoiding any language that would go over their head or, even worse, seem like you are "talking down" to them.

This is something all YA writers need to be concerned with—but it is of particular importance when it comes to nonfiction. Because you are often dealing with facts and figures, you may almost automatically fall into "lecture mode," where you come across sounding like a college professor. With all due respect to the college professors out there, this probably will not score you any points with young readers. You need to find a way to make your nonfiction book informative, while at the same time interesting and entertaining to young readers who have notoriously discriminating tastes. This is not so easy—and it is one major area in which new YA nonfiction authors often run into trouble.

Pen Pal

For general research into the minds of teens, reading major magazines that target this age group can be helpful. But when you are trying to find the right "voice," publications such as *CosmoGirl, Girls Life,* and *Elle Girl* can be a treasure trove of insights. These publications often have first person essays or "as told to" pieces, in which teens share their story, in their own words, with a writer. These stories are written by teens, for teens. That means they are written the way teens really talk, often including current slang and phrases or terms popular with young people. Study these pieces carefully, and before long you may find yourself talking like a 13-year-old (which, in this case, would be a good thing).

From Nonfiction to Fiction

Suppose you have a burning desire to be a successful novelist. You get the opportunity to write a YA book—but it's nonfiction, so you are ready to say, "Thanks, but no thanks."

Not so fast. Although nonfiction may not be your life's calling, this can still be an excellent opportunity. For one thing, it is an excellent chance to get your feet wet in the YA realm. You would gain valuable writing experience and get a firsthand glimpse of the good and bad parts of writing for the YA reader. You would get to flex your creative muscles, and develop important writing habits that would be a huge help for any type of book project you do in the future. Plus you get your initiation into the YA world, making those first-time mistakes (and yes, we all make them) with a work that may not be as near and dear to your heart as that novel you've been dying to write. Fiction tends to be a much more personal creation—especially debut novels, which agents and editors say often have a lot of autobiographical elements. As a result, mistakes—or worse, bad reviews—sting much more when it comes to your fiction book. Many writers prefer experiencing their book-related "baptism by fire" with a less-personal nonfiction work, which helps them develop a thicker skin before exposing their fictional writings to the world.

And don't worry that writing one nonfiction book will doom you to a lifetime on the nonfiction shelves. Just the opposite, having a book credit under your belt will often make it easier to get your next book project, whether you seek fiction or nonfiction opportunities. The next publisher you approach will know that you are a talented writer who can handle a book-length project, which will make them much more likely to feel confident offering you a deal.

Many writers (in both the YA and adult realm) frequently jump back and forth from fiction to nonfiction projects with no problem, so there's no need to worry that by writing one book of a certain type you will be permanently pigeonholed into that category.

Pen Pal _____

Most major publishers—and even specific editors within those companies—handle both fiction and nonfiction. By doing a good job with a nonfiction book, you get your foot in the door at that company and earn some valuable contacts that can help you get more work, in both fiction and nonfiction areas. Plus publishing is a small world, and editors tend to be friends with other editors. If your editor likes you, he may sing your praises to his editor friends at other publishers, possibly paving the way for you to get more projects in the future.

The Least You Need to Know

♦ The YA nonfiction market is thriving, meaning lots of opportunities for writers.

♦ By building a successful track record as a YA nonfiction author, writers can get a head start on a fiction career or establish themselves as an expert.

♦ Do your research: study other YA nonfiction books and note who the major publishers are.

♦ Pay careful attention to your voice and tone, and make sure your writing is geared toward the teen reader.

Chapter 25

Questions of Ownership

In This Chapter

- ◆ Copyright basics
- ◆ Ownership of work
- ◆ The danger of plagiarism
- ◆ Obtaining use permissions

Just because you write a work doesn't mean that you own it. Confusing? You bet. The legal side of literary work can be a bit mind-boggling. Still, it's important to know the basics about rights and permission so that you don't get yourself in hot water. This chapter spells out the legal do's and don'ts you need to know to protect your work.

What Is Copyright?

Copyright is a form of government protection of creative work. It's different from a patent or trademark, which protect inventions or discoveries. According to the United States Copyright Office's website, the United States provides protection to the authors of "original works of authorship, including literary, dramatic, musical, artistic, and certain other intellectual works. This protection is available to both published and unpublished works." The 1976 Copyright Act was passed to protect works of authorship and allows the owner the right …

- To make copies of the work in print or audio recordings.

- To prepare "derivative works" based on the original.

- To distribute copies or recordings for sale, rental, lease, or loan and to otherwise transfer ownership.

- To authorize or conduct public performances of the work.

- To display works publicly.

- To perform sound works publicly by means of an audio transmission.

What follows is a sample taken from a short-form copyright registration. Note that the information requested is fairly basic, but does require finished copies of your manuscript:

1. Title of This Work

2. Name and Address of Author and Owner of the Copyright

3. Year of Creation

4. Publication

5. Type of Authorship in This Work

6. Signature of Author

7. Person to Contact for Rights and Permissions

If the work is unpublished, send one copy. If published, send two copies of the best published edition. (If first published outside the United States, send one copy either as first published or of the best edition.) Copies submitted become the property of the U.S. Government.

Pen Pal

Derivative work means a work that is based on another piece of work. For instance, an abridged version of a book or a movie that is based on a short story or magazine article are both derivative works.

Use this form if 1) you are the only author and copyright owner of this work, *and* 2) the work was not made for hire, *and* 3) the work is completely new (does not contain a substantial amount of material that has been previously published or registered or is in the public domain). Note: *"Short Form TX" is not appropriate for an anonymous author who does not wish to reveal his or her identity.*

For a full explanation of copyright provisions, visit the U.S. Copyright Office's website at www.copyright.gov.

What's Fair Is Fair

Copyright provisions are not without exception, however. The law provides for "fair use," which allows a portion of copyrighted works to be used without authorization in certain circumstances. The law states that these circumstances include "purposes such as criticism, comment, news reporting, teaching (including multiple copies for classroom use), scholarship, or research."

To use the work in any of these ways does not constitute an infringement of copyright. To determine whether the use falls under the "fair use" provision, the law states that the use must meet the following criteria:

◆ The purpose and character of the use, including whether such use is of a commercial nature or is for nonprofit educational purposes

◆ The nature of the copyrighted work

◆ The amount and substantiality of the portion used in relation to the copyrighted work as a whole

◆ The effect of the use upon the potential market for or value of the copyrighted work

According to the U.S. Copyright website, the law also states that "the fact that a work is unpublished shall not itself bar a finding of fair use if such finding is made upon consideration of all the above factors."

Although the author or creator of a work, by definition, owns the copyright of the work by virtue of creating it in a tangible form—such as a manuscript or a recording—defending copyright is not that simple. To exercise an author's or creator's rights under the law, the copyright needs to be registered with the U.S. Copyright Office. Another exception to the intrinsic copyright of a piece is whether the work was written under an agreement that provided for the transfer of rights, which we cover later.

> **Slush Pile!** _____
>
> Although the law provides for fair use, there aren't any hard-and-fast rules about what constitutes "fair." So instead of risking getting in hot water, you're usually better off to ask permission.

Registering Your Rights

Although you don't have to register copyright, it is necessary that the work be registered if the owner of the copyright intends to bring a lawsuit against a violation, such as unauthorized reproduction. Registration provides a public record that you are the owner of the work and gives you a greater number of options under the law when it comes to enforcing your rights should the work be used in an inappropriate manner or one that violates your ownership. Registered works, according to the U.S. Copyright Office, may be eligible for statutory damages and attorney's fees if it is found that the work was used in an unauthorized manner. The USCO further says on its website that "if registration occurs within five years of publication, it is considered prima facie evidence in a court of law." That means that such evidence indicates the case is strong enough to justify further discovery and possibly a full trial.

You can register your work by going to www.copyright.gov and downloading the appropriate form for the type of work which you are registering, filling it out, and sending it in with the indicated number of copies of the work and the appropriate fee. It's an easy process.

> **Pen Pal**
>
> Copyright registration can take a while. Expect your certificate anywhere from six to eight months from your date of mailing, even though a successful copyright application is effective from the date of mailing.

> **Slush Pile!**
>
> Some people refer to "poor man's copyright," which references sending a copy of a work to yourself in a sealed envelope. The fact that the seal isn't broken proves that the work was created before the date of postmark. However, this type of "copyright" provides no protection under the law.

Copyright Ka-ching

Fees for registering your copyright range from an average of $30 to $60 per filing—and the good news is that you can file a batch of work at a time, saving on fees. Some fees are significantly higher, such as a $200 fee for the office to reconsider a work that has been previously refused, and $500 for a second reconsideration fee. Registration is retroactive to the date of the postmark of your application. Be sure to review the various forms carefully and fill them out in their entirety to ensure that your copyright application is processed as quickly as possible.

How Long Does It Last?

The U.S. Copyright Office says that for works created after January 1, 1978, copyright protection lasts for the author's lifetime, plus 70 years. Works for hire, or those created anonymously, or under a pen name or pseudonym enjoy copyright protection of 95 years from the year the work was first published, or 120 years from the date of creation, whichever is sooner.

Pen Pal

After your work is registered with the U.S. Copyright Office, it will appear in the database of work approximately three months later. You can search the database at the USCO website at www.copyright.gov.

Can I Copyright It?

The U.S. Copyright office specifically lists the original works that can be copyrighted, but qualifies the list with the statement that each category is viewed broadly. The copyrightable works that the USCO lists on its website include the following:

◆ Literary works

◆ Musical works, including any accompanying words

◆ Dramatic works, including any accompanying music

◆ Pantomimes and choreographic works

◆ Pictorial, graphic, and sculptural works

◆ Motion pictures and other audiovisual works

◆ Sound recordings

◆ Architectural works

Not everything that is conceptualized or even written can be copyrighted. Copyright protection does not extend to ideas, so if you have a great concept for a novel in your head, and tell it to someone else who then uses that idea to write a best-seller, copyright laws won't be of much use to you. However, if you wrote the concept on paper and registered the text, which was then used in the unscrupulous author's version of the book, you may have protection.

So what else is off-limits when it comes to copyright? The U.S. Copyright Office is quite clear about that and lists the following provisions on its website:

- Works that have not been fixed in a tangible form of expression (for example, choreographic works that have not been notated or recorded, or improvisational speeches or performances that have not been written or recorded)

- Titles, names, short phrases, and slogans; familiar symbols or designs; mere variations of typographic ornamentation, lettering, or coloring; mere listings of ingredients or contents

- Ideas, procedures, methods, systems, processes, concepts, principles, discoveries, or devices, as distinguished from a description, explanation, or illustration

- Works consisting entirely of information that is common property and containing no original authorship (for example, standard calendars, height and weight charts, tape measures and rulers, and lists or tables taken from public documents or other common sources)

Pen Pal

Because the U.S. government has copyright agreements with other countries, registering your copyright protects you in many international markets as well as in the United States.

Who Owns What You Write?

Of course, the determination of who owns what you write—and who is entitled to the copyright to the work—lies in the contract that you sign for your book. Publishing contracts are often complex documents that assign various rights to the work to the publisher, and along with that the benefits that those rights carry. So although you may write a brilliant novel that tops the best-seller lists for weeks, if you've signed a contract that assigns all the rights to the publisher for a flat fee, you'll reap none of the benefits of the big sales numbers. In addition, if you write a nonfiction YA work on the history of pencil production and sign an all-rights contract, you cannot sell excerpts from the book for publication—those profits go in the pocket of the publisher, unless otherwise stipulated in your contract.

That's why it's critical to have an experienced agent or lawyer who can help you navigate the choppy waters of negotiating the rights you sell in exchange for your advance.

What Type of Rights?

There are many types of rights provisions within contracts, and sometimes contracts that may provide for one type of rights assignment in one section may have additional rights assignments in another section, so it's important to approach the contract as a whole and not assume that it only requires assignment of one type of rights based on one section of the document.

Again, you really should have an experienced attorney and/or agent to guide you through the process of negotiating your contract to best protect your interests. However, in the interest of sharing some of the more common contract provisions when it comes to rights, you should be aware of the following terminology:

First-publication rights. This type of contract assigns the publisher the right to be the first to publish the document. This provision may mean the first to publish the document in book form or it may mean the first to publish the story in any form. For instance, if you have published your novel in an abridged format in a magazine, or serialized the chapters on a website, you need to clarify whether the first-publication rights provision is for book format or any format whatsoever. Failure to make that determination could leave you in breach of your contract.

All-rights or work made for hire. These types of contracts have slight differences but essentially mean that you are transferring all rights and interest in the work to the publisher. They mean that after you sign the contract, the publisher owns what you have written. Depending on the contract's provisions, the publisher may be able to resell, abridge, serialize, or otherwise distribute your work, and you may not receive additional compensation. This also means that you cannot resell or reuse the work in any way (unless you have a contractual provision for doing so).

Slush Pile!

It's usually a good idea to retain as many rights as possible when it comes to publishing your work. If, for instance, you sell all rights to your novel and Hollywood comes calling to make a movie about it, you may not see a dime of the fee paid to option the work if you have relinquished your rights, unless your contract specifies that you will.

Exclusive publication rights. This means that the publisher—and only the publisher—will be able to publish the book. Exclusive distribution rights means that the book may only be distributed and sold by the publisher.

Foreign rights. The publisher may also purchase or include the right to publish the work in foreign countries and in other languages. It is common for the contract to provide an additional fee schedule should the publisher exercise that right.

Electronic rights. Increasingly, publishers are looking for the right to republish the work in an electronic format. That may include publication as an e-book or audio book, or excerpts from the book to be published on the Internet or in other electronic formats. There may or may not be an additional fee schedule for this type of use.

There are many other rights that you must consider when negotiating a contract. Again, it is strongly recommended that you have a competent agent/attorney review any publication contract before you sign.

Referring to Others

Sometimes you may find that your project would benefit from referring to or excerpting other works. As mentioned earlier in this chapter, some such references fall under the domain of fair use. However, to truly protect yourself from accusations of plagiarism and potentially violating the copyright of another author, you should use proper literary citation methods and attribution to indicate that you are referencing the work of another writer or copyright owner.

One way to reference the attribution is to indicate the reference within the text. For instance, if you're referencing a definition from a particular dictionary, you may write, "*The Oxford English Dictionary* says that the meaning of the word ...." The attribution is embedded in the text of the narrative.

Another way to properly reference material that is drawn from other sources is with a footnote or endnote. A passage that includes historical references might read as follows:

 Pen Pal _____

An endnote is found at the end of a chapter or in a special section at the end of the book. A footnote is found at the bottom of the page or the end of a chapter.

Tarrymore Castle is an imposing structure built by Lord Balderdash in 1749.[1]

The footnote or endnote would then have the details about the literary reference:

1 Balderdash, Sonny, *The History of My Family*, Castle Story Publishing House, pp. 45–46.

Of course, there are many different formats for proper citations and you should find out your publisher's preference for which format is best.

Even with attribution, there is a limit to the amount of material that can be used without the express permission of the original author. Generally, if you're using more than a few short references, you should ask the owner of the copyright for permission.

The Danger of Plagiarism

Plagiarism is the unauthorized use of another author's work or the act of taking material created by another writer and passing it off as an original work. In addition to being unethical, if the infringed work is protected by a copyright registration, the owner of the violated work may seek statutory damages of up to $10,000 per infraction. In addition, other penalties may be imposed by your publisher if the infraction is discovered after your book is published.

So it's critical to take great care that your work is original and, when another author's material is referenced, that it is properly attributed or annotated. Failure to do so can be a costly mistake.

Asking Permission

To gain appropriate permission that authorizes you to reuse or extensively reference work in the body of another work, you first need to find the owner of the copyright. This may be the author or it may be the publisher, depending on the agreement that was signed. If the author was the owner of the copyright and is deceased, the owner of the copyright may be the author's estate or a particular heir to the estate.

After you've tracked down the owner of the copyright, you must explain what you intend to use and how you intend to use it. It's then up to the owner to grant you permission or not. Generally, the more well known the work is, the more difficult it may be to get permission to reuse it. For example, lyrics to songs by The Beatles may be very difficult to get permission to reference. Even if you're lucky enough to get permission, you will likely also be required

Pen Pal

It's a good idea to indicate copyright ownership on your work. Simply including the copyright symbol as well as the reference to the owner and the year is often sufficient. For example, ©2006 Sonny Balderdash.

to pay a fee, which could potentially range from a few hundred to thousands of dollars. Depending on the circumstances of your book and its publication, such requirements may make it cost-prohibitive to include the material in your book.

Release Me

If you're successful in your request for permission, you'll want to confirm it in writing so that you have a binding authorization for you to use the work. The entity that is granting permission may have a form that you need to fill out. Otherwise, you need to draft your own release form or letter.

This document should include the material that you intend to use, the format and work in which you intend to use it, confirmation of the copyright holder's authorization, an assurance that the individual signing the document is authorized to grant permission to use the work, and other provisions, depending on how you intend to use the referenced work.

The following sample release letter is intended to be an example for illustration only and is not intended to be a legally binding document. Please consult your attorney/agent for the proper provisions for a release letter based on the circumstances of your project.

Date

Mr. Sonny Balderdash
123 Main Street
Anytown, USA 12345

Dear Mr. Balderdash

This letter confirms our conversation in which you agreed to allow Ima Y.A. Writer to reproduce material from *The History of My Family*, a work of nonfiction by Sonny Balderdash, in her new book, *Scary Daughter*, the story of a young female wizard who routinely startles her parents. Following are the details of this authorization:

◆ Sonny Balderdash is the owner of this copyright and is able to assign the right to reference this material.

◆ The material referenced will be primarily factual data about the Balderdash family castles. However, some other facts may also be referenced.

◆ Such references will be made without compensation to Sonny Balderdash or any entity associated with *The History of My Family*.

- Ima Y.A. Writer agrees to fully attribute the work referenced by annotating references within the text of the book and providing reference material throughout.

- This permission extends through the life of the published work and cannot be revoked.

- Sonny Balderdash indemnifies and holds harmless Ima Y.A. Writer, her agents, publisher, and associates, for any cost, litigation, claim, or judgment that results as a breach of this agreement.

Please indicate your agreement to these terms by signing two copies of this agreement and returning one to me at the address indicated.

Thank you for your permission to use material from *The History of My Family* in my book.

Sincerely,

Ima Y.A. Writer

I authorize reproduction of the above-referenced material, according to the terms outlined.

_____   _____

Signature   Date

_____

Print Name

Right On

Copyright, ownership, and permissions can be confusing, but it's critical that you have a basic understanding of them so that you preserve as much of the rights to—and profits from—your work as possible, and so that you don't inadvertently break the law. Take some time to visit the U.S. Copyright Office website, and don't skimp when it comes to asking an attorney for advice on contracts, rights, and permissions. The money you spend for good legal counsel could save you a great deal of trouble, headaches, and money in the end.

The Least You Need to Know

- Copyright is a government-created protection of the authorship of your work.

- To take legal action to protect your rights, you need to register your copyright with the U.S. Copyright Office.

- "Fair use" allows copyrighted works to be excerpted without permission in very specific circumstances.

- Proper citations are essential to avoid plagiarism issues when work from one source is referenced or otherwise used in another source.

- Understanding your publication contract is essential to preserving the rights to your work.

Appendix A

Glossary

advance   Payment made to an author upon signing a publishing contract; advances are paid assuming that a book will earn additional money in sales, thereby earning back the money advanced to the author.

antagonist   The villain of the story; a character who represents an idea (corruption, outdated social rules, corporate greed, prejudice, etc.) or a series of events that bring trouble to your protagonist.

arch nemesis   Ultimate enemy; arch = denoting the highest level of importance; nemesis = enemy; an opponent or rival.

audience   Readers of any particular book or books.

author   The creator or writer of a manuscript; also the writer of a published book.

best-seller   Book cited on any of several lists of top-selling books, usually listed by various categories (fiction, nonfiction, children's, etc.).

bible   Information gathered about a fictional character for the author's own reference. See *dossier*.

chapter book   A children's book that is broken into distinct sections or chapters; usually refers to books intended for beginning readers.

character(s)   The person or people represented in a work of fiction; also those traits (characteristics) that define the morals, attitude, strengths, and weaknesses of a particular individual.

character list A list of the people (characters) appearing in a work of fiction.

cliffhangers Endings designed to leave a reader hanging (as in hanging over the edge of a cliff) and to lure readers on to the next chapter. May refer to chapter endings or story endings.

commission Fees taken by an agent for selling your work to a publisher; based on a percentage (usually 15 to 25 percent) of advances and/or royalties earned by a book or title.

cover copy Text on book covers giving story and marketing information such as story synopsis, author information, age level, etc.

dossier Information gathered about a fictional character for the author's own reference. See *bible*.

easy reader Children's book designed for beginning readers; book containing simple vocabulary and short, uncomplicated sentences.

episodic Stories consisting of a series of events (episodes) not necessarily related by theme or chronological order, and whose resolution doesn't necessarily depend on them.

fiction Any piece of writing that is not factual; stories derived from an author's imagination. Stories, including those that are fact-based, that are presented in an imaginative way; i.e., not strictly limited to the actual people, places, or events or a particular incident.

footnote Commentary or reference information about a particular passage or detail in a work of nonfiction that is found at the bottom of a page.

foreshadowing Information that lays the groundwork for upcoming plot developments; details that hint at future events.

format The physical presentation of a manuscript (i.e., font, margins, spacing, etc.). The presentation of a work referring to genre (i.e., horror young adult, mystery, etc.).

galley(s) Also known as page proofs; the printed text of a manuscript released to authors and editors for proofing prior to a book's publication; also refers to their format: long, uncut strips of paper containing text.

genre Categories of books such as fantasy, mystery, romance, sci-fi, thriller, etc.

guidelines Refers to rules of content and format regarding the submission of manuscripts to publishers. Also manuscript guidelines; publishing guidelines.

head popping Inadvertently switching from one character's point of view (head) to another's, breaking the cardinal rule of POV: never switch POV within a scene.

illustrations Artwork accompanying text, especially as in children's picture books.

in print Published books that are currently available in libraries or for purchase; books that are out of print are no long actively being marketed.

internal conflict Problems generated by a character relating to him- or herself.

level Above or below level; refers to vocabulary, sentence construction.

list Books to be published during a particular season; usually spring/summer, fall, or winter lists.

manuscript An unpublished completed draft of a fiction or nonfiction work.

manuscript guidelines Requirements of content, format, and submission procedures specified by individual publishers.

middle grade Children's books geared toward readers aged 8 to 12.

misleads False clues or any kind of deliberately false information. In mysteries, also known as red herrings.

nonfiction Factual and research-based works.

omniscient narrator Being everywhere at once, all-knowing and all-seeing. An omniscient narrator knows the private thoughts and motives of every character.

option The right to purchase, acquire, or represent a written work.

page count The number of pages in a manuscript.

permission Authorization obtained by a copyright holder to quote, cite, or otherwise use a published work.

picture book Heavily illustrated children's books.

pitch letter A letter containing information designed to attract the interest of an agent or publisher.

point of view (POV) Refers to the character who's telling or seeing the story and its events.

proposal Part of or the whole of submission materials designed to interest an agent or publisher in a specific book project.

protagonist The hero or heroine of the story. We like protagonists; we are pro-protagonist.

public domain Works of fiction (or any individual, creative work; i.e., songs, plays, symphonies, etc.) that are no longer protected by copyright. Creative works in the public domain may be quoted from, adapted, or used without incurring permissions, royalties, or other fees.

query Publishing term referring to a writer's initial inquiry to an agent or publisher; query letters describing a manuscript are often part of a proposal or submission package.

reader Any person who reads a piece of writing.

reading level The degree of difficulty of a book, suggesting the age and grade level of appropriate readers. Most children's books are assigned a reading level based on factors such as content, subject matter, word length, word count, vocabulary, etc.

rejection letter A written response from an agent or publisher declining to take on a particular project or writer.

royalty or royalties Payments to an author made by publishers; a percentage paid to the author for each book sold.

series Fiction or nonfiction books sharing common authors, genres, characters, subjects, or themes (e.g., Agatha Christie's mysteries series).

slush pile Stacks of unsolicited (unagented) manuscript submissions; usually read by assistants or interns.

submission A piece of writing sent to an agent or publisher for their consideration.

summary A condensed telling of a story or plot in third person present tense; also called a synopsis.

synopsis A condensed telling of a story or plot in third person present tense; also called a summary.

text The words on a page (as opposed to artwork, illustrations, charts and graphics, etc.).

unsolicited manuscripts Manuscripts sent to publishers by authors without going through an agent. Also called unagented manuscripts.

voice Refers to the tone of your writing; the way a piece sounds (e.g., formal, casual, intimate, formal).

word count   The number of words in a sentence, paragraph, chapter, or manuscript; one of the factors in determining reading level.

young adult (YA)   Books targeted to teen readers; variously designated 10 and up, 12 and up, 12 to 14, 10 to 16, etc.

Online Resources

General Resources for Writers

Agent Research
www.agentresearch.com/agent_ver.html

Agent Query
www.agentquery.com

Authorlink
www.authorlink.com

Go Publish Yourself
www.go-publish-yourself.com

Predators and Editors
www.anotherealm.com/prededitors

Publishers Marketplace
www.publishersmarketplace.com

Writer's Market
www.writersmarket.com

Writers Net
www.writers.net

Associations, Societies, and Online Schools

Absolute Write University
www.absoluteclasses.com
P.O. Box 93273
Rochester, NY 14692
866-974-8399
801-409-9167 (fax)

American Booksellers Association
www.bookweb.org
200 White Plains Road
Tarrytown, NY 10591
1-800-637-0037, 914-591-2665
914-591-2720 (fax)

American Library Association
www.ala.org
YA website: www.ala.org/ala/yalsa/yalsa.htm
50 East Huron Street
Chicago, IL 60611
1-800-545-2433

American Society of Journalists and Authors (ASJA)
www.asja.org
1501 Broadway, Suite 302
New York, NY 10036
212-997-0947
212-937-2315 (fax)

Authors Guild
www.authorsguild.org
The Authors Guild
116 West 23rd Street, Suite 500
New York, NY 10011
212-563-5904
212-564-5363

Blue Phantom Writers
www.bluephantomwriters.com

BOOST
www.boost4writers.com

Children's Book Council
www.cbcbooks.org
12 West 37th Street, 2nd Floor
New York, NY 10018-7480
212-966-1990
212-966-2073 (fax)

Coffeehouse for Writers
www.coffeehouseforwriters.com

Gotham Writers' Workshop
The Writers Room
www.writingclasses.com
1841 Broadway, Suite 809
New York, NY 10023
877-WRITERS (877-974-8377)
212-307-6325 (fax)

Mediabistro.com
www.mediabistro.com
494 Broadway
New York, NY 10012
212-929-2588

National Writer's Association
www.nationalwriters.com
· 10940 S. Parker Road, #508
Parker, CO 80134
303-841-0246
303-841-2607 (fax)

National Writers Union
www.nwu.org
113 University Place, 6th Floor
New York, NY 10003
212-254-0279
212-254-0673 (fax)

Poynter
www.poynter.org
801 Third Street South
St. Petersburg, FL 33701
1-888-769-6837

Society of Children's Book Writers & Illustrators
www.scbwi.com
8271 Beverly Boulevard
Los Angeles, CA 90048
323-782-1010
323-782-1892 (fax)

The Writer's Croft
www.writerscroft.com

Write 101
www.write101.com
32 MacDonnell Road
Margate Beach, QLD 4019
Australia
+61-7-3284-3077

Writers on the Net
www.writers.com

Writing World
www.writing-world.com

General Resources for Writers

Library of Congress
www.loc.gov
101 Independence Avenue, S.E.
Washington, D.C. 20540
202-707-5000

Publishing Law Center
www.publaw.com
1163 Vine Street
Denver, CO 80206

U.S. Copyright Office
www.copyright.gov
101 Independence Avenue, S.E.
Washington, D.C. 20559-6000
202-707-3000

Writer's Store
www.writersstore.com

Magazines and Websites

AuthorsDen
www.authorsden.com

Book Spot
www.bookspot.com

Cynthia Leitich Smith
www.cynthialeitichsmith.com

Novel Talk
www.noveltalk.com

Publishers Weekly
www.publishersweekly.com
Publishers Weekly, 360 Park Avenue South
New York, NY 10010
646-746-6758
646-746-6631 (fax)

The Children's Literature Web Guide
www.acs.ucalgary.ca/~dkbrown

The Writer Magazine
www.writermag.com
Kalmbach Publishing Co.
21027 Crossroads Circle
Waukesha, WI 53186
262-796-8776

Writer's Digest
www.writersdigest.com
4700 E. Galbraith Road
Cincinnati, OH 45236
513-531-2222

Writer's Break
www.writersbreak.com

Voice of Youth Advocates
www.voya.com
4501 Forbes Blvd., Suite 200
Lanham, MD 20706
1-888-486-9297

Young Adult (& Kids) Books Central
www.yabookscentral.com

Nonfiction Resources

Bella Online
www.bellaonline.com/articles/art1861.asp

Deadline Online
www.deadlineonline.com

eServer
www.eserver.org

Internet Resources
www.internet-resources.com

Journalism Net
www.journalismnet.com

RefDesk
www.refdesk.com

Street Tips
www.Sreetips.com

Writing Instruction

2006 Guide to Literary Agents by Kathryn S. Brogan

Art of Dramatic Writing: Its Basis in the Creative Interpretation of Human Motives by Lajos Egri

Beginnings, Middles & Ends by Nancy Kress

Bird by Bird: Some Instructions on Writing and Life by Ann LaMott

Art of Creative Writing by Lajos Egri

Artist's Way: A Spiritual Path to Higher Creativity by Julia Cameron

Characters and Viewpoint by Orson Scott Card

The Complete Idiot's Guide to Publishing Children's Books by Harold Underdown

Creating Characters Kids Will Love by Elaine Marie Alphin

The Creative Writing Handbook by Jay Amberg, Mark Larson

The Elements of Storytelling: How to Write Compelling Fiction by Peter Rubie

The Everything Creative Writing Book: All You Need to Know to Write a Novel, Play, Short Story, Screenplay, Poem, or Article by Carol Whiteley

Fiction First Aid: Instant Remedies for Novels, Stories, and Scripts by Raymond Obstfeld

The First Five Pages: A Writer's Guide to Staying Out of the Rejection Pile by Noah Lukeman

How to Write a Damn Good Novel: A Step-by-Step No Nonsense Guide to Dramatic Storytelling by James N. Frey

How to Write a Damn Good Novel, II: Advanced Techniques for Dramatic Storytelling by James N. Frey

How to Write a Film by Geoff Evans

Immediate Fiction: A Complete Writing Course by Jerry Cleaver

Jeff Herman's Guide to Book Publishers, Editors & Literary Agents, 2006: Who they are! What they want! How to win them over! by Jeff Herman

On Directing Film by David Mamet

The Plot Thickens: 8 Ways to Bring Fiction to Life by Noah Lukeman

Write Away by Elizabeth George

Write Source 2000: A Guide to Writing, Thinking & Learning by Patrick Sebranek

Writing Books for Kids and Teens by Marion Crook

Writing Down the Bones by Natalie Goldberg

Writing Fiction: The Practical Guide from New York's Acclaimed Creative Writing School by Gotham Writers' Workshop

Writing for Young Adults by Sherry Garland

Writing with a Purpose by Joseph F. Trimmer

YA Books of Note

Anne of Green Gables by Lucy Montgomery

Best Books for Young Adults by Betty Carter

Black Beauty by Anna Sewell

Both Sides of Time by Caroline B. Cooney

The Catcher in the Rye by J. D. Salinger

The Chocolate War by Robert Cormier

A Day No Pigs Would Die by Robert Newton Peck

Dear Mr. Henshaw by Beverly Cleary

Dicey's Song by Cynthia Voigt

Driver's Ed by Caroline B. Cooney

The Face on the Milk Carton by Caroline B. Cooney

Forever by Judy Blume

The Giver by Lois Lowry

A Hero Ain't Nothing but a Sandwich by Alice Childress

Holes by Louis Sachar

Island of the Blue Dolphins by Scott O'Dell

Johnny Tremain by Esther Hoskins Forbes

Kidnapped by Robert Louis Stevenson

To Kill a Mockingbird by Harper Lee

A Light in the Forest by Conrad Richter

The Lord of the Rings series by J. R. R. Tolkien

Maniac Magee by Jerry Spinelli

Nancy Drew series by Carolyn Keene

The Outsiders by S. E. Hinton

The Princess Diaries by Meg Cabot

The Sisterhood of the Traveling Pants by Ann Brashares

The Secret Garden by Frances Hodgson Burnett

Tuck Everlasting by Natalie Babbitt

Walk Two Moons by Sharon Creech

Watership Down by Richard Adams

Where the Red Fern Grows by William Rawls

A Wrinkle in Time by Madeleine L'Engle

The Yearling by Marjorie Rawlings

Index

C

Check Out These
Best-Sellers

Grammar and Style
SECOND EDITION
Laurie E. Rozakis, Ph.D.
1-59257-115-8 • $16.95

Buying and Selling a Home
FOURTH EDITION
Shelley O'Hara and Nancy D. Lewis
1-59257-120-4 • $18.95

Being a Groom
SECOND EDITION
Jennifer Lata Rung and Mark Rung
0-02-864456-5 • $9.95

Learning Spanish
THIRD EDITION
Gail Stein
0-02-864451-4 • $18.95

Personal Finance in Your 20s & 30s
SECOND EDITION
Sarah Young Fisher and Susan Shelly
0-02-864374-7 • $19.95

Organizing Your Life
FOURTH EDITION
Georgene Lockwood
1-59257-413-0 • $16.95

Total Nutrition
FOURTH EDITION
Joy Bauer, M.S., R.D., C.D.N.
1-59257-439-4 • $18.95

Positive Dog Training
Pamela Dennison
0-02-864463-8 • $14.95

The Bible
THIRD EDITION
James Stuart Bell and Stan Campbell
1-59257-389-4 • $18.95

Calculus
W. Michael Kelley
0-02-864365-8 • $18.95

Music Theory
SECOND EDITION
Michael Miller
1-59257-437-8 • $19.95

The Perfect Resume
THIRD EDITION
Susan Ireland
0-02-864440-9 • $14.95

Playing the Guitar
SECOND EDITION
Frederick Noad
0-02-864244-9 • $21.95

Manga Illustrated
John Layman and David Hutchison
1-59257-335-5 • $19.95

Knitting and Crocheting Illustrated
SECOND EDITION
Barbara Breiter and Gail Diven
1-59257-089-5 • $16.95

More than *450 titles* available at
booksellers and online retailers everywhere

www.idiotsguides.com

ALPHA